Civic Education

Civic Education

What Makes Students Learn

Richard G. Niemi and Jane Junn

Yale University Press

New Haven and London

Designed by James J. Johnson and set in
Melior Roman type by Running Feet
Books, Durham, North Carolina.

Printed in the United States of America
by BookCrafters, Inc., Chelsea, Michigan.

A catalogue record for this book is available from the British Library.

The paper in this book meets the guidelines for permanence and durability of
the Committee on Production Guidelines
for Book Longevity of the Council on
Library Resources.

Library of Congress Cataloging-in-
Publication Data

Niemi, Richard G.
    Civic education : what makes
students learn / Richard G. Niemi
and Jane Junn.
        p.   cm.
    Includes bibliographical references
and index.
    ISBN 0–300–07247–3 (alk. paper)

    1. Political science—Study and
teaching (Secondary)—United States.
2. Civics—Study and teaching (Secondary)—United States.   I. Junn,
Jane.   II. Title.
JA88.U6N54   1998
320.4'071'273—dc21   97–32807

10 9 8 7 6 5 4 3 2 1

To our spouses, Shirley Niemi and David Champagne

Contents

Acknowledgments

A project of this magnitude is never the work of the named authors alone. This is especially true in our case, for the data set on which the analyses in the book are based—the National Assessment of Educational Progress (NAEP) 1988 Civics Assessment—was designed and executed by many individuals, including primary, secondary, and college teachers; curriculum specialists; test specialists; and sampling statisticians. To all of the individuals who participated in that effort, we offer our thanks. In addition, we thank the many people who compiled the various transcript studies, which we use in chapter 4. We hope that the conclusions we draw from the NAEP data underscore the relevance and usefulness of such data collections to scholarship that has traditionally been considered outside of the field of education.

We have also benefited greatly from Niemi's participation in the planning phases for the next NAEP Civics Assessment, currently scheduled for fieldwork in 1998. Although the many individuals involved in this effort may not recognize specific ideas as having come from them, we can assure them that the book profited from the many discussions, questions, suggestions, and even casual comments made during the course of our meetings. Don Vetter, who supervised the "consensus" project, was always helpful. Mary Crovo, Assistant Director for Test Development of the National Assessment Governing Board, was supportive and full of useful insights. Margaret Branson shared with us her wisdom and her many years of work on civic education. John Ellington assisted us in making the necessary contacts to carry out the nationwide survey of civics requirements.

Junn's year as a Visiting Scholar in the Educational Policy and Research Division of the Educational Testing Service helped the progress of this book along in many ways. We are grateful to the NAEP Visiting Scholar program and the staff at ETS, especially to Paul Barton, Charles Davis, Linda DeLauro, Eugene Johnson, and Molly Joy, who provided important help throughout her year there. We would also like to thank Al Rogers, Tom Jirele, and Steve Lazer for facilitating our analysis in various ways, big and small. Robert Clemons and Sharif Shakrani at the National Center for Education Statistics enabled us to gain access to the precise wording of unpublished assessment items that are reserved for future test purposes.

Two anonymous readers for Yale University Press and M. Kent Jennings provided detailed critical comments on an earlier version of the manuscript. We thank the reviewers, and especially Kent, for their suggestions and questions, which strengthened both the quantitative analysis and the substantive conclusions of the book.

Amy Makinen at the University of Rochester proved to be an able and cheerful research assistant, and we could not have done the work without her quick and accurate responses to our requests for data analysis. Michael Heel also ably assisted us early on. Finally, at Yale University Press, we would like to thank Susan Laity for a terrific editing job and John Covell, our editor, for his support and encouragement.

Dick and Jane

Civic Education

CHAPTER ONE

Civic Education and Students' Knowledge

Political theorists have long maintained that in order for a democratic polity to make good decisions, the decision-makers must understand the political world. As such, for ordinary citizens to have political knowledge has frequently been considered one of the most important qualifications for self-governance. It is reasoned that democratic citizens should have a minimum understanding of the political system in which they express preferences and elect representatives. Political deliberation and consent among citizens who understand their own interests and are informed of their options contribute to the production of good government and the legitimacy of the democratic regime, as well as to the development of each individual's full potential.

A politically knowledgeable citizenry is, however, a goal rather than a reality. Data gathered from surveys of citizens on their knowledge of American government and politics over the past half century are often cited as evidence that it is unrealistic to expect informed political deliberation from the mass public. Although a small proportion of American voters are knowledgeable and sophisticated about politics, the vast majority of the population fails to reach the standards of political knowledge that are espoused by political theorists. In the United States, political enfranchisement is a birthright; there is no political-knowledge test—no "cognitive poll tax"—that citizens must pass in order to be included among the decision-makers in a democratic polity. As a result, political observers have wondered about whether American citizens have enough

political knowledge to make good decisions, in other words, how quali-
fied the mass public is to engage in self-rule.

The incongruity between the empirical findings of low levels of knowledge and the normative expectations of a high degree of political awareness among citizens leads theorists to offer solutions that traverse the
spectrum from anti-democratic elitist models that place power in the
hands of experts and elites to participatory-democratic models that seek
to transform the democratic capabilities of ordinary citizens. The first argument suggests that citizens who lack knowledge and understanding of
political candidates, issues, and rules and principles of governance in
American democracy should be restricted from engaging in politics. One
could argue that elite leadership in the political sphere is necessary to
counteract the uninformed opinions and actions of the mass public. Although popular, this model has been criticized as antithetical to the spirit
of the American liberal-democratic tradition: its solution of elite domi-
nation is characterized as worse than the problem. In the second model,
the political knowledge and awareness of citizens need to be increased
through education so that those citizens can engage in informed deliberation and consent.

The belief that there is a causal connection between formal education
and the creation of good democratic citizens—including their acquisition
of political knowledge—has a venerable legacy in both political philoso-
phy and political science. The American tradition is best exemplified
by the educational writings of John Dewey ([1916] 1966) and the work
of Charles Merriam (1931; 1934), who both followed the tradition of En-
lightenment theorists, most conspicuously John Locke and John Stuart
Mill. Common among these perspectives is the argument that education
has transcendent importance in the development of the qualities essential
to citizenship in a democratic polity. This emphasis on the responsibility
of American schools to teach the facts and principles of American democracy to the largest group of new and emerging citizens—high school students—continues unabated in contemporary American politics. The call
for education to alleviate political as well as social and economic ills is
a familiar refrain of politicians and policymakers alike, exemplified by
public-health officials who advocate education programs to stem teenage
smoking and pregnancy, by business leaders who call for training programs to prepare the next generation for an increasingly technologically
advanced workplace, and by academics, reformers, and politicians who
call for greater civic knowledge and participation as an antidote to collective ennui and growing political cynicism.

Schools, along with their teachers and curricula, have thus long been identified as the critical link between education and citizenship, as the locus from which democratic citizens emerge. As a result, the popular prescription for the problem of a powerful yet politically ignorant electorate is to increase political knowledge through education. This solution is supported by evidence culled from the same surveys that document low levels of political knowledge—evidence demonstrating that those with more formal education are also more knowledgeable about politics (Campbell et al., 1960; Converse, 1964; Neuman, 1986; Zaller, 1992; Delli Carpini and Keeter, 1996; Nie, Junn, and Stehlik-Barry, 1996).

At first glance, it appears unarguable that formal education increases political knowledge; the more years a student spends in school, the more likely he or she is to understand the political world. Yet although the findings of the "transcendent importance" of education (Converse, 1972: 262) appear consistently in survey after survey, companion findings from research at the intersection of political science and education cast a shadow upon the view that more education will create better-informed citizens. Studies conducted from the mid-1960s on concerning what impact high school classes in American government and civics have on political knowledge have, for the most part, found that there is little or none. In other words, level of schooling attained makes a difference to what citizens know about politics, but classes in American government and civics do not appear to be responsible for this knowledge. These "non-findings" of the impact of the civics curriculum on political knowledge are puzzling. If civic knowledge cannot be attributed, even in part, to course work itself, what is it inside the "black box" of formal education that makes those with more formal schooling know more about politics than those with less? In addition to education, what determines citizens' knowledge of politics? To the extent that Americans are knowledgeable about government and politics, how do they get that way? If they lack knowledge, what can we do to enhance their learning?

One way to answer these questions might be to focus on the production of information by candidates and elected officials and the flow of that information through the media to citizens. If candidates are unclear about their intentions, even attentive citizens may have trouble understanding what options are available to them. If representatives and other elected officials fail to provide adequate information about costs and consequences of proposed policies, citizens will find it difficult to evaluate policy choices. And even if candidates are clear and officials forthcoming, few citizens receive that information directly. The media thus take on a crucial role in sorting, interpreting, and clarifying the activities and pronouncements of political actors and, more generally, of making sense of the political world.[1]

Our focus in this book differs from such an approach in two important ways. First, instead of concentrating on knowledge of current political activities, we look at knowledge of the foundational aspects of the American political system, including structures and processes of government and principles of American democracy. Although both types of knowledge are important, our premise is that one can be well-informed about the day-to-day aspects of politics only when one understands the context in which government operates.[2]

The second distinctive feature of our study is the population of citizens we analyze. Rather than looking at the adult population as a whole, we concentrate on high school seniors, who are in the process of becoming adult citizens. Specifically, we shall draw on an important nationwide study of high school seniors conducted in 1988, the National Assessment of Educational Progress (NAEP) Civics Assessment. Focusing on a population with identical levels of formal education limits the inferences we can draw about citizens in general, yet there are several features of the NAEP data that make the assessment particularly useful for the questions at hand. Perhaps most important, unlike typical national surveys of a representative sample of the U.S. population, the NAEP data provide a wide range of measures of the students' backgrounds, including their school and home environments. These measures allow us to account simultaneously for these various factors as competing explanations of political knowledge. In addition, the NAEP data include a large number and wide range of substantive measures of political knowledge. With 150 questions on American government and politics, this data collection exceeds by more than a factor of ten the factual questions on politics available in most other surveys.[3] Finally, the portion of the NAEP data that we analyze includes enough cases to enable us to conduct separate analyses of politically relevant subgroups, in particular, African-American and Hispanic students. These features of the data set allow us to ask a broader range of questions about students' sources of political knowledge and to pinpoint more accurately some of the answers.

Although we focus in this book on the the sources of civic knowledge, we consider two additional issues in the broader debate about political knowledge and democracy. First, how much do Americans know about politics and their government? Second, what types of political knowledge are necessary, and under what circumstances is such knowledge important?

Levels of Political Knowledge

Over the past half-century, there have been numerous attempts by political scientists and others to determine how politically knowledgeable ordinary Americans are. These efforts have entailed surveys on a wide assortment of topics, including current political issues, names and functions of elected and appointed officials, structures and institutions of national and state government, and rules of the democratic system. The surveys have involved quizzes about specific facts and figures as well as tests of understanding of public policies and political processes, and they have utilized both closed-ended questions (where respondents choose among answers provided), and open-ended questions.

The results of these surveys have usually been interpreted as somewhere between disappointing and disastrous. Most Americans know little about current issues; few can name their state or congressional representatives; many are uncertain of how their government works; and a large proportion are ill-informed about or unable to apply the basic principles on which our political system is based to hypothetical situations. In one of the earliest studies of the American public, Hyman and Sheatsley (1947: 412–14) identified a "hard core of chronic 'Know-Nothings,'" whose size was "of considerable magnitude," and who were "generally uninformed" about issues of the day. Drawing on numerous surveys over the next fifteen years, Erskine (1963) reported similarly discouraging data on the knowledge held by Americans about "textbook," domestic, and international matters. More recently, demonstrating the ignorance of the public has become something of a cottage industry, with one researcher after another trying to find a more absurd example of what Americans do not know about politics and government or a more apt metaphor to express their collective ignorance.[4]

The lack of knowledge among American citizens is indeed striking to those of us who deal with political life daily. What is most significant, however, is not so much the inability to recall isolated facts and figures but the breadth and depth of the ignorance. When first confronted with survey results showing low levels of knowledge, one might assume that this applied only to certain types of subjects. Many Americans, for example, find foreign policy somewhat incomprehensible. But an ignorance of foreign affairs might be seen as understandable and even "excusable" if one thinks about the lack of immediate relevance of international matters to most people's lives and if ignorance about international topics far from home were matched by greater knowledge about domestic politics. But citizens are equally ignorant about domestic politics (Delli Carpini and Keeter, 1996: 68).

Acquiring empirical evidence of the depth of the public's political ignorance became a focus in the 1950s, when sociologists and political scientists set out to explore the ideological and issue-based foundations of American voting behavior. In *The American Voter* (Campbell et al., 1960), for example, the authors speak of "widespread lack of familiarity with prominent issues of public policy, along with confusion on party position that remains even among individuals familiar with an issue" (188). In an analysis of the electorate's use of ideological concepts that are common to elite political discussion—in particular, the notions of liberalism and conservatism—the authors concluded that "the concepts important to ideological analysis are useful only for that small segment of the population that is equipped to approach political decisions at a rarefied level" (250). In a later study, one of the authors of that volume coined the term *nonattitudes* to express voters' frequent and extreme lack of issue awareness and political understanding (Converse, 1964).

Nor have young people been spared this sharp critique. A variety of surveys have found that teenagers and young adults are ignorant of American history, geography, and politics (not to mention literature, on which see Ravitch and Finn, 1987; "Pop Quiz," 1988). These studies have been less systematic than those of adults, but the findings and conclusions are often as pointed. In 1993, for example, a survey showed that students at elite colleges were often ignorant of basic political facts, such as the names of their senators, the line of presidential succession, the name of the prime minister of Great Britain, and so on ("General Knowledge," 1993). In the same year, in Great Britain, a study reported that one in ten seventeen-year-olds could not locate England on a world map and almost half could not find New Zealand (Preston, 1993: 3). Increasingly, stories of such gaps in young people's learning have come from the NAEP assessments (Vandermyn, 1974; Ravitch and Finn, 1987; Paul Williams et al., 1995).[5]

In general, young adults have been found to be less knowledgeable than older adults (Delli Carpini and Keeter, 1996: 159). It is difficult to sort out the reasons for this. In some instances, greater ignorance is clearly associated with life experiences: young adults in the 1980s and 1990s could less often identify President Truman's party, the New Deal, or World War II concentration camps (Delli Carpini and Keeter, 1996: 158–59; "Polling on the Holocaust" 1993). Yet overall, it is unclear how much of the knowledge gap can be attributed to generational differences and how much to learning associated with age per se; it is also uncertain whether in recent years any of it is due to problems in the schools.[6]

The matter of voter knowledge has been the subject of many theoretical and empirical analyses. On the theoretical side, some writers explain why the lack of information makes sense and why it might, to some degree at least, be compatible with democratic government. On the empirical side, an effort was made to see how widely the political ignorance extended. Early forays abroad, focusing on voter awareness of issues and ideology rather than on factual knowledge, emphasized the similarities in mass electorates across disparate political systems, thus suggesting that citizen ignorance was endemic to mass electorates (see, for example, Converse and Dupeux, 1962; Butler and Stokes, 1969: chaps. 8–9).

In the 1960s, after the initial shock of these findings wore off, analysts tried to restore the reputations of voters. They introduced the concept of "issue publics": individuals learn about issues and candidates that are of particular importance to them while remaining ignorant of other matters (Converse, 1964). The point was also made that people recognize and understand concepts that they do not spontaneously bring up in answer to survey questions (Converse, 1964; Barnes, Kaase, et al., 1979), and that they recognize names that they cannot spontaneously recall (Mann and Wolfinger, 1980). In addition, evidence showed that voters' knowledge and ideological perspectives depend to some extent on the nature of the party system (Barnes, Kaase, et al., 1979, part 2; Niemi and Westholm, 1984), on the extent to which candidates take clear and distinctive positions on issues (Page and Brody, 1972), and on the length of time that an issue has been before the public (Page and Shapiro, 1992: 12–13). In addition, methodological questions were raised about the basis for some of the more extreme conclusions about voter ignorance (Achen, 1975; Green, 1988; Krosnick, 1991).

Nonetheless, at its simplest level, both adults and adolescents are demonstrably ignorant of many facts about American government as well as about contemporary politics and policies. This pattern remains true despite large, nominal increases in levels of education, a movement toward a more inclusive politics for women and minorities, and a vastly improved capacity for transmitting information (Delli Carpini and Keeter, 1996: chap. 3). Given the relative constancy in levels of knowledge since the 1950s despite a considerable increase in the proportion of people finishing high school and college, it is important to analyze the sources of political knowledge, and in particular, the role of schools and civic education in supplying that knowledge. We turn first, however, to the question of political knowledge itself: When is it necessary in a democracy, and what kind is needed? Is all of the fuss about public ignorance warranted?

The Necessity of Political Knowledge

Various arguments have been forwarded to counter the notion that political knowledge is either necessary or desirable. In particular, one might suggest that political ignorance is an indicator of the rationality of the public: instead of asking why Americans are so ill-informed about politics, scholars have suggested that the interesting question is, Why does anybody become informed about politics? (See, for example, Downs, 1957: chaps. 11–13; Fiorina, 1990.) A second argument, in the pluralist tradition, might be that a knowledgeable public is not necessary because special-interest groups will represent citizens' preferences and interests. Far less information on the part of individual citizens is necessary to choose a group that will organize and represent their interests than to influence politics personally. A third argument relies on the notion of issue publics: people are specialists in areas that serve their interests; they need only know how to function with respect to those interests. Alternatively, it is said that knowledge is situational, in the sense that citizens will learn all they need to know when they need to. Finally, a more elitist argument holds that the mass public cannot become knowledgeable because most citizens view politics as a "great sideshow of life" and are neither capable of nor interested in following politics in such a way as to acquire a thorough understanding of it (Kinder and Sears, 1985).

Yet another argument, which has been promulgated in the 1990s, suggests that the widespread lack of political knowledge among citizens is not cause for alarm because individuals are information misers who use judgmental heuristics that allow them to make meaningful, sensible decisions with relatively little information (Page and Shapiro, 1992; Popkin, 1991; Sniderman, Brody, and Tetlock, 1991; Zaller, 1992). Cue-taking—relying on the positions of political parties, groups, national leaders, or various experts—is an especially prominent method of forming attitudes and making political decisions. Thus, for example, voters may not know where a candidate stands on the matter of welfare reform, but they can make reasonably accurate inferences on the basis of the candidate's political party.

These are persuasive theories. Even political junkies cannot know everything about politics; some specialization is necessary; some things one learns only when necessary; some short-cuts to decision making are essential. But none of these arguments states that democratic citizens are better off if they are ignorant. Even cue-taking from presumably trustworthy sources can sometimes be problematic and can mislead the public, as Kuklinski and Hurley (1994) point out. Nor do these arguments suggest

that a society in which citizens are largely politically ignorant will operate as well as one in which they are better informed.[7] Delli Carpini and
Keeter (1996: 61) expressed it well: "We are not arguing that contemporary
democracy requires that all citizens be expert on all facets of national [or
other levels of] politics, but we do suggest that the more citizens are pass-
ingly informed about the issues of the day, the behavior of political leaders, and the rules under which they operate, the better off they are, the
better off *we* are."

Thus, while these arguments raise important issues, we believe that
civic knowledge is necessary and useful for citizens in a democracy and,
indeed, that democracy is incompatible with widespread ignorance about
government and politics on the part of the citizenry.[8] We are persuaded by
three arguments—one that takes an individualistic, instrumental perspective, one a collective and principled outlook, and the last a more
abstract, philosophical viewpoint. Consider first the perspective of the
individual.

For democratic decision making to be meaningful and legitimate, citizens must be capable of understanding what is at stake in politics, what
their alternatives are, and what their own positions are. Theoretically, at
least, individuals in a democracy have a good deal of power over collective decisions that affect them. Thus, one might say that from an *instrumental* standpoint, knowledge is a prerequisite to successful political engagement—that is, to pursuing and defending one's interests in politics
(Nie et al., 1996: chap. 2). To assume otherwise is to believe that some individuals need not or cannot speak for themselves, that another set of citizens should and can represent them accurately. At the extreme, it suggests that some individuals are actually better off if they let others look
after their interests. From a perspective purely of external rewards, this is
clearly the case in some instances. But to presume that we should disre-
gard civic education because individuals are often politically ignorant is
to accept a strongly anti-democratic standard of representation. To dis-
count or disallow voice on the basis of political ignorance effectively de-
nies citizens the liberty to pursue individual interests.

Nevertheless, an argument based on instrumental knowledge is not
enough. Democratic politics is not the unbridled exercise of individual
rights or the unqualified pursuit of individual (short-run) interests; it is
also an acceptance of the responsibilities and limits of collective political life. Thus, it is also necessary that citizens have knowledge of political
principles, especially an understanding of the basic rules of the democratic game. It is clear that democracy does not require complete agreement
on all matters and that consensus cannot be expected. But tolerating dis-

agreement over interpretations of important principles of democratic governance is very different from saying that widely shared beliefs are unnecessary. Critics might object that we are now straying into the realm of attitudes or beliefs about proper behavior in a democracy and not about knowledge as such. Empirically, however, as has often been noted, there is a close connection between level of education and support given to basic democratic norms (Stouffer, 1954; Sullivan, Piereson, and Marcus, 1982; McClosky and Zaller, 1984; Sniderman et al., 1989, 1991; Nie et al., 1996). Evidently, those who fail to understand the significance of democratic norms often fail to believe in them.[9]

Civic knowledge is important from yet a third perspective. Democracy assumes that there is some degree of equality among citizens. In the private sector, resources and ability are variously rewarded. But the government ought not to be systematically more responsive to some than to others. The phrase "one-person, one vote," derived from legislative redistricting cases in the 1960s, aptly sums up the principle that all citizens should be equal in their ability to influence the initiation and application of laws. This, too, is an ideal that is only approximated, but a democratic society should not sanction anything that reduces the ability of citizens to participate with equal effectiveness. Ability and willingness to participate depend on a host of factors, but knowledge is prominent among them. Failure to understand what is at stake or how best to influence collective decision making can, in Delli Carpini and Keeter's words, "combine to produce a stratified political system that affords different access to political power—and thus one that is more or less democratic—depending on where in the knowledge hierarchy one falls" (1996: 3–4).

There is, of course, no set of guidelines that lays out how much knowledge is necessary or how widespread it has to be. Democracies surely can tolerate the presence of some who are completely ignorant (and proud of it) and some who do not understand or do not share the dominant beliefs about democratic functioning. Popular surveys as well as academic studies also make it clear that democracies can function effectively even though most citizens fall short of being what civic educators or political scientists would call well-informed. But the absence of a minimum level of acceptable political knowledge or of a maximum number of uninformed citizens that can be tolerated does not mean that knowledge is inconsequential, either from an individual or a collective point of view.

In these days of heightened cynicism, a further argument might be made for greater civic knowledge. Citizens who are more highly educated appear to hold more positive views about American society and government in general and about governmental responsiveness in particular.

Ironically, this does not come about because of naive optimism. On the basis of surveys conducted in late 1995, Morin (1996: 6) reported that the more people knew about government and politics, the more mistrustful they were of government. "But at the same time, more knowledgeable Americans expressed more faith in the American political system. They were far more likely to see their vote as a remedy for that they believed was wrong with government."

In short, political knowledge helps citizens operate effectively in a democracy, heightens their awareness of the limits of both governmental and citizen behavior, increases attainment of democratic goals by promoting more equal access among citizens, and contributes to the extent to which citizens regard their government with confidence and satisfaction.

Having accepted that some civic knowledge is needed, one might next ask what kind of knowledge is desirable. Indeed, the relevance of the general political ignorance of American citizens has sometimes been dismissed precisely on the grounds that political knowledge has been measured in the wrong way (see, for example, Graber, 1994: 341–42; Popkin, 1991: 20–21). That is, most tests given to large populations ask for isolated bits of information, such as the number of justices on the Supreme Court, the length of a senator's term, and the name of the respondent's representatives in Congress. Is it essential that citizens know these facts? And more to the point, is the NAEP test an adequate measure of what young adult citizens should know?

The answers to both these questions are equivocal. As to what citizens should know, there is no "canon" that defines what students (or adults) should know. One might identify broad themes—such as Delli Carpini and Keeter's (1996: 65) "*the rules of the game, the substance of politics, and people and parties*" or the detailed lists of facts, concepts, and principles in the voluntary national standards for civics (Center for Civic Education, 1994). But, in truth, there exists no list of essential political facts. At the same time, it is important for citizens to know some facts and, in general, the more the better. Almost any single piece of information by itself seems unessential. One can live one's daily life without knowing that the president is the commander-in-chief of the armed forces or, for that matter, without knowing the name of the president. But how many political discussions and how many news reports would be incomprehensible without this information? And the more political information citizens have, the more sense they can make of those discussions and news reports and the more they can contribute to such discussions.

As to how best to measure political knowledge, several recent analysts have made strong arguments for the use of a battery of factual items. Delli

Carpini and Keeter (1996) argue that "factual political knowledge is the most important component of a broader notion of political sophistication" (294); in their study, as in ours, the "analyses are limited to a finite set of facts, but this set includes a very large number of survey questions on a very wide range of political topics" (15). Similarly, Luskin (1987: 890), after considering various classes of measurement of political sophistication, argues that "because they are more direct than abstractness-based measures, I suspect that information-holding measures represent the best *single* existing approach." Zaller (1992: 21) also argues that "political awareness" is, "for both theoretical and empirical reasons, best measured by simple tests of neutral factual information about politics. The reason, in brief, is that tests of political information, more directly than any of the alternative measures, capture what has actually gotten into people's minds, which, in turn, is critical for intellectual engagement with politics."

As to the NAEP test specifically, the absence of a canon of civic knowledge means that no test can hope to cover all the information that might be considered important. Nonetheless, because of the process by which it was constructed, the NAEP test is an excellent, if imperfect, assessment of the goals and standards for civic education. Civics by its very nature is a controversial subject, and there is imperfect agreement on both its meaning and how to test whether students are well informed about it. The 1994 publication *National Standards for Civics and Government* (Center for Civic Education, 1994), for example, was generally well received, but it was not exempt from sharp criticism (Dry, 1996; Merelman, 1996).[10]

Because of the controversial nature of their topics, NAEP assessments are the product of an extensive series of meetings and even more extensive consultations concerning the appropriate test content and manner of testing. Teachers, curriculum specialists, administrators, university faculty, and others are brought together to consider what students ought to know about each subject. Clearly there is an effort to test what students are being taught. As stated (in somewhat negative fashion) in the Civics Committee's description of the development process (*Civics*, 1987: 5), the guidelines were "reviewed extensively by teachers, curriculum specialists, and school administrators to ensure that the assessment topics do not diverge substantially from current instructional practice or expectations." At the same time, NAEP assessments are not strictly confined to what is presently taught in average or representative classrooms. Or, more precisely, they are not geared strictly to showing what students have learned but rather to what they *ought to* know. This is most clearly seen in the fact that the assessments seek to determine "levels of proficiency" in the subject being tested (see Anderson et al., 1990, chaps. 2–3). Thus, the assessment on which this book is based is intended to evaluate what a large and varied group of individuals believed to be representative of what is being taught and of what should be taught about civics and U.S. government.[11]

Sources of Political Knowledge

In spite of the controversy over how much and what types of political knowledge are necessary in a democracy, as well as disagreement about actual observed levels of such knowledge in the mass public, there is virtual unanimity on one point: formal education is the strongest, most consistent correlate (and is widely considered the central causal determinant) of political knowledge. This finding has been replicated in study after study (Hyman, Wright, and Reed, 1975; Delli Carpini and Keeter, 1996; Nie et al., 1996). Regardless of how political knowledge is measured, formal education is the single most important factor differentiating those who know more about politics from those who know less. Citizens who spend more years in school simply know a lot more about politics.

There is far less certainty, however, about what components of formal education make citizens more knowledgeable. Even the massive report by Coleman and his colleagues (1966) could not pinpoint the specific educational factors that contributed to student achievement. True, the Coleman report focused on variations among schools and not on variations in levels of schooling (see Hyman, Wright, and Reed, 1975: 112–13); but it nonetheless suggests the difficulties associated with trying to assess exactly how education leads to greater political knowledge.

Some argue that it is not education itself that makes the difference, but rather that a process of selection bias leads smarter and more motivated students to acquire more formal education. In this case, schooling itself has little effect; rather, the differences between those with more or less formal education can be attributed to such correlates as intelligence, social class, parental involvement in learning, and other life circumstances. Precisely this argument was made in Luskin's (1990) study reporting that, once intelligence and other variables were taken into account, education had no effect on "political sophistication" about political candidates and parties. Luskin then asks: If this is true, why do so many studies show a correlation between education and sophistication? His answer: "The simplest explanation is the paucity of [statistical] controls. The studies showing an education effect do not always partial [i.e., control] on interest, and never on intelligence or occupation qua political impingement. So 'education's' effect may really be intelligence's, occupation's, and interest's.

Education may be taking credit for other variables' work. Students must pick up some political information in school, but apparently do not wind up knowing much or more, other things being equal, the longer they spend there" (349). Smith (1989: 210–19) makes a similar point, although for him the crucial variable left out of the equation is selection of who attains lower or higher levels of education. His data, collected in part by Niemi, concern education at the college level; he concludes that education had little effect on political knowledge because "those who went on to higher education were more knowledgeable in the beginning" (218).

The argument that schooling really makes no difference might still seem far-fetched until one considers the variety of in- and outside-of-school factors that might affect political knowledge. Let us begin with civics courses. Just as students learn about chemistry in chemistry classes and literature in English classes, we might initially assume that they learn about civics in civics classes. But setting the matter out in this fashion points to the first difficulty. Many classes are potentially sources of education about politics and government; assessing the contribution of civics classes alone does not capture all of the potential curricular influences on students.

The problem is complex. In addition to courses labeled civics or government, American history classes are important venues for lessons about politics. Indeed, as we discuss in chapter 3, statewide requirements for civics training are often formally carried out in these history classes. But even courses in literature are sometimes mentioned as a source of political learning. Take, for example, disagreements over what literature should be included in the curriculum. In some instances, students may be unaware of these disagreements, but in other cases they will be directly involved. A classic case is Mark Twain's work, in which the characters frequently use a demeaning racial epithet. There have been many arguments about whether his works should be read in school and what, if anything, should be said about language and race when they are. To the extent that such matters arise, and especially when they generate controversy or classroom discussion, students may well learn some political lessons, which may or may not involve learning specific political facts.

Given this complexity, it would be nearly impossible to identify all curricular influences without a detailed study of every school district involved, something that is impossible in a large-scale, nationally representative data collection. Even focusing on the most relevant courses, however, does not exhaust the possible sources of student information about government and civics. This is because civics lessons involve much more than imparting factual material or even ways of learning about the world.

An important part of civics courses involves exploring modes of decision making. This has at least two implications. First, it means that attitudes or values immediately become relevant. That is, it is almost impossible to separate knowledge and values entirely in teaching about politics and government. Unless one discusses only written rules or laws (such as Senate rules about invoking cloture or constitutional procedures involving presidential vetoes), discussions about decision making will almost invariably involve judgments. Are the procedures by which decisions are made fair? Are the decisions good ones? By whose standards? What happens to those who disagree with the rules? We shall see shortly that the close connection between knowledge and values is reflected in research about the effects of civics courses.

The second implication is that classroom and school procedures can themselves be an important part of the learning process. What is variously referred to as the context of instruction or the hidden curriculum (Patrick, 1977: 204–6; Patrick and Hoge, 1991) may be a major force in the development of political attitudes among students, especially of their feelings about and willingness to participate in the political process. (For a contrary view, see Merelman, 1980.) The context includes not only the method of interaction and discourse in the classroom (Wilen and White, 1991) but also the overall "school climate" (Jennings, Ehman, and Niemi, 1974: 221–25; Ehman, 1980: 110–14; Leming, 1985: 156–63). Likewise, participation in extracurricular activities has sometimes been cited as a contributor to more participatory attitudes, as well as to actual participation (Beck and Jennings, 1982; Holland and Andre, 1987; Verba, Scholzman, and Brady, 1995: chap. 15). While the effects of school climate and procedures are usually thought to be attitudinal, a few studies suggest that they may also be related to levels of knowledge as well, especially if knowledge is defined as the acquisition of certain kinds of conceptual frameworks and skills, as opposed to the accumulation of basic facts (Patrick, 1977: 206–12).

Finally, there is a strong presumption that learning about politics and government also takes place outside the school. In some curricular areas, this is less likely to be true. Some parents may have the expertise and inclination to help their children with calculus and chemistry, but it is probable that families infrequently involve themselves with these subjects. In the case of civic knowledge, such an assumption is untenable. Few parents may consciously direct the political learning of their children, but parental attitudes about government and politics are often expressed in daily conversations. Even if these attitudes are merely expressions of overall likes or dislikes, they can alter youthful interest, which in turn can affect the amount of attention students pay to the subject. More-over, politics surrounds us; students cannot avoid confronting govern-ment issues in the form of taxes, bureaucracies (the Department of Motor Vehicles, for example), laws, and appearances by candidates on television (Bill Clinton's appearance on MTV, for example). Finally, families, like schools, have different modes of decision making, which may influence students' attitudes toward it, if not their knowledge of how government decision makers operate (Almond and Verba, 1963: chap. 12; Chaffee, McLeod, and Wackman, 1973).

Perhaps because curricular effects are so difficult to verify, previous studies have often found few that can be attributed to the civics curricu-lum. Indeed, the accepted wisdom in the political science profession is that civics classes have little or no effect on the vast majority of students. Beck, for example, concluded his view of the role of "agents" of political socialization by saying that "social studies teachers, civics courses, and extracurricular activities seem to have little impact on students' political views" (1977: 131). He attributed these largely null findings to the possi-bility that "the messages they [school-related agents] contain have already been communicated to the students by other agents (or by earlier school experiences)."

This theme is echoed over and over in the literature. Morrison and McIntyre (1971: 174), reviewing much the same material as Beck, con-cluded that "there is virtually no evidence of a primary independent ef-fect arising from education, and most of the educational studies indicate that such effects as arise do so from individuals being in educational com-munities rather than from processes of school or further learning." On knowledge specifically, they note the "relative ineffectiveness of educa-tion" (174). Gutmann (1987: 105–7) offers a hopeful note about the pos-sibilities inherent in civics teaching, but she recites the familiar line that history and civics courses "are not a major source of political socializa-tion" (107). Erikson and Tedin (1995: 131), in the fifth edition of their pop-ular text on public opinion, claim that "the thrust of the empirical re-search seems to indicate that schools have little if any effect on teaching of the democratic creed or political values in general." They also cite neg-ative findings about the effects of course work on knowledge (131–32; see also Corbett, 1991: 214–15).

Works in the field of education are more mixed. Patrick and Hoge (1991: 432–33), for example, cite positive effects of school variables on civic knowledge, although they also report that school factors are much less effective in creating civic attitudes. Wilen and White (1991: 485–87) cite both positive and negative results in studies of the relationship between teaching styles and students' cognitive skills. But the most visible works in the field are perhaps the criticisms launched in the 1980s against the overall quality of U.S. education (most notably *A Nation at Risk,* 1983). These attacks focused primarily on science and reading and their relationship to job productivity and economic competitiveness, but civics and such related fields as geography and history were not spared (Murphy, 1990: chap. 1).

In one of the more visible of these attacks, Hirsch (1987: chap. 5) placed the blame for young Americans' lack of "cultural literacy" (about historical and political facts and personalities, among other things) on the schools. Ravitch and Finn (1987), on the other hand, in summarizing the results of their large-scale survey, pointed away from students in arguing that "youngsters are not the causes of their own ignorance" (203) and pointed toward the schools by suggesting reforms and improvements that focused prominently on the educational system. In a 1996 study, schools of education and school districts across the country were blamed for the failure to establish and uphold teacher standards (National Commission on Teaching, 1996). If, in addition, one equates good citizenship with such qualities as self-discipline, interest in government and politics, and participation in civic life, there is a prima facie case for the failure of civic education in the widespread political cynicism of American adults (Stanley and Niemi, 1995: 157). Whatever the effects of schooling might actually be, attacks on contemporary education suggest that they are insufficient or misguided.

In fact, the literature—at least about political knowledge—is neither as one-sided nor as conclusive as these views would suggest. (For a general, broad-ranging critique, see Berliner and Biddle, 1995.) Schools in general and individual classes in particular have often been found to have significant effects on student learning. We have already pointed out, for example, that some studies suggest a connection between teacher style and student knowledge. Torney, Oppenheim, and Farnen (1975: 158) also looked at teacher style, along with other classroom and school characteristics; they found that even after controlling for home environment (parental education and occupation, number of books in the home), gender, age, and a proxy for general verbal competence, "knowledge about the school attended makes possible a better prediction of performance on the IEA Civic Education cognitive test." Their conclusion is noteworthy because it is based on the largest cross-national study of civic education so far completed.

With respect to civics classes per se, many small-scale studies—which have had the corresponding advantage of experimental design—have found positive effects. Patrick (1972) reported that a course created to introduce modern political science in high schools had an impact on the political knowledge and skills of students. Likewise, an evaluation of an experimental course developed in the context of the American bicentennial evidently had a great impact on student knowledge (Stretcher, 1988). Elsewhere, Westholm, Lindquist, and Niemi (1990) found a significant impact of both civics and history courses in Sweden; Denver and Hands (1990) established the effects of civic training in Great Britain; Morduchowicz and her colleagues (1996) described positive effects of a newspaper program on the political knowledge of Argentine youth; and Wormald (1988) reported effects of civics courses in Papua New Guinea. Even Ravitch and Finn (1987), despite their negative conclusions about student achievement, indicate that the number and kind of history courses taken by students are related to history knowledge (174–78)—results that they find "unremarkable" (174) and "unsurprising" (176).

Why, then, does the conventional wisdom hold that school, and civics courses in particular, have no effect on political knowledge, and what does this belief suggest for the inquiry in this book? The answer to the first probably lies in the fact that there are prominent studies in which researchers failed to find anticipated effects. For political scientists, the most important such study was conducted in the 1960s as part of a large-scale investigation of political socialization (Jennings and Niemi, 1974). The initial report on school effects was published by Langton and Jennings in 1968. The researchers obtained self-reports from students on the overall number of social studies courses taken, number of history courses taken, and specific government courses taken, such as Problems of Democracy and American Government. No matter how they analyzed the course work, they found almost no relation between civics courses and political knowledge or other political orientations. Langton and Jennings's conclusion minced no words; they argued that results gave no support to the notion that the civics curriculum is "even a minor source of political socialization" (865). Reinforcing their view were results from a number of college-level studies in the late 1950s and early 1960s that also failed to establish a connection between courses in political science and how much students knew (Somit et al., 1958; Robinson et al., 1966).

Studies in the education field have also shown no effect of course work on political knowledge. Despite its basically positive conclusion about educational effects in the IEA study, under close examination, Torney, Oppenheim, and Farnen's (1975) work reveals that in the United States, the apparent effects of "learning conditions" were vanishingly small (155). And Farnen (1990, 66) himself later argued that the effects reported in their joint work were related to the nature of classroom instruction but not to exposure to civic education as such. NAEP studies themselves have lent little support—and that equivocal—for the significance of the school curriculum. Regarding the effect of civics curricula on knowledge, a report describing the 1988 NAEP data highlighted the puzzling finding that "the amount of civics instruction received appeared to be unrelated to students' proficiency" (Anderson et al., 1990: 74).

In addition to these negative results, pronouncements deriding the importance of the curriculum and other school characteristics to political knowledge have almost certainly been influenced by the findings of attitudinal studies. Such studies have tended to find fewer positive effects than have purely cognitive studies. Jacob (1957), for example, in his summary of research on college students in the 1940s and 1950s, was highly skeptical about the effects of the curriculum, teachers, or methods of instruction on such values as political tolerance. Hyman and Wright (1979: 65–67) take pains to explain why the effects of education on values are significant, even though "their cumulative weight in the mind's scales does not appear as great as that observed in the realm of knowledge" (65). Patrick (1977: 215), in writing about innovative curricular practices of the 1970s, notes that "for the most part, the project evaluation studies report little or no impact on attitudinal learning." Ferguson (1991: 392) notes that social studies instruction has few effects, and where they occur, they are "more instrumental in promoting knowledge . . . [than] participatory attitudes and skills." And studies by political scientists have often found only limited effects of civic education on students' values (Langton and Jennings, 1968; Merelman, 1971).

Nevertheless, even here the studies have been anything but uniformly negative. Indeed, a large number have found that all levels of schooling influence many types of attitudes. This includes studies of specific courses (Button, 1974; Liebschutz and Niemi, 1974; Goldenson, 1978; Avery et al., 1992; Brody, 1994) and kinds of instruction (Hahn, 1991); meta-analyses of colleges and of education generally (Feldman and Newcomb, 1969; Hyman and Wright, 1979); studies at the elementary (Tolley, 1973; Targ, 1975), high school (Litt, 1963), and college (Newcomb, 1943) levels; cross-sectional and longitudinal studies (Newcomb et al., 1967); and comparative studies (Almond and Verba, 1963; Torney et al., 1975; Wittebrood, 1995). (See also the host of studies on "values clarification" and its effects on attitudes, such as Leming, 1985.)

Thus, despite the negative position of the political science profession, the chorus of complaints about schools in general, and the equivocal findings of the NAEP study, there are reasons to reassess the effects of schooling on knowledge of government and politics. The ambiguous and contradictory conclusions of past research, combined with the putative role of education as the central causal determinant of political knowledge, compel us to make a better effort to understand both what high school students know and what in the context of their educational experiences assists them in gaining political knowledge.

In our efforts to solve some of the mysteries surrounding this issue, we have been helped considerably by the availability of the NAEP data and by the research strategy that they make possible. Researchers have often been stymied in their efforts to analyze the underlying effects of formal education by the absence of adequate data. The majority of the results, whether from political scientists or from educators, come from small-scale, often experimental studies, where Hawthorne effects and generalizability are key concerns, or from cross-sectional samples of the adult population, where there are few measures of either political knowledge or educational experience and background. As a consequence, scholars have generally found it difficult both to assess the validity of competing explanations of educational effects and to isolate the effects of specific elements of the educational experience.

To overcome these limitations and to identify and analyze the mechanisms hidden inside the "black box" of the education variable, it is necessary to use measures of political knowledge and educational experiences that are both broad and deep. Only good measures of political knowledge, the civics curriculum, individual achievement and motivation, parental and familial characteristics, and other individual background traits can help us ascertain the validity of competing explanations of why education has such a large impact on political knowledge. The 1988 NAEP Civics Assessment provides an unparalleled opportunity to isolate and sort out these effects because it includes all these measures applied to a representative sample of high school seniors.

In particular, the set of test items available to us is far superior to that in other studies of civic knowledge. As noted earlier, the 1988 NAEP Civics Assessment includes 150 multiple-choice items, covering a wide variety of topics about American government and politics. Other studies have had far fewer. Langton and Jennings's (1968) study contained only six factual questions; Rodgers's (1973) had four; Sigel and Hoskin's (1981) fifteen; Bachman's (1969) five; Westholm, Lindquist, and Niemi's (1990) eight. Torney, Oppenheim, and Farnen's (1975) study was much broader, but even it had only a third of the number of items available in the NAEP study.

The 1988 NAEP Civics Assessment

The National Assessment of Educational Progress is an ongoing, congressionally mandated project that was established in 1969 to obtain comprehensive data on the educational achievement of American students. NAEP studies cover a wide range of subjects; in each case, the core of the assessment is a test given to a nationally representative sample of students in grades 4, 8, and 12. In the winter and spring of 1988, approximately 11,000 students were tested as part of the Civics Assessment. We draw on the sample of 4,275 twelfth graders who took part in the study.

The civics test was developed on the basis of recommendations of an advisory committee consisting of university professors, elementary and secondary school teachers, school administrators, and curriculum specialists. Three objectives, related to context, cognition, and content, guided the design and selection of test items. Context was the most straightforward of the test areas. Most questions at the twelfth-grade level focused on national and state governments, although some emphasized local communities, were more theoretical in nature, or, in a few instances, dealt with comparative perspectives.

By *cognition,* the planners of the Civics Assessment meant that questions were to be divided into two major categories. The first concerned what students know. This was defined as "the ability to recall specific facts and concepts, to show familiarity with relevant terminology, and to recognize basic procedures and ideas" (*Civics,* 1987: 10). Second, students were to be tested as to their ability to understand and apply. This required them "to examine their own views, to determine the validity of information and arguments, and to make judgments and decisions based on the comparative merit of available alternatives" (10).

Finally, question content was designed to cover four substantive categories: Democratic Principles and the Purpose of Government (principles underlying the Constitution, changes in interpretations of concepts and value, and so on); Political Institutions (including principles, structure, and operation of the U.S. government, and organization and functions of state and local governments); Political Processes (how laws are passed, implemented, and reviewed; influences on government; how conflicts are resolved); and Rights, Responsibilities, and the Law (the Bill of Rights, civil and criminal law, responsibilities of citizenship). In the actual set of test questions, there was a greater emphasis on some topics, such as government structures and rights and responsibilities, than on others, such as political parties.

For our purposes, the important point about these objectives is the breadth of coverage, both in terms of subject matter and skills required to answer the questions. We shall say more about this in the next chapter, but it is important to emphasize at the outset that the wide variety of questions in the 1988 Civics Assessment makes it possible to identify the specific subject areas in which students are well-versed and those in which they are ignorant. Moreover, we can assess, to some degree at least, student performance on questions with a more demanding format than simple recall—questions that ask about comprehension of texts and the interpretation of charts and figures, for example.

The actual study design was complicated. In order to avoid problems of fatigue, no student was given the full set of 150 questions; instead, each received a subset in a so-called spiral design. This and other aspects of the design are described in Appendix A. One subset of students was asked to name the current U.S. president and then to write one or more paragraphs about the president's responsibilities. Two other multiple-choice items dealt with perceived government responsiveness to people and electoral results. It is unfortunate that so little of the test consisted of open-ended, or constructed-response, items. On the other hand, the reliance on brief items meant that a large number of individual topics could be covered. We take advantage of this by grouping the items, not into the four broad categories used by the test designers, but under a variety of subject-specific headings, such as Criminal and Civil Justice, State and Local Government, Political Parties, and Women and Minorities. For this reason, as well as for interpretability, we shall use the percentage of correct answers as our criterion of success for the 150 factual items, rather than the proficiency score of plausible values used in the NAEP reports.

In addition to the test itself, all students were given a background questionnaire (this is common to all NAEP studies), along with a short civics questionnaire, in which they answered questions about their interest in civics and government, their course work, and their participation in student government. Characteristics of the schools were supplied by a principal or other school administrator, who filled out another questionnaire. Information from these three questionnaires allows us to describe how test scores vary across important groups defined at both the individual and school or community level and to make inferences about the likely sources of higher and lower scores.

A final note concerns the reporting of test items. Working with what amounts to an ongoing test raises an unusual problem for those, like political scientists, who analyze public surveys. We are bound to maintain the confidentiality of many of the individual test items in order to retain their utility for future civics assessments. Short descriptions of almost all items are provided by Anderson and colleagues (1990: 108–10), but these are not always a reliable guide to exact content. We were given access to the complete wording of all questions, so we are confident about the subject-matter classifications we report in chapter 2. Some twenty-five questions that were designated for public release by the assessors are provided in Appendix B.

CHAPTER TWO

What High School Students Know (and Don't Know) about Civics

It is fashionable these days to argue that students fail even the most basic tests of geographic, historical, political, and other knowledge. A report on the 1988 Geography NAEP, for example, concludes that students "lack an understanding" of locations and population distributions and fall short in map reading and other geographic skills (Allen et al., 1990: 23, 31). Ravitch and Finn (1987: 46) begin their review of the 1986 History NAEP by saying that "the amount of 'commendable' performance on this assessment is exceedingly sparse. Barely a tenth of the questions reveal A or B level knowledge on the part of American eleventh grade students." With respect to government and politics, *The Civics Report Card* (Anderson et al., 1990: 40) notes with "disappointment" that only half of the high school seniors reached a level of competence described as "understanding specific government structures and functions." Further disappointment is expressed over the fact that only 6 percent achieved a "broader and more detailed knowledge of the various institutions of government."

It would be easy to take this line and fill these pages with examples of students' inability to answer "basic" questions about civics and government. Take, for example, the matter of representation in Congress. On a question about the number of representatives from each state in the U.S. House of Representatives, nearly 40 percent of the seniors answered incorrectly, believing that each state has two or three representatives or that the number varies according to the area of the state. A similar proportion did not know how many senators are elected from each state (many of

them thinking that the number of senators varies according the population of the state). An even larger proportion—just over half of the students—did not know that "under the United States Constitution, the
power to tax belongs to Congress" (rather than to the president, the
Supreme Court, or the Department of the Treasury). And nearly two-thirds
did not know that a political action committee (PAC) is "an organization
set up by a special-interest group to raise money for a candidate."

Our purpose, however, is not to add another demonstration of the in-
adequacies of contemporary American education. We especially do not
wish to add an "undifferentiated" voice to that choir. That is, we think
that it is more useful to indicate what students do know along with what
they don't, rather than emphasizing only the latter. Therefore, we concentrate on the *relative* ability of high school seniors to answer political-
knowledge questions. In some instances, we find that their knowledge is
considerable, while in other instances it is woefully lacking.

Identifying students' relative abilities provides insight into the areas
that need more emphasis in civics and American government classes. But
it also gives us clues about young people's interests in matters related to
government and politics, as well as indicators of the alternative sources of
their knowledge, a subject we shall only begin to explore in this chapter.

To determine students' relative levels of knowledge, we divide the test
questions into a number of substantive categories. We make no claim that
the items under any given heading exhaust the subject matter or even that
they address all the components that could be included under that heading. Nor do we assert that each of the categories is separate in the sense
that it taps a differential ability on the part of students. Indeed, a recent
study of adults indicates that individuals tend to be generalists when it
comes to civic knowledge: those who are knowledgeable in one area tend
to be knowledgeable in others (Delli Carpini and Keeter, 1996: 294–95;
also see below). But it does not follow from this that they have equal
knowledge of all topics. Therefore, by categorizing items according to
subject matter, we can reach a more detailed understanding of the kinds of
subjects that students have learned about as well as where their knowledge is most deficient.

The categories do not have strict boundary lines. Several questions
about minorities, for example, could be included in the category Rights
of Citizens rather than in Women and Minorities. Nonetheless, we have
treated the categories as mutually exclusive, including each test item in
only one group. Not surprisingly, a large number of the items deal with
the Constitution, particularly, various provisions or applications and interpretations of those provisions. Rather than lumping these items to-

gether, we have grouped them by the subjects they refer to—criminal and civil justice, state and local government—with a residual, catch-all category on the structure and functioning of the national government. Using these guidelines, we were able to classify nearly all of the 150 multiple-choice questions; only a few miscellaneous items defy classification.

One category is substantially different from the rest, in that the questions ask students to make inferences from textual or tabular material rather than to choose answers based on memorized facts. Were there more than a handful of such questions, we would deal with them in a separate chapter, as the ability to work with written and pictorial material is to some extent distinct from and at least as important as the memorization of facts. But there are only a few such questions. Indeed, in this case as in some others, we base our conclusions in part on an assessment of the questions as well as on the answers.

Overall, the items—and therefore our categories—place a heavier emphasis than we would like on formal rules and procedures and on structural aspects of government. At times we criticize the questions precisely on the grounds that they reflect civics classes that are too limited in their focus. At the same time, it is reasonable that a test given to seventeen-year-olds, who have only begun to take politics seriously, should not place too great an emphasis on contemporary public figures or policy issues. In addition, the creators of the Civics Assessment will probably want to use some of the questions in future tests, perhaps a decade or more later, in order to gauge educational progress.

The question about presidential responsibilities—the only one requiring students to provide a written answer—will be handled separately toward the end of the chapter. Finally, we shall briefly discuss the two questions on government responsiveness. By themselves these questions can only provide a glimpse into the civic attitudes of high school seniors; still, they are of intrinsic interest, and they allow us to generalize in a small way our understanding of the role of school factors and other influences on the political world of high school seniors.

For each of the subject areas in this chapter, we shall organize all the items into a single table, arranging them from high to low according to the percentage of correct answers. The 1988 NAEP employed a complex sampling scheme rather than a simple random sampling technique. Each individual student is therefore assigned a sampling weight that reflects his or her probability of being selected. Analyses of these data must utilize these weights. The computation of standard errors of estimates of descriptive and inferential statistics employs a jackknife technique. In this chapter, the proportions giving a correct answer to each question are based on weighted *N*s ranging from 211,162 to 227,729, with raw *N*s ranging from 1,701 to 1,850.[1] The standard errors of these proportions range from 0.4 to 1.8; as a general rule, extreme proportions have low standard errors and proportions near the middle (50 percent) have higher standard errors. (For exact values of standard errors, see Appendix C.) The average percentage correct, shown at the bottom of the table, gives a rough indication of the level of knowledge in that area. One should not infer too much from these summary figures, however, as it will become clear that apparent levels of knowledge are greatly affected by the precise questions asked as well as by the plausibility of the incorrect answers. Public-release items are denoted with an asterisk; the complete wording of these questions is available in Appendix B. The remaining questions are either secured release or nonrelease questions; under certain conditions of confidentiality, the wordings are made available to researchers by application to the National Center for Education Statistics.

Criminal and Civil Justice

We begin by looking at two topics on which students are well-informed, at least in some respects: the criminal and civil justice system and the general (noncriminal) rights of citizens. Table 2.1 shows how knowledgeable high school seniors are about our system of justice. To begin with, they are especially well-versed in criminal rights. Ninety percent or more knew that Americans have the right to a lawyer, to know what they are accused of, and to remain silent when they are arrested and that a person cannot be kept in jail indefinitely without proof of guilt. Almost all students, we suspect, are also aware that police must read suspects their rights before questioning them about a crime; nearly three-quarters correctly answered a question about this right even though the question identified it only by reference to the Supreme Court's Miranda ruling.

Somewhat fewer students know about other aspects of the criminal and civil justice system. Nonetheless, more than 70 percent were able to answer most questions on this issue, even when the questions dealt with such things as the rights of a landlord to sue a tenant—something that students are unlikely to have encountered in their own lives and something that is not the stuff of television dramas. When the question involved "second-order" or less immediate considerations—the right to appeal a case to a higher court, say—the number of students who answered correctly dropped farther.

It is not hard to find explanations for the high level of student knowledge about the justice system. For one thing, movies and television pro-

Table 2.1 Knowledge of Criminal and Civil Justice
(Percentage Correct)

Right to a lawyer	98
Right to know what one is accused of	97
Right to remain silent	94
No right to go free	92
The right to counsel means the right to be represented by a lawyer*	91
Accused cannot be kept in jail indefinitely without proof of guilt	90
Duty of a jury in a criminal trial is to determine guilt	87
Police can do nothing unless a law is broken	84
Defendants in criminal cases are innocent until proven guilty	79
Suing someone in court is legal	76
Invoking the Fifth Amendment means avoiding self-incrimination*	75
Miranda ruling means reading rights to an arrested person before questioning	73
Landlord may bring lawsuit against tenant	73
Appeal criminal case in higher court	67
Ban on double jeopardy	47
Average	82

Note: Results in tables 2.1–2.8 are based on weighted *N*s ranging from 211,162 to 227,729; raw *N*s range from 1,701 to 1,850. Standard errors of the proportions range from 0.4 to 1.8; extreme proportions have low standard errors and proportions near 50 percent have higher standard errors.
*Public-release item.

grams are filled with such information, especially about individual rights. It is hard to imagine a seventeen-year-old who has not watched scenes of the police arresting a suspect and "reading him his rights." From this perspective, it also makes sense that fewer students (though still a high percentage) know that the police can "do nothing" unless a law is broken; similarly, a reasonable percentage know that one can appeal a case in a higher court. These ideas have also formed the bases of movie and television plots, which gives them considerable visibility. Yet they occur less frequently in these venues than do ordinary arrests. And the sight of a lawyer appealing a ruling before a higher court is not as exciting for most of us as that of a cop running down and arresting a fleeing suspect.

Rights of the accused are also likely to be remembered because they are personally relevant. We live in a time in which young people are committing many crimes. The ubiquitousness of weapons and drugs in society, and the fact that these have become issues in the schools themselves, mean that students are likely to have personal knowledge (directly or through friends and acquaintances) about matters of search and seizure and police procedures. But even apart from such factors, it is likely that every student has encountered the police in one way or another. Driving—a major event in teenage life—immediately brings to mind traffic tickets, drunk driving, and accidents, all of which involve the police and often the courts.

Yet another explanation for relatively high levels of knowledge about the justice system is the infusion into the curriculum of "law-related education" (LRE) in the ten years prior to the NAEP assessment. A number of nationwide surveys indicate a rapid growth in LRE courses between the mid-1970s and mid-1980s (Patrick and Hoge, 1991: 428). The goal of LRE is not specialized legal education; nevertheless, its emphasis on "the knowledge and understanding, skills, attitudes and appreciations necessary to respond effectively to the law and legal issues in our complex and changing society" (Study Group on Law-Related Education, 1978: 50) surely places a much greater emphasis on the justice system than is found in more general civics and American government courses. But the impact of LRE should not be overestimated. Despite its rise in popularity, LRE was offered in fewer than half the nation's states, and then only as an elective. Moreover, students do not learn everything they are taught. Leaving for later the question of the overall impact of the curriculum, we have only to note here that most seniors have been exposed to course work covering facts about provisions of the U.S. Constitution, yet their ability to answer questions on these provisions is markedly lower than their knowledge of the justice system (see table 2.6, below, and the related discussion).

Finally, note that despite the generally high level of knowledge about the justice system, less than half of the students recognized the ban on double jeopardy. It may be that students understand the concept and are simply unaware of the term. But this degree of unfamiliarity cautions us that students' knowledge may be somewhat shallow even in the areas they know best.

General (Noncriminal) Rights of Citizens

Students are also likely to know about the noncriminal rights of citizens, although they are much less secure in their knowledge of where those rights are spelled out (table 2.2). Not surprisingly, students are most likely to know about rights in a very general sense. Thus, for example, more than 90 percent know that presenting one's views to the media and writing protest letters are legal activities. They also know that various other actions, such as choosing one's neighbors, refusing to obey laws, and refusing to pay taxes, are illegal.

When it comes to specific applications of these rights, there is greater uncertainty. One question inquired whether citizens had to allow neither, one, or both of two mainline advocacy groups should be allowed to speak in their community. Only three-quarters of the students answered that

Table 2.2 Knowledge of General Rights of Citizens
(Percentage Correct)

Choosing neighbors is not a constitutional right	96
Refusing to obey laws is illegal	95
Refusing to pay taxes is illegal[a]	94
First ten amendments of the Constitution deal with individual rights*	93
Presenting views to media is legal	91
Writing protest letters is legal	91
Constitution protects individual freedoms	91
Citizens cannot refuse to pay taxes[a]	86
Congress cannot restrict freedom of press	85
Congress cannot establish national church	83
Yelling "fire" in a crowded auditorium not an expression of freedom of speech	77
Two advocacy groups should both be allowed to speak in community	77
First amendment to the Constitution guarantees freedom of religion*	64
Hunger strikes are legal	64
Participating in a boycott is legal	62
Organizing a recall election is legal	62
The right to religious freedom is in the amendments to the Constitution	52
Average	80

[a]There were two different questions on this subject.
*Public-release item.

both groups should be allowed to speak, suggesting that general lessons about freedom of speech have not been thoroughly internalized. Such findings have their counterpart in studies of adults. But adult studies have usually asked about speeches by unpopular groups—communists, those against churches and religion, those who favor government ownership of railroads and big industries, and racists (Prothro and Grigg, 1960; Niemi, Mueller, and Smith, 1989, chap. 4). In the question asked of seniors, the groups were nonsubversive and nonthreatening to conventional norms.

Students were also uncertain about "unconventional" or even conventional but less typical political behavior: less than two-thirds, for example, knew that it is legal to go on a hunger strike or to organize a recall election. Significantly, only about the same proportion knew that participating in a boycott is legal, despite the fact that this point is likely to have been made in history lessons (about the Montgomery bus boycott in the 1950s, for example) as well as in civics classes. Ironically, as we discuss later, a large proportion (nearly 85 percent) of the twelfth graders taking the 1988 history NAEP were able to identify Rosa Parks as the woman who sparked the Montgomery boycott.[2]

As with criminal and civil justice, students' relatively high levels of knowledge about individual rights might be attributable, in part, to their own experience and that of their friends (as well as to the existence of law-related education). Certainly the need to obey laws is something that everyone has personal experience with. In addition, many seventeen-year-olds work for pay, which makes even those who have not heard their parents complaining aware of the obligation to pay taxes. And nothing in their experience is likely to suggest that they have a right to choose their neighbors. It is when matters are outside their experience—such as participating in a boycott, for most students—that they are less aware and unable to apply lessons they presumably learned in the classroom.

Although students know about freedoms at a general level, their ability to explain the origins of those rights is less certain. Sometimes this results in seemingly contradictory responses. More than 90 percent of the students correctly noted that the first ten amendments to the Constitution deal with individual rights (rather than with methods of electing the president, powers to tax, or powers of the Supreme Court). Yet when asked what the First Amendment guarantees (freedom of religion, the right to vote, the right to an education, freedom from slavery), a third could not do so. (More than a fifth picked the right to vote.) And when asked the same question in another form, almost half could not identify the amendments to the Constitution as the source of our religious freedom. Students may have a tenuous hold on how our freedoms are guaranteed, but they do understand that Congress cannot abridge them.

State and Local Government

At an operational level, high school seniors are relatively well-informed about the division of power between the national government, on the one hand, and state and local governments, on the other, and apparently even of divisions between the latter two (table 2.3). It is not surprising, perhaps, that 90 percent or more were aware that the federal government makes treaties and that state governments regulate automobile licensing. But more than four-fifths were also aware that the federal government prints money, regulates international trade, and controls the military. Nearly three-quarters were aware that local governments run the public schools; inasmuch as there are *state* curricular guidelines, *state* graduation requirements, *state*-operated universities, and so on, this proportion seems quite high.

That the Constitution is the basis for the division of powers is also well known. On a general level, nearly three-fourths of the students recognized this point. On the other hand, examination of the incorrect answers reveals that a quarter of the students think that power belongs entirely to the federal government (11 percent) or that it is divided between the states and the federal courts (16 percent).

Table 2.3 Knowledge of State and Local Government
(Percentage Correct)

State governors are usually elected	93
Federal government makes treaties	92
State governments regulate automobile licensing	90
Federal government prints money	87
Federal government regulates international trade	85
National defense is not a responsibility of local government	82
County government is the highest level of local government in most states	82
Local government does not regulate military	81
The Constitution divides power between states and federal government*	73
Local government operates the public schools	73
The governor is the chief executive of the state	71
Federal government does not set marriage laws	66
The legislative process for a bill in most states	63
Local governments do not issue passports	58
Building interstate highways is an example of federal and state cooperation*	55
The state assembly is in the legislative branch	52
The governor is in the executive branch	50
Referendum means voting on a ballot question	50
The Constitution sets the qualifications for Congress	46
Citizens may remove officials by a recall election[a]	45
Local government does not license lawyers	39
The county sheriff is in the executive branch	27
Average	66

[a]This question emphasizes the recall election as a structure for removing elected officials; the "recall"
question in table 2.2 emphasizes the right to organize such an activity.
*Public-release item.

Students' knowledge of the division of powers also has its limits.
There was some confusion in students' minds about who issues pass-
ports. Many were unaware that the federal government does not set mar-
riage laws. A fifth thought that the states determine the qualifications for
election to Congress (this was before the term-limit movement got under
way), and about 15 percent thought that making treaties (as opposed to
building interstate highways) is a cooperative activity between the states
and the federal government. (A substantial minority also picked the
postal system as an example of federal-state cooperation.) Still, these gaps
will generally be filled in as the students get older and begin traveling,
marrying, moving. Compared to other areas of knowledge, their sense of
what is done by each level of government is good.

The limits to students' knowledge become more apparent when the inquiry turned to the structure of state government. One might think that
because 75 percent recognized Congress as belonging to the legislative
branch (see table 2.6), an equal number could properly associate state executive and legislative branches with the governor and the state assembly.
In fact, only about half are able to do so (see table 2.3). Even fewer were

able to assign the county sheriff to the executive branch, which is lower than the percentage that were able to locate the president's Cabinet (46 percent; see table 2.6). Similarly, given the considerable classroom emphasis placed on how a bill becomes a law in Congress (the subject of a question analyzed later), one might expect a large proportion of the seniors to be able recognize a description of the process used in most states. In fact, less than two-thirds were able to do so.

What is significant about these results is not so much the students' inability to answer these specific questions about state and local government. The more important point is that the students have evidently learned discrete facts (Congress belongs to the legislative branch; how a bill becomes a law in Congress) but not concepts (executive versus legislative functions; how bills become laws in bicameral legislatures). One would suppose that it is a small step from classifying and describing Congress to doing the same for state legislatures. Perhaps so, but for many high school seniors it is a leap they cannot make.

Overall, students possess a relatively good knowledge of the division of powers between the various levels of government, with the gaps in their understanding that are likely to be filled as they move into the adult world. The only disconcerting note is that they seem unable to apply what they have learned about one level to the other levels. This suggests that they lack a conceptual understanding to go along with the facts.

Parties and Lobbying

When we turn to such nonconstitutionally defined organizations and processes as political parties and lobbying, high school seniors are less well-informed. At least it would appear that way. In fact, using the NAEP Assessment to judge students' knowledge of political parties and lobbying is a difficult undertaking. Presumably reflecting the lack of in-depth coverage in civics and government courses, the NAEP questions were mainly limited to rules and procedures and to items that asked for little more than basic definitions.

A relatively high proportion of students was aware that political parties choose candidates in primary elections (table 2.4). That their knowledge was not very deep, however, is apparent in responses to additional questions. Several dealt with the presidential nomination process. Depending on how the question was phrased, only about 40–55 percent of the students correctly answered questions about the process in general, and only 40 percent knew that the parties themselves establish the procedure. More than half of the seniors were unable to say who was allowed

Table 2.4 Knowledge of Political Parties and Lobbying
(Percentage Correct)

Political Parties	
The Constitution does not define the activities of political parties	77
Parties choose candidates in primaries	74
The United States has more than two political parties	58
National convention selects presidential candidate	57
Only registered voters with a party affiliation may vote in a closed primary*	45
The procedure for nominating presidential candidates is established by the parties*	39
How presidential candidates are nominated	38
Average	55
Lobbying	
Lobbying is a legal way to change laws	84
Lobbying is legal	74
Lobbyists are known as the Third House	67
National Rifle Association activity is known as lobbying	61
The Supreme Court is the least influenced by lobbying*	57
PACs are set up by special interests to raise money for candidates*	35
Average	63

*Public-release item.

to vote in a closed primary. And many were unaware that there are more than two political parties in the United States (although given the dominance of the Democratic and Republican parties, one might regard this as something of a "trick" question).

Fewer and equally unpenetrating questions were asked about lobbying. Most of the students agreed that lobbying is a legal way to change laws. But the question construction made this an easy one to guess, as the other alternatives seemed obviously inappropriate. Another question, asking for essentially the same information but in a less weighted manner, showed that a quarter of the students were uncertain as to whether lobbying was legal. Questions about the National Rifle Association and about Political Action Committees (PACs) suggest that students have a weak grasp of who lobbyists are and what they do. Indeed, close to half could not pick out the Supreme Court as the branch of government least influenced by lobbying.

We can only wonder how much students know about the workings of contemporary American politics, in which parties and interest groups are essential ingredients. We get no sense from the NAEP questions that students are expected to do more than recognize formal structures and processes, such as the names of the political parties (a question asked of eighth graders in the NAEP history survey), the number of parties (where the answer is "more than two"), a bit about primary elections, the fact that lobbying exists and is legal, and so on.

There is nothing at all in the NAEP test concerning partisanship in the electorate: its distribution and strength, its variation across time or between groups, its role in voting. Nor are there any questions on the parties' traditional or contemporary stands on issues—or or any that ask whether the parties do, in fact, differ. Nor is there any sense that partisanship is a factor in congressional debates and voting or that it affects the judicial system. There are no questions about how lobbyists work, other than the one that showed that they "lobby," and few about who they are and what interests they represent. Thus, in addition to including only a few questions on these topics, the NAEP test suggests through the questions that are asked that seniors should be expected to know about government (structures and formal processes) but not about politics.

The absence of material on contemporary problems and conflicts found in the civics questions also characterizes the questions in the NAEP history survey. Students are expected to know the names and positions of some recent and contemporary government leaders—Gerald Ford and Sandra Day O'Connor appeared on the 1988 test—but not their partisan affiliations, ideological tendencies, or positions on issues. Likewise, partisan conflict is largely ignored; for example, there are questions about Nixon and China and about the expansion of government during the New Deal, but they make no reference to partisanship. The only reference to political parties on the history test is in a question about the Populist Party and farm support.

In part, of course, the emphasis on structures and formal processes is both understandable and appropriate. As we pointed out at the beginning of this chapter, a test designed for seventeen-year olds and for use over time cannot emphasize current events and personalities. Yet, at least judging from both the history and civics assessments, the role of parties and groups in contemporary politics plays a small role in civics teaching. Presumably, the conflicts underlying partisan and group activities are also minimized.

The nature of the material has something to do with the level of knowledge attained, as we can see if we compare students' knowledge of individual and criminal rights with their understanding of political parties and interest groups. In the first case, much of the material is directly relevant to students' lives. When it is not—when it concerns appealing cases before a higher court, say—their level of knowledge was not especially high. How knowledgeable would students be about political parties and group politics if there were more emphasis in civics courses (an emphasis that would presumably be reflected in the NAEP test) on matters of contemporary policy and politics than on structures and functions?

Women and Minorities

As with political parties and lobbying, what is most surprising about the
NAEP assessment as it pertains to women and minorities is the nature of
the items themselves (table 2.5). First, there are only a few questions. This
is so even though we have been generous in our interpretation of what
constitutes a relevant item. The question about a poll tax, for example, is
completely divorced from its historical roots; one could reasonably answer without knowing that poll taxes were once used to prevent African-
Americans from voting.

Second, the items are mostly historical in nature, ignoring (with one
exception) any contemporary references to gender and racial or ethnic
problems or concerns. Even the question about *Brown v. Board of Education* addresses only the legal point that segregated schools are unconstitu-
tional, without hinting at problems of enforcement subsequent to the decision or such current complications as segregated communities. Indeed,
the entire civil rights movement of the 1960s and beyond is ignored. This
makes the questions bland and "safe." That certain laws at one time prevented some people from voting is factually correct, but it hardly taps students' knowledge of past discrimination. And even the one contemporary
question (ignoring the poll tax item), about gender discrimination, is
phrased as an inquiry about legal principles.

Our critique of the questions should not lead readers to believe that
the questionnaire designers were biased or that they were inattentive to
matters of multiculturalism. Questions not explicitly about gender and
race or ethnicity demonstrate a concern for these matters. Note, for example, the skills question we quote below, in which "Juan" and "Faye" express points of view about order versus freedom of speech. Rather, our
point is that almost nothing is asked about women and minorities that is
of contemporary relevance. Questions about affirmative action, representation, immigration, language, and so-called glass ceilings, not to mention
problems of the inner cities, differential poverty rates, and domestic violence, are nowhere to be found.

Answers to the questions that *are* asked support an argument we made
earlier—namely, that information of direct relevance to students is usually absorbed while other material is rarely remembered. Roughly 90 percent were able to answer questions about poll taxes and sex discrimination. Since the poll tax question was actually a question about current
eligibility requirements for voting, and since many of these students would
soon turn eighteen, it is not surprising that this item was widely known.
Similarly, sex discrimination was a visible issue even in 1988. The truly

Table 2.5 Knowledge of Issues Relating to Women and Minorities
(Percentage Correct)

Payment of a poll tax is not required to vote in national elections*	91
U.S. courts can decide sex discrimination cases	89
In *Brown v. Board of Education,* Court held racially segregated schools unconstitutional	68
At one time, laws prevented some people from voting	58
Authors of a quotation were delegates to the 1848 Seneca Falls Convention*	35
Average	68

*Public-release item.

"historical" questions were correctly answered by no more than two-thirds of the twelfth graders.

Whether students have much of an appreciation of the history of race relations in the United States is hard to divine, but it would appear that their knowledge is spotty at best (judging largely from the history assessments). We noted earlier that most high school seniors (83 percent) who took the 1988 history test were able to identify Rosa Parks. Even more, 88 percent, correctly associated Martin Luther King, Jr., with the "I have a dream" speech. About the same percentage (84 percent) knew that slaves had no civil or political rights and associated the Ku Klux Klan with the use of violence to oppose minorities. Yet fewer than 60 percent claim to be aware that people were sometimes legally prevented from voting (see table 2.5). And students were frequently uninformed about the Dred Scott decision (30 percent correct), "Jim Crow laws" (30 percent), and Reconstruction (20 percent). Regarding the Jim Crow laws, over a third chose answers suggesting that such laws were adopted to *protect* the civil rights of former slaves (Ravitch and Finn 1987, 62).

With respect to women, it is clear that students could connect a number of female figures like Harriet Tubman (81 percent) and Susan B. Anthony (73 percent) with their respective movements. Yet fewer were able to identify Eleanor Roosevelt (68 percent) or Sandra Day O'Connor (66 percent), who was appointed to the Supreme Court only seven years before to the 1988 assessments. And their grasp of women's history and political involvement is called into question by the finding that many students chose Anthony and Elizabeth Cady Stanton as leaders of the women's movement in the 1970s (Ravitch and Finn 1987, 59). The only other insight we gain from the NAEP data is that students were largely ignorant of the 1848 Seneca Falls Convention (see table 2.5; only 27 percent identified it on the history test).

Structure and Functioning of the U.S. Government

Whatever their differences, courses in civics and government always involve students' memorizing facts about the structure and functioning of the U.S. government, mostly as embodied in the Constitution. How many senators does each state elect? How are members of the Supreme Court chosen? How does a bill become a law? We dealt with a number of such questions above because they fell into other categories, concerning individual rights, the powers of states, and so on. There remains a motley collection of "Constitution" items that do not fall into any of these categories. These deal with the basic structure and functioning of the U.S. government and are distinguished by the fact that they involve almost nothing in the way of interpretation or inference. We show the results for these items in table 2.6.

The first thing that strikes us is the wide variance in the ability to answer these questions. Some questions can be answered by almost everyone; others by no more than a third of the seniors. In certain cases, it is easy to see why. It is unsurprising, for example, that 94 percent of the students know that presidential elections are held every four years. Nor is it surprising that only 36 percent of seventeen-year-olds know that the Department of State is the office that deals with foreign affairs. (The job was not created by constitutional provision; and the name of the department, unlike "Foreign Ministry," is not self-explanatory.) Nor that teenagers (and even adults, for that matter) are largely unaware that it took a constitutional amendment (more than 80 years ago) to allow the imposition of income taxes.

Some of the variation can also be attributed to the precise questions asked. A question on the power to declare war, for example, was answered correctly by a large proportion of the students (71 percent). It is easy to see why when one notes that the *incorrect* alternatives were the Supreme Court, the United Nations, and the Joint Chiefs of Staff (each of which was chosen about 10 percent of the time). If the alternatives had been the president, the Senate only, and the president with the approval of the Senate, we can well imagine that less than half of the students would have answered correctly. Similarly, the question about impeachment could have been phrased in such a way that more than a third of the students could have answered correctly. It is presumably the subtle point that the House alone impeaches the president, with the Senate then conducting a trial, that is frequently misunderstood. Still, there are some surprises, at both extremes. The question about the presiding officer in the House had four reasonable alternatives—the whip, the speaker, the chair, and the presi-

Table 2.6 Knowledge of Basic Structure and Functioning of the
U.S. Government
(Percentage Correct)

Presidential election held every four years	94
Courts decide copyright disputes	84
The secretary of defense is appointed	83
Treason is making war against the United States or giving "aid and comfort" to the enemy	82
Constitution is the basis for Supreme Court cases	81
U.S. courts cannot declare war	78
Congress consists of House and Senate	77
Senators are elected[a]	77
Congress belongs to the legislative branch	75
Senators are elected[a]	75
The president belongs to the executive branch	74
The presiding officer of the House is called the Speaker*	73
A declaration of war must be approved by Congress*	72
The Supreme Court belongs to the judicial branch	71
The Supreme Court can declare an act of Congress unconstitutional	69
The Supreme Court can declare a law unconstitutional	68
Checks and balances involve powers of three branches vis-à-vis one another	68
The Supreme Court can declare a war unconstitutional	66
The Chief Justice is appointed by the president, approved by the Senate*	66
Separation of powers	66
The most recent amendment lowered the voting age to 18	64
The Electoral College permits a candidate who did not win a majority of popular votes to be declared president*	64
The attorney general heads the Department of Justice	63
The number of representatives in the House varies by the state population*	63
Each state has two senators*	62
The secretary of state is a member of the president's cabinet	58
The president nominates federal judges	56
Example of checks and balances	55
Judicial review is the authority of courts to decide the constitutionality of actions of other branches*	55
Checks and balances include certain congressional actions	54
The Senate approves Supreme Court appointments	54
A two-thirds vote of House and Senate is required to override a veto	54
Federal judges must be approved by the Senate	52
Under the Constitution, the power to tax belongs to Congress*	50
Courts settle disputes	47
The Cabinet belongs to the executive branch	46
Treaties must be ratified by the Senate	45
Supremacy clause is used to resolve conflicts between state and federal laws	45
When states have more senators than representatives	43
Method to replace the vice president	41
Congress can double the income tax	39
Senator's term is six years	37
The House can impeach a president; Senate then conducts trial	36
The Department of State deals with foreign affairs	36
A constitutional amendment authorizes the income tax	33
Candidate gets 100 percent of the electoral votes in a state	29
A majority of the Supreme Court can strike down laws	15
Average	59

[a]There were two different questions on this subject.
*Public-release item.

dent pro tempore—yet more than 70 percent chose the correct answer. In contrast, the fact that a majority of the Supreme Court can strike down laws—presumably in contrast to a supermajority or a unanimous Court— was known by only one in seven students.

Perhaps the most important point we wish to make is again just how many questions were of this type—stripped of any controversial/ comparative (even across states)/partisan context and devoid of any contemporary referents (except in the sense that most Constitutional provisions apply now just as they have for the past two hundred years). These features make the questions bland and uninteresting and the information hard for students to remember. Nonetheless, many students *can* remember that the number of representatives varies by the state population, that treaties must be ratified by the Senate, that a two-thirds vote of the Senate is required to override a presidential veto, and even that it is the Supremacy Clause of Article VI that is used to resolve conflicts between state and federal laws.

Students' Inferential Skills

Some of the questions on the Civics Assessment went beyond asking students to recall specific facts. Students' ability to answer these questions varies greatly, but it more closely resembles their modest understanding of political parties or lobbying than their considerable knowledge of the criminal justice system and the rights of citizens. The tasks that were asked of students required making inferences from textual items or from tabular or pictorial material. Although there were only a few questions of each type, we can infer that students are better equipped to deal with textual than with other kinds of material.

Consider the following textual item from the public-release portion of the test:

> *Juan:* "I think it's important that governments maintain order. All of these protests are disturbing the peace. People tend to be too critical of the government and that is very disruptive. How can elected officials ever do their work if people are criticizing them all the time?"
>
> *Faye:* "I think it's important that people let their opinions be known. Protests are okay as long as they aren't violent."

The conflict expressed in the dialogue is between
    A the maintenance of order and freedom of speech
    B union protests and student protests

C a representative government and a true democracy

D dictatorship and authoritarian rule

This question asks students to read the statements and make an inference about the conflict expressed by them. Students need only a vague understanding of such terms as "dictatorship" and "democracy." They do not need to remember specific facts. Even so, 27 percent answered incorrectly (table 2.7).

It is impossible to be certain whether the problem these students had with the question was one of reading ability, reasoning ability, or time pressure. Time pressure is not likely, however. Another question, of the same type but requiring twice the reading (about conflict over a proposed project), was correctly answered by a slightly larger number of students. Yet another textual question, about an informed citizenry, was shorter than the question quoted above, but fewer students answered it correctly. Reading ability may have played a minor role, in that the question about an informed citizenry used sentence construction that made it more difficult than this question. On the other hand, the item displayed above was the only one using such "specialized" terms as "true democracy," "dictatorship," and "authoritarian rule," and yet the proportion answering correctly was about the same as for the other two text-interpretation questions. These factors seem to indicate that a substantial minority of students cannot make relatively simple inferences from textual material.

Another item had a different format but also required reasoning skills. Students were asked which of a set of questions could best be addressed through a public opinion poll. Examples were given in the stem of the question to clarify what kind of polling data were under consideration. Students could not have memorized the answer beforehand; they had to make a reasoned determination about what can be gleaned from asking questions of the public. Here, student performance was especially weak,

Table 2.7 Ability to Make Inferences from Texts, Tables, or Charts (Percentage Correct)

Bill must pass both House and Senate (chart)	88
Supreme Court can protect individual rights (text)	80
Community must consider pros and cons of a proposed project (text)	78
Conflict between maintaining order, freedom of speech (text)*	73
Bill goes first to House committee (chart)	70
Madison believed in informed citizens (text)	69
More educated people are more politically active (table)*	63
Kind of question for which one would conduct a public opinion poll	49
Average	71

*Public-release item.

with just under half answering the question correctly. The problem may lie, in part, in the unfamiliar context. Some students may have given up simply because they thought that they knew nothing about polling. But others are likely to have been unfamiliar with the distinction between factual and normative statements, an essential ingredient to answering the question. Patrick (1972: 175) found precisely this inability fifteen years earlier among students in a variety of social studies courses, although his test subjects were primarily ninth graders. It now appears that twelfth graders have the same difficulty.

Tables appear to give students greater problems, although it was somewhat difficult for us to judge. Below is the only example on the test requiring interpretation of data in a table:

Percentage of People Engaged in Political Activity,
by Educational Level in Year 19XX

Educational Level	Very Active	Fairly Active	Fairly Inactive	Very Inactive
College Education	28%	30%	30%	12%
High School Education	9	17	40	34
Grade School Education	5	11	33	51

Which of the following best summarizes the information presented in the table above?
  A The more education people have, the more likely they are to be politically active.
  B The more education people have, the less likely they are to be politically active.
  C The kind of education people have is more important than the amount of education in influencing political participation.
  D There is no relationship between educational levels and political activity.

To those skilled in reading tables, the question is a simple one; it is difficult to see how students could fail to answer it correctly.[3] Yet those of us who teach college undergraduates know that students even at that level are frequently stymied by tabular presentations. They are often unaware that some sort of comparison is called for—here, between people with varying levels of education. Particularly difficult is figuring out which numbers to compare and how to compare them. Thus, it is not surprising that many high school seniors have trouble with even as simple a table as this.

The difficulty that students have with tables may extend to other pictorial material. Two test questions were based on a chart showing how a bill becomes a law in Congress. It is a "standard" chart of the sort that would appear in textbooks that explained the constitutional process. The chart consists of words and pictures; it has no numbers. One of the questions—about the need for a bill to pass both the House and Senate—was answered correctly by a large percentage of the students (see table 2.7). Perhaps this was because students already knew this, or perhaps the alternatives were unpersuasive. In any event, only 70 percent of the students correctly answered the second question—about the assignment of a bill to a committee of the House—even though, if anything, the answer to the question was more apparent in the figure than was the first answer.

These findings about students' skills can be interpreted in two ways. On the one hand, it is disconcerting that many students were unable to answer what we regard as easy questions. Those who dismiss low scores on the other items as meaningless, because they indicate only an inability to recall isolated facts, cannot do the same with these results. Only the most rudimentary statistical skills—basically, understanding percentages—was required to read the table, for example, and yet students could not do it. On the other hand, given the limited attention at the high school level to inferential skills, and especially to data presentation and interpretation, the fact that many students *were* able to answer these questions suggests that the problem is resolvable. With practice, even the ability to read tables and charts is well within the reach of many, perhaps most, seventeen-year-olds. Either way, more instruction and practice are needed for high school seniors to perform well at these tasks.

Comparative and Theoretical Perspectives

Although the NAEP questions focused almost exclusively on American government, a half-dozen items dealt with other nations or called for a comparison of the United States and other countries. The questions were so few and so simple that they are not as revealing as the other dimensions. Nonetheless, we present the results in table 2.8 to show that students have learned some basic comparative information. Most students know that countries other than the United States elect their national leaders and that these countries have political parties. Many were able to choose (from a set of plausible alternatives) the country that has had the most influence on the American way of life. And clear majorities correctly answered the other questions, including what seemed to be a fairly difficult question about the purpose of the United Nations.

Table 2.8   Knowledge of Comparative and Theoretical Perspectives
(Percentage Correct)

Comparative Perspective	
Many countries have elected national leaders	85
Many countries have political parties	82
Country with most influence on U.S. way of life	78
Many countries have a written constitution	68
Main purpose of the United Nations	62
Soviet Union has only one political party	61
Average	73
Theoretical Perspective	
The United States has a representative democracy	64
Definition of bicameralism*	37
Statement reflects the theory of a social contract*	28
Average	43

*Public-release item.

On the other hand, students were largely unequipped to deal with theoretical perspectives about politics. When asked to identify the United States as a representative democracy, only two-thirds of the seniors were able to do so. Only one-third could associate bicameralism with a legislative system composed of two houses. And only a quarter could identify words from the Declaration of Independence—"Governments are instituted among men, deriving their just powers from the consent of the governed"—as expressing a theory of social contract (28 percent) as opposed to one of federalism (42 percent), the rule of law (22 percent), or absolutism (7 percent).

Miscellaneous Questions

The questions discussed above account for almost all of the items on the 1988 Civics Assessment. The remaining items are sufficiently distinct from the preceding questions and from one another to preclude generalizations. In one case, however, several similar questions are suggestive of a point we made earlier and that we shall return to in the conclusion—namely, that which facts are remembered depends, in part, on whether the subject matter is directly relevant to the students: in a series of questions, students were asked whether the federal government ensures that everyone has a job, regulates food and drugs, assists farmers, and helps people buy homes. Correct answers were 83, 83, 73, and 35 percent, respectively.

The other miscellaneous items include the following:

- Ninety-four percent of the students were able to name the president.
- Ninety-two percent knew that the voting age is eighteen.

- Seventy-one percent were able to answer the sole question about political behavior (apart from the "table-reading" item already discussed). This was a question about which group—middle-aged professionals, college students, the unemployed, or factory workers—is likliest to vote in U.S. presidential elections.
- Fifty-six percent know that the income tax is the chief source of income for the federal government.
- About half could identify selected quotations as having come from the Declaration of Independence (58 percent recognized the right to "life, liberty, and the pursuit of happiness").
- Slightly less than half recognized that the Louisiana Purchase was an example of an action performed according to powers not specifically granted by the Constitution.

Presidential Responsibilities

The presidential responsibilities question, given to a subset of the seniors in the Civic Assessment, serves as a useful validation of and supplement to the multiple-choice questions reviewed so far. It consisted of a single question and related essay, as follows:

> What is the name of the President of the United States?
> In one or more paragraphs, discuss the most important responsibilities that the President has. Before you begin, take a few minutes to write down the main ideas you want to discuss. Then write your answer on the lines in your answer book.

Students were given fifteen minutes to complete the essay. The essays were then scored by readers into four levels, ranging from "elaborated" to "unacceptable." Considerable care are was taken in the training of readers so that the scores would be reliable; every fifth essay was scored twice, with exact agreement reached 91 percent of the time (Johnson, Zwick, et al., 1990: 142).

The levels were labeled and identified as follows: "1) *Elaborated:* Provides a thoughtful response with a mix of specific examples and discussion; 2) *Adequate:* Provides one or two examples of responsibilities with little discussion; 3) *Minimal:* Answers in generalities or provides a list of responsibilities that contains errors; 4) *Unacceptable:* Digresses from the topic, provides incorrect information, or does not attempt to list responsibilities." Exemplary student responses were offered for each level. We quote some of these responses verbatim from *The Civics Report Card* (Anderson et al., 1990: 60, 61–63).[4]

Elaborated

The most important responsibility of the President is to govern and oversee the events of the government while keeping the people in mind. It is his responsibility to ensure that all actions taken by the government and that all laws made protect the rights and interests of the American people. It is, more specifically, his responsibility to conduct foreign relations properly in order to ensure harmony between the United States and other countries in order to protect the welfare of the American Citizens. The President must not rely wholly on himself and his knowledge; he must be able to use his Cabinet in order to keep a constant flow of new ideas and also to remain in touch with the concerns of the people. The office of President is a very important position. I believe that the President must always consider the American citizens in order to be successful. The rights of the people must *always* be protected.

He has the power to veto a bill. If the house or senate passes a bill it goes to the President, he then can veto it or he can hold it for ten days and this makes a pocket veto. He serves as secretary of war and he greets foreign visitors when they come over here to the United States. He has the power to declare war, if he feels it would be in the best interest of the United States. The President has the power to appoint judges to the Supreme Court. He serves also as a spokesperson for foreign affairs. These are some things the President has power to do.

His duties are to be the spokesperson for the United States, he is Commander-in-Chief of the Armed Forces, and he has the power to accept or veto proposed bills that are passed to him from Congress. The President also has the power to appoint his own cabinet members and top White House clerks. Supreme Court Justices are appointed by the President of the U.S., with the approval of the Senate. Referring back to my first point, if the President disapproves of a Bill and vetos it, he must give Congress a statement as to why he vetoed the bill. The President is chosen to represent the U.S. with dignity and respect. He is a symbol of leadership that this nation can be proud to look up to.

Minimal

To me, I think the most important responsibilities that the President has is to make sure that there is peace here in the U.S. and to keep good relations with the other countries. I guess he just has to keep the country in order (legally) or else there's another scandal. Anyways, the President has to be able to look at both sides of the issue before he makes any decisions in everything that he has to decide upon.

Table 2.9 Students' Performance on the Presidential Responsibilities Essay

Scoring of response	Percentage correct on 150 multiple-choice items	Percentage of students
Elaborated (Provides a thoughtful response with a mix of specific examples and discussion.)	80	19
Adequate (Provides one or two examples of responsibilities with little discussion.)	69	40
Minimal (Answers in generalities or provides a list of responsibilities that contains errors.)	60	35
Unacceptable (Digresses from the topic, provides incorrect information, or does not attempt to list responsibilities.)	56	7
Raw N = 1,793 Weighted N = 221,901		

He has the greatest responsibility of anyone in our nation. He makes major decisions that effects us and our government. His job is very dangerous. But without one in control our country would be in trouble. Thanks to many of our presidents and government we've been out of war since world war II. The president cuts down on pollution and so fourth in our country. We should respect this man for what he stands for. He represents the people of the United States.

The presidential responsibilities item potentially serves two purposes. First, requiring that students write an essay as well as answer multiple-choice questions helps validate each type of measure. If performance measured by ability to write a good essay were unrelated to students' knowledge of specific facts (and vice versa), this would raise more questions about the test than about the students' abilities. In fact, the evidence indicates that the two kinds of measures are strongly related. Those who wrote better essays answered more of the multiple-choice questions correctly overall (table 2.9) as well as in each of the subject areas above.

It is especially noteworthy that the essay responses relate to multiple-choice items on such topics as lobbying, women and minorities, and comparative and theoretical perspectives. The content of these categories overlaps little, if at all, with the specific subject matter of the essay. Yet students who wrote better essays knew considerably more in each of these areas. Clearly, then, what is being measured by the essay and by the multiple-choice items is not narrowly restricted to the tasks at hand. This point will be particularly important to subsequent chapters, when we make inferences about the sources of student knowledge. We assume there that we are not speaking solely of students' ability to answer the specific questions in the NAEP test or only questions given in a multiple-choice format.

In addition, the presidential responsibilities essay helps us judge the *adequacy* of students' preparedness, at least with respect to one kind of civic information. In labeling some responses unacceptable, the test designers have incorporated judgments about the kinds of answers students ought to be able to give. With the multiple-choice items, it is always better to give more than fewer correct answers, but we have avoided making sweeping statements about the adequacy of students' overall levels of attainment. With the presidential responsibilities question, judgments are built into the scoring.

In our opinion, the presidency question is most useful for the first purpose—as a check on the inferences we make using the multiple-choice items. As an absolute measure of student quality, we are concerned that some of the apparent inadequacy in the responses derives from the minimal instructions given in the test of what was expected. An "elaborated answer," for example, required both specific examples and some discussion. But the instructions did not indicate that students should provide both examples and discussion, so it is unclear whether the failure to include both was due to the students' inability or to a lack of clarity in the test. Thus, although we report the overall distribution of answers here, we shall return to them in later chapters, where we shall use them to validate the effects of a variety of characteristics on students' *relative* performances.

In any event, as table 2.9 shows, more than half of the nation's high school seniors wrote essays that were judged to be adequate or better, but less than 10 percent gave detailed, or elaborated, descriptions of the president's responsibilities. More than 40 percent of the students gave minimal or, in some cases, unacceptable answers. While this may represent too harsh a judgment about student capabilities, as we have noted, it reinforces the point that civic education cannot be taken for granted. Just as students are unable to answer many factual questions, they are also unable to give thorough descriptions of the responsibilities of the chief executive.

Government Responsiveness to People and Elections

As we noted in the chapter 1, NAEP tests are now limited exclusively to cognitive material. Nevertheless, there were two questions in the 1988 Civics Assessment that gauged students' feelings about the responsiveness of the government:

Table 2.10   Government Responsiveness to People and to Elections

	Attention government pays to people		Percentage correct (150 items)	Elections make government pay attention		Percentage correct (150 items)
	NAEP (Percentage of Respondents)	Adults[a]		NAEP (Percentage of Respondents)	Adults[a]	
A good deal	17	13	70	43	38	69
Some	60	58	68	46	45	65
Not much	23	29	61	10	18	58
Raw N	4,206	4,212		4,212	1,742	
Weighted N	517,722			518,708		

[a]*Source:* 1988 American National Election Study.

> How much do you feel that having elections makes the government pay attention to what the people think?

> Over the years, how much attention do you feel the government pays to what people think when it decides what it wants to do?

Overall responses from the high school seniors are shown in table 2.10. For comparison purposes, we include the responses from a cross-section of American adults tested in the same year. The comparison shows that the seniors were a bit more sanguine about government responsiveness. Based on repeated high school and adult surveys on the related concept of political trust (Jennings and Niemi, 1981: 174; Stanley and Niemi, 1995: 157), this hopefulness is probably a life-cycle phenomenon, and the seniors' expectations will likely decline after graduation.

Although only two questions cannot serve as a basis for extended analysis, we shall draw on them to provide clues as to whether our conclusions about political knowledge extend beyond the cognitive realm. As we noted in chapter 1, however, attitudes are not entirely divorced from knowledge. This is obviously the case here, as students who felt that the government is more responsive were also more knowledgeable about government and politics (see table 2.10)—much as Morin (1995) reported for adults. Although there is no way to be certain of the causal relationship, this finding is consistent with the argument that lack of knowledge leads to greater cynicism. If as these students age they come to think of government as less responsive, we expect the change to be most concentrated among those who are least knowledgeable, perhaps because of their lack of knowledge. Even if the knowledge levels displayed in this chapter are deemed adequate or irrelevant (because of the assessment's stress on factual questions), here is another reason to be concerned about the effectiveness of civic education.

* * *

The outlines of what high school seniors know about civics and government emerge clearly from our analysis of the items in the Civics Assessment. As students leave high school, they are well-versed in many aspects of the criminal justice system, especially as it pertains to their individual rights. They are also well-informed about citizens' rights in general. Although they have only begun to encounter government directly, through paying taxes, registering to vote, and obtaining drivers' licenses, they are well-informed about the division of powers among the various levels of government and about state and local governments. They are also able to make rudimentary comparisons of the government of the United States and that of other countries. In all of these instances, although students are somewhat hazy on details, they nonetheless perform relatively well on these aspects of the test.

Seniors know less about political parties and lobbying, subjects that are not mentioned in the Constitution. What they do know about these subjects appears to be limited to bare-bones facts. With respect to women and minorities, the evidence is less clear, though it appears that students have been introduced to some of the relevant historical figures. However, judging as much from the history as from the civics surveys, students know little about the context in which those individuals operated. Here are substantive areas in which much more should be expected of—and conveyed to—graduating seniors.

Finally, high school seniors appear to have considerable difficulty working with civics material. Making inferences from short textual passages and interpreting simple visual and data presentations proved beyond the abilities of many of them. Similarly, few seniors seemed to have a grasp of even the simplest theoretical concepts concerning government. Here are areas where there is vast room for improvement.

Beyond these specifics, our analysis of individual items and categories of items from the NAEP survey leads to two observations, both of which will be the foundation for later recommendations. The first is that civics classes, to judge from what students were examined on, deal sparsely with contemporary events, problems, or controversies. We see this in the small number of questions, as well as in the kind of questions, asked about political parties, lobbying, and women and minorities (not to mention the absence of any references to current political issues). We shall return to this point in chapter 4, when we consider student reports of teacher emphases. There, we shall relate those reports to students' overall test scores.

The second observation is that students seem to have retained knowledge on aspects of civic information that were already familiar to them from other contexts or that were meaningful to them in some direct way. Although it may seem obvious, this elementary fact also suggests ways civic education might be improved. In particular, it suggests that students might better learn about government—at all levels—if greater attention were paid to local politics. We shall elaborate on this point in chapter 7. Before doing so, we need to show that the patterns of student knowledge observed in this chapter are not simply due to random variations; rather, despite the findings of some earlier studies, civics course work and other elements of the school environment do influence high schools students' civic knowledge.

CHAPTER THREE

How Students Learn about Government: The Exposure-Selection Model

In chapter 2 we detailed differences in levels of knowledge across types of political knowledge among a nationally representative sample of high school seniors. Although these results reveal a lot about what this group of new and emerging citizens knows and does not know about American government and politics, and consequently, how prepared they are to assume the rights and responsibilities of democratic citizenship, they tell us little about the causes of the variation among students.

As we have seen, opinions about which causal mechanisms are behind the acquisition and retention of political knowledge are sharply divided. Those concerned with secondary school curricular reform focus on the relevance of exposure to particular subjects and teaching styles; students of political socialization direct their attention to other aspects of the school and to the student's home environment; and those more concerned with cognitive aspects of student learning emphasize the relevance of individual behavior and attitudes like student achievement and tastes. But these competing hypotheses are rarely tested simultaneously against one another. In particular, what difference, if any, does the school environment, including the civics curriculum, have on high school students once social and economic background characteristics are taken into account? What happens when additional factors, especially those involving student motivation like achievement and interest in a particular subject, are accounted for? With respect to the forces most often presumed to encourage learning about American politics and government, we have little comprehensive and systematic evidence to either confirm or reject these competing paradigms.

In this chapter, we introduce what we call the exposure-selection model of the acquisition and retention of political knowledge. This model synthesizes various theoretical explanations of political knowledge, combining aspects of contextual situations in which students are located with individual student differences. In other words, the exposure-selection model incorporates both structural and motivational interpretations of the sources of political knowledge. The model hypothesizes that in order for students to learn and retain information about government and politics, they must first be exposed to relevant political information and then select that information for retention. In short, both exposure and selection are necessary conditions for political knowledge; neither is sufficient alone.

In addition to explicating the exposure-selection model, we specify a range of measures of the school, the home, and students themselves that are available in the 1988 NAEP civics data and that potentially affect civic knowledge. We classify this range of factors as either measures of the exposure students have to information about American government and politics or indicators of selection. The former focus on the context of the school and home environment and will be examined in detail in chapter 4. Characteristics of selection focus on individual student behavior, interests, and ascribed characteristics. They act as indicators of the extent to which students find certain types of political information relevant and interesting. These measures and their relationship to civic knowledge will be considered in detail in chapter 5.

How Students Learn about Civics and Government

Two general sets of features determine what and how much students learn about government and politics.[1] The first set, exposure characteristics, determines the political information that students are exposed to. The second set, selection characteristics, regulates what information is retained. Although these characteristics are theoretically distinct and identifiable, they are most meaningful to political learning when considered together. In order to understand what knowledge students hold about politics and government and why they know what they do, it is vital to analyze these two processes together.

The importance of both exposure and selection is perhaps best conveyed with an example. A person with neither a background nor interest in violent contact sports watches a television commercial advertising a major prize fight repeatedly over a series of days. Because the viewer has no interest in the spectacle or motivation to watch, the broadcast time of the event and the names of the participants will simply wash over him or her, unremembered. Simple exposure to information does not guarantee retention of the names of the fighters and the location of the fight. The event is of little or no relevance and interest to this particular viewer; and regardless of the number of times the advertisement is broadcast, the viewer is unlikely to select it for retention. On the other hand, a person who likes boxing but does not watch television and has no other means to get information about the event, is also unlikely to know the details of the broadcast, as this person has not been exposed to the relevant information. In our example, neither exposure nor interest and motivation, by themselves, are sufficient for the retention of information.

Although we do not equate watching television commercials with receiving formal education, the point remains: to be politically knowledgeable, students must both be exposed to political information and value it sufficiently to select it for retention. Failure to consider the importance of exposure characteristics like the school curriculum implies that much of what happens in school is irrelevant. On the other hand, emphasizing only structural characteristics while ignoring characteristics of selection implies that members of any given class of students will have the same levels of political knowledge. Taken together, the two processes offer a general analytical framework for what and how students learn about civics and government. It is the interaction of exposure and selection that determines what students know.

The distinction between these two processes is useful in another way. How much and in what ways students are exposed to political matters is determined largely by *structural* factors; that is, features primarily of the home and of the school civics curriculum, broadly interpreted. Students have relatively little control over these characteristics. In contrast, what students select for retention is determined most heavily by *individual* or *motivational* factors. These are more obviously under the control of the student. Structural features, however, such as the amount of civic instruction, are unlikely to substitute for individual attributes.

Table 3.1 outlines the exposure-selection model and specifies which of four sets of factors are structural characteristics regulating the exposure students have to political information and which are individual and motivational characteristics determining the selection students make of different kinds of civic knowledge. We consider the four general areas of civics curriculum, home environment, individual achievement, and background or demographic factors. Some contribute primarily to exposure

Table 3.1   The Exposure-Selection Model

Factor	Exposure (Structural)	Selection (Individual)
Civics curriculum		
Amount of course work	X	
Recency of course work	X	
Subject matter coverage (variety of topics studied)	X	
Instructional approaches (teaching techniques)	X	
Home environment		
Reading and reference materials at home	X	
Language spoken at home	X	
Two-parent household	X	
Educational level of parents		X
Amount of television viewing		X
Individual achievement		
Participation in student government		X
How much one likes to study government		X
Four-year college planned after graduation		X
Background/demographics		
Race	X	X
Gender		X

while others mostly affect motivation and selection. The distinctions are not sharp, and all of the characteristics probably contribute, to some degree, to both processes. Although the educational background of parents may help determine which school district a student lives in, for example, thereby affecting the amount of exposure to civics courses, we argue that the primary importance of parental education to students' civic knowledge is its effect on the extent to which parents motivate and encourage students to learn. The analytical framework of the exposure-selection model is nonetheless useful as a heuristic to separate and identify steps in the complicated process by which students learn about American government and politics.

Exposure

The structural factors listed in table 3.1 regulate, to a substantial degree, the formal exposure of students to facts about civics and American government. Of the eight characteristics listed, the first four are aspects of the school, specifically, of the civics curriculum. The amount of civics course work—the most studied of this set of explanatory variables—should in theory have a positive impact on how much students know about government. Students who have taken more civics courses have been exposed to more information about civics and government. Yet because of the contradictory findings of empirical research regarding the importance of course work, a finding of a positive relationship is far from certain. In addition, and apart from questions about civics courses per se, we also know that most information learned has a limited shelf life. Facts about government organization and processes, which tend not to be cumulative or mutually reinforcing, may be especially likely to be forgotten if they are not constantly reiterated. Thus, the *recency* of student course work should be a factor in student knowledge, although, as we shall note in chapter 4, recency may have another interpretation in the context of students who are in or approaching their first year of adulthood. In any event, how recently students studied civics in the classroom is a second important structural factor.

Two other features of the curriculum deserve independent study. We know that courses vary widely in the amount of subject matter they cover, perhaps at least as much in civics as in other subjects, inasmuch as civic content may be packaged into separate courses or formally combined with the study of American history. Educators have also long been concerned with the relevance of instructional approaches, and, for reasons noted in chapter 1 concerning the relationship between classroom participation and evaluation of political and social decision making, methods of teaching may be especially important for civic learning. In addition, the close connection between civic knowledge and current political debates implies that the extent to which students discuss current events in their classrooms may greatly affect their intake of information (through exposure, but also, in part, through the selection mechanism of increasing their interest). Thus, we anticipate that how students learn about American politics and government will also enhance student knowledge.

Of course, exposure to civic information is not determined exclusively by what happens in the school. The home environment encompasses another set of factors that are almost certain to be related to how often and in what way a young person hears and reads about American government and politics. The greatest influence of the home may be motivational. But we have identified three aspects of the home environment that are more likely to affect the exposure students have to information about government and politics: the availability and variety of reading and reference materials in the household, whether the student lives in a two-parent household, and whether only English is spoken at home.

Having easy access to reading materials at home, including newspapers, magazines, books, and encyclopedias, should bring the world of politics closer to the student. Availability does not guarantee exposure— a teenager could studiously avoid rather than study these materials—so, again, individual characteristics must also be incorporated into our analysis. However, it is likely that a greater presence of reading and reference material means that students are exposed to more information about American government and politics. Having two parents in the household is relevant because it increases the likelihood that students will hear adult conversations. Some of these conversations may involve politics and government, thereby enhancing the student's exposure to political issues and topics. Finally, if only English is spoken at home, it is more likely that students will be exposed to both the language and substance of issues particular to *American* politics.

Finally, we characterize race or ethnicity as both structural and individual factors. That they are individual characteristics is obvious. And it seems likely that, for a variety of historical and other reasons, they affect the selection of politically relevant cues that students and other citizens pay attention to and are likely to remember. Yet race and ethnicity are not direct measures of individual achievement or motivation, as are such characteristics as considering American government a favorite subject. Being a member of a racial or ethnic minority implies a contextual, structural environment that may have a significant exposure influence on civic knowledge. For example, African-American and Hispanic students typically go to school in lower-income districts than non-Hispanic whites; and often they must make do with inferior classroom materials. Through such means, being African-American or Hispanic is likely to affect the student's degree of exposure to civics and government material. Hence, we categorize race and ethnicity as structural as well as individual factors, recognizing that the two are somewhat different from the other factors under their respective headings.

Selection and Retention

Individual characteristics of the home environment, individual achievement, and background characteristics affect the selection of civic and political information students choose to store. Unlike the structural characteristics, the individual characteristics primarily influence the *retention* of political facts by determining how students *select* which political facts are more or less likely to be remembered. These factors measure the incentives students have to learn about politics and government.

We consider two aspects of the home environment relevant: the educational level of the parents and the amount of television watched by the student. The educational level of parents often indicates the expectations they have for their children; better-educated parents typically expect their children to learn as much as or more than they themselves know. As a result, it is likely that students with better-educated parents have a greater incentive to remember what they have been taught about government (as well as other subjects). In addition, these students will more often look forward to continuing their formal education beyond high school and are therefore likely to feel the need for a greater storehouse of knowledge to prepare them for the next stage of their formal education. Level of parental education is likely to be related to student learning in yet another way. Given the relative homogeneity of many American neighborhoods, students are likely to have classmates whose parents have similar educational backgrounds and aspirations. Being surrounded by like-minded souls will tend to reinforce motivational lessons learned at home.

In contrast, frequent television viewing is likely to be an indicator of a lack of motivation to understand and remember political information. In principle, watching television does not have to indicate low interest in civic affairs. Students could be watching news and other public-affairs programs. But data on viewership demonstrate that young people are unlikely to watch such news and issues-oriented channels as C-SPAN and Court-TV, or even the nightly news (*Television Audiences Report,* various years). Watching television may also signal less interest in school work in general rather than in political material per se, or television viewing may be as much a consequence as a cause of lack of political interest. Regardless, we would expect students who watch a lot of television to know less about many subjects, including politics and government. In addition, frequent television viewing may have some spillover effect on exposure; the more hours students spend watching television, the less time they can spend reading, doing homework, and interacting with adults—activities that are likely to involve more political content than the average television program.

In addition to characteristics of the home environment that contribute to the selection of political information for retention, we consider three characteristics that collectively represent individual achievement: participation in mock elections, student government, and the like; an interest in studying government; and the intention of attending a four-year college. Participation in school activities like student government indicates at least a modicum of interest in collective concerns, as does a student's enjoyment of civics and government classes. Both characteristics demonstrate as well as create incentives for students to select political knowledge for storage and retention.

Intention to study at a four-year college serves at least two purposes. First, it is likely to be a relevant factor in selection in a direct sense. Students who intend to continue their education in college have a greater incentive to retain the information they were exposed to in high school, if for no other reason than to do well in college. In addition, intention to study at a four-year college is a measure of individual ability and achievement in a broad sense. General ability and achievement presumably contribute to knowledge in many ways: they make it easier for students to read and absorb material outside the classroom; they may make it more likely that students will do so. In the absence of a more direct measure, such as scores on standardized tests, inclusion of this measure helps account for general ability and achievement. In its absence, we might falsely attribute the effects of general ability to civics classes and other aspects of the school.

A final characteristic we categorize as individual in nature is gender. Students obviously do not choose their sex, but males and females do develop somewhat distinctive tastes in academic subjects. Previous research has shown that girls have traditionally favored humanities subjects over hard sciences, whereas boys have gone in the opposite direction.[2] With respect to civics and American government, the NAEP data show that boys are more likely than girls to say that government is their favorite subject and that they enjoy civics classes more than other classes. These data lead us to suspect that because of their enhanced interest, boys are more likely to be motivated to pay attention to and remember the material they study in their civics courses.

As noted earlier, the distinction between structural characteristics that influence exposure to political information and individual characteristics that motivate selection of political knowledge for retention are not as clear in practice as they are in theory. All the factors we have identified could be considered both structural and individual in some ways and in some circumstances. Nonetheless, the analytical framework we have outlined serves as a useful guide through the complicated process by which students learn.

Coverage, Emphasis, and Importance

Learning—even if limited to one subject and only to factual items—is a highly complex process. Our listing of factors affecting exposure to and retention of civic information is surely not a complete compilation of all that underlies individual differences in levels of political knowledge as measured by the NAEP assessment. With regard to the curriculum, for example, it would be helpful to know whether students obtained their civic instruction in history or in civics classes and even to know the names of specific courses students were enrolled in. With regard to the home environment, a direct measure of interaction between parents and child would be helpful, or a report on the level of interest in politics shown among parents. Unfortunately, the 1988 NAEP data do not include such measures.

Yet as it stands, we have considerably more to analyze than is typically the case in studies of civic knowledge. Indeed, we shall not attempt to analyze in detail all the factors noted. Of the structural factors, we focus exclusively on the civics curriculum in the next chapter, although factors in the home environment will be included in the multivariate analysis in chapter 6. Of the individual factors, we consider one in the home environment—amount of television viewing—as well as two of the three reflecting individual achievement, plus race or ethnicity and gender, in chapter 5. The remaining factor, level of parental education, will be discussed in chapter 6.

The relative emphases are to some degree an indication of our own interests, but mostly they reflect our sense of the kinds of factors that have been more of less thoroughly studied, along with considerations of their general interest and perceived importance to education policy. It has been frequently and consistently reported, for example, that knowledge of civics, history, and geography is strongly correlated with parental education levels (Anderson et al., 1990: 52; Ravitch and Finn, 1987: 124–25; Hammack et al., 1990: 37; Paul Williams et al., 1995: 23; Allen et al., 1990: 71). In contrast, the civics curriculum has received little attention, and the results have often been contradictory. Moreover, parental educational achievement is fixed, at least in the short run, while the curriculum is at the heart of educational policy and reform. As a consequence, it is important to study civic education, for much can potentially be gained from doing so, while there is little reason to repeat what has been shown elsewhere about parental education.

This relative emphasis in our coverage should not be taken as an indication of the importance, in an overall sense, of each factor to the development of student knowledge. In fact, describing the set of factors that influence student learning allows us, in the end, to bring them all together to make judgments about their relative weight.

CHAPTER FOUR

Exposure to Learning: Civic Instruction

As we observed in chapter 1, the presumption that academic knowledge is gained entirely or even primarily in the classroom may be a truism for some subjects but not for civics. For mathematics or the natural sciences, it is hard to imagine things being otherwise for the vast majority of students. It is difficult to visualize students doing word problems or reading chemistry texts on their own—and few of us would want our children experimenting in our kitchens. Many, perhaps most, parents are disinclined to work systematically with their children on advanced mathematics or physics, even if they are able to do so. And although friends may discuss various aspects of animal behavior, they are not likely to form discussion groups about molecular biology. The media are of little help either. We hear daily reports about advances in medical research, but no one pretends that monitoring the news is a way to learn basic science.

In the case of civics (and perhaps such subjects as English as well), the matter is not so simple. Government and politics affect our daily lives in innumerable ways. Young people—and adults, for that matter—can choose to ignore much of what goes on, but it would take a conscious and concerted effort to ignore or avoid involvement with government in all forms. It is nearly impossible to miss the fact every fourth year that a presidential election is taking place. It is thus difficult to avoid knowing that one can vote, and other political information is likely to follow on this. That one can vote for officials other than the president is likely to reach all but the most dedicated of the uninvolved, and from this, some understanding must follow of the structure of government (or at least that there are many government officials).

Most students, of course, cannot vote before the twelfth grade, which could lead them to ignore election information. But as we noted in chapter 2, teenagers who want a driver's license, who get a job, who travel abroad have to deal with government forms or bureaucracy. In most states, making simple purchases makes one aware of taxation. And virtually no one can be unaware that there are laws (especially traffic laws) and official enforcers of those laws. It is also difficult to avoid hearing, if not expressing, opinions about government and politics. Parents may not talk about the periodic table of the elements, but they are likely to express their feelings about government, candidates, bureaucracy, taxes. And when presidential candidates show up on popular television shows, and when the government attempts to regulate movies, television, and the Internet, it is hard to imagine that a high school senior could be completely unaware of his or her political surroundings.

Given the press of politics and government on citizens, it is not inconceivable that much civic knowledge is learned outside the school. Students may develop most of their knowledge of government and politics from parents, friends, the media, and through direct contacts with government. Indeed, political scientists have largely ignored the high school civics curriculum, having concluded that efforts to teach civic knowledge in the schools are largely redundant and therefore ineffectual.

We feel, in contrast, that the case for the ineffectiveness of the civics curriculum has not been proven and that prima facie evidence as well as some scholarly research suggest the contrary. Therefore, it behooves us to investigate the nature of civic education in America's schools and to consider what contributions curricula and the school environment make to student knowledge. We shall look at several aspects of civic instruction in the schools: overall amount of civics course work and when the course work is taken, breadth of subject matter, and kinds of instructional approaches. We shall draw on several sources—including a nationwide survey about course requirements, a nationally representative student transcript study, and, primarily, data from the 1988 NAEP study.

We concentrate on these aspects of civic instruction because they seemed to us and to the NAEP planning committees to be the relevant factors determining students' exposure in school to information about American government and politics. We recognize, however, that curriculum and course content are not uniform across schools and that the opportunities to learn through civics course work might vary across types of schools and according to the resources available to each school. Thus, we go on in this chapter to investigate whether differences between schools in terms of sponsorship (public versus private), financial resources, teacher-student ratios, and ethnic or racial homogeneity also play a part.

We shall relate each aspect of the civics curriculum to levels of student knowledge and measure knowledge both by the percentage of correct answers across all 150 multiple-choice questions and by the percentage of correct answers within each of the categories of political knowledge laid out in chapter 2. Political knowledge tends to be unidimensional—people usually do not specialize in knowledge about specific domains (Delli Carpini and Keeter, 1996: 135–42). Nonetheless, examining the results for knowledge within each of the subject areas will increase our overall confidence in the patterns observed. And we will find that the effects of school factors vary depending on the kinds of material involved. We shall also use the item on presidential responsibilities in order to demonstrate that our main results are not dependent on the multiple-choice format. Finally, we shall look at attitudes toward government expressed by students on the two questions in the 1988 NAEP test.

Civic Instruction in the High School

If the civics curriculum and its effect on students have been understudied, one of the reasons might be the difficulty of determining how much and what kinds of relevant course work students have had. Instruction about civics comes in a bewildering variety of forms. In many schools, there are obvious primary courses—conveniently titled "American Government" or "Civics" or perhaps "The American Political System." But in other schools, courses with titles like "Contemporary Issues" or "Economic, Legal, and Political Systems in Action" are the most relevant. In others, explicit instruction in government and civics is incorporated into history courses (in addition to what is routinely learned about politics and government through study of various episodes in American history).

Elective courses are even more varied. Those that focus on the United States come under such names as "Street Law," "Political Processes," "American Heritage," and so on, as well as the more standard "Problems of Democracy" or "Political Science." Courses with a comparative or international focus can include "Comparative World Government" and "American Foreign Policy." Still other titles do not readily convey their content: "Decision Making in a Crisis," "Writings Influencing Government." In addition, there are Model U.N.s, Model Senates, and assorted internships.[1]

Most states have a requirement for some form of study of civics or American government in grades 9–12. In response to a questionnaire sent to social studies curriculum specialists in all fifty states and the District of Columbia, forty-two (82 percent) reported that their state had such a requirement. However, in only twenty of those states does the requirement demand that there be a separate course; most states simply require that the material be covered in some way during the high school years. State requirements usually do not specify the grade at which civics must be taught. Specific courses are primarily offered in the later grades, especially grade 12, but in some instances, the last formal civic instruction a student receives may occur as early as the ninth grade.

Separate civics courses rarely last more than a semester (or sometimes a quarter), though in a few states (like Virginia) a year-long course covering the state and national governments is required. Courses in American history are typically full-year courses, but the amount of time devoted to civics in history classes is nearly impossible to determine. An additional factor is that school-based programs involving participation in the community often stress civic learning; these became more extensive in the 1980s (Patrick and Hoge, 1991: 428), but we are only now beginning to get firm estimates of the proportions of students involved or of the content and nature of such programs (National Center for Education Statistics, 1995).

A detailed study of student transcripts provides additional insight, but it leaves many gaps in our knowledge of student course work. We find, for example, that 72 percent of the 1987 high school graduates (78.1 percent of 1994 graduates) had at least a half a credit (that is, a 45–60 minute class at least once a day for half a year) in the general heading "American Government and Politics" (Legum, 1997: A-199), but there is no report of when students took this course. In addition, nearly all graduates took at least a year of American history (A-199), though, again, there is no way of estimating the amount of civics work in such courses. Moreover, information from the transcript study could not be linked to individual students taking the NAEP civics test.

Faced with a multiplicity of sources for civic instruction and the helpful but limited information from the transcript study, the NAEP designers opted for inquiring of students directly about the amount and nature of their course work. Students were asked two questions:

Did you take or do you expect to take a course in American government or civics in the following grades? [Answers: Ninth, Tenth, Eleventh, Twelfth][2]

Since the beginning of ninth grade, how much American government or civics course work have you completed up to now? [Answers:

None, Less than half a year; half a year; Between half a year and one year; one year; More than one year][3]

Given the ambiguities about what constitutes civics, as well as the frailty of memory, it is not surprising that student-generated estimates contain some error. In particular, a comparison with the transcript data suggests that students slightly overestimated the number of civics courses they had taken, at least if we interpret their responses as referring to separate courses of at least a semester's length. Nonetheless, if used with caution, the reports allow us to draw some broad conclusions.

By their own estimates, nearly nine out of ten students received a half-year's study or more of civics or government by the end of their senior year (table 4.1).[4] Close to half the students reported from a half to a year of course work. Based on the amount of instruction available, it is likely that those reporting more than one year meant no more than a year and a half. Thus, unlike English, science, and language training, civics and American government course work is narrowly bounded, with a high proportion of the students evidently receiving between a half and one and a half years of training.

Not surprisingly, given the frequency of statewide requirements and the relatively narrow range of the number of course taken, the amount of civic instruction is relatively uniform across students in varying kinds of high school programs. Table 4.2 shows a comparison of the amount of civic instruction taken by students in vocational, general, and college preparatory programs. This comparison is notable for its lack of differentiation; the differences are so small and irregular that they have no practical significance, and this is precisely the point. To the extent that the goal of secondary education is to expose American youth of all ability levels and interests to their civic heritage and to their responsibilities as citizens, the schools have met it to a remarkable degree insofar as the distribution of high school course work is concerned. Of course, a corollary of this result is that high-ability students—those who intend to go on to four-year colleges, for example, or those who have earned high grades—receive no more instruction in government and civics than others do.

While most students appear to receive comparable *amounts* of training, there is variation in *when* they receive their civic instruction. The student reports indicate, as expected, that there is a U-shape to the distribution of civic instruction over the high school years. Despite recent declines in civics requirements for grades 7–9 (Patrick and Hoge, 1991: 428), more ninth graders than tenth graders take such classes. Civics course-taking picks up in the junior year (in part owing to work embedded in his-

Table 4.1 American Government/Civics Course Work That Students Report Taking in Grades 9–12

Amount of Course Work	Percentage of Students
None	8
Less than a half-year	5
A half-year	14
Between a half-year and one year	11
One year	23
More than one year	40
Raw N = 4,257 Weighted N = 523,694	

Table 4.2 American Government/Civics Course Work Taken in Grades 9–12, by Type of School Program

Amount of Course Work	School Program		
	Vocational	General	College Preparatory
		(Percentage of Students)	
None	12	10	6
Less than a half-year	3	4	5
A half-year	13	14	15
Between a half-year and one year	10	11	11
One year	18	24	23
More than one year	43	38	41
Raw N	389	1,470	2,384
Weighted N	43,810	176,212	302,463

Table 4.3 Grade in Which the Most Recent American Government/Civics Course Was Taken

Grade	Percentage of Students
No civics course	8
Grades 9–11	31
Grade 12	61
Raw N = 4,204 Weighted N = 517,254	

tory courses), and the highest proportion of students report taking a course of this kind in the senior year.[5]

Table 4.3 shows the distribution of the civics courses taken most recently by students. This distribution is important because we shall find below and in chapter 6 that course work in the twelfth grade plays a more important role in the retention of political knowledge than work done earlier. If students' reports are correct (and, as noted, they appear to be an *over*estimate), 61 percent of students take a civics course during their senior year in high school. Thus, even though almost all students receive some civics and government instruction in high school, the amount of course work dedicated to the subject in the senior year is far from universal.

Civics Courses and Knowledge of Politics and Government

If minimal levels of course work in civics are nearly universal and maximum levels quite low, we must ask whether the amount of civics course work is sufficiently variable and meaningful to explain differing knowledge levels of high school seniors. In seeking to relate course work and levels of knowledge, an obvious place to start is with the amount of instruction. That is, does more course work—whenever taught, whatever the instructional method, and so on—translate directly into greater knowledge of government and politics?

The *Civics Report Card*—the "official" report on the 1988 NAEP Civics Assessment—is ambivalent about this question, while trying to support the commonplace expectation that civics courses make a difference (Anderson et al., 1990). Reflecting on results for the fourth, eighth, and twelfth grade tests, the *Report* highlights the conclusion that "there appears to be a positive relationship between students' average civics proficiency and the amount and frequency of instruction they received in social studies, civics, or American government" (75). Yet it also describes as "puzzling" the fact that in twelfth grade, "the amount of instruction received appeared to be unrelated to students' proficiency" (74). In reality, do high school civics courses make a difference? Or is it possible that "life experiences" or other factors suffice for learning about government? And does it matter which specific questions or tasks are considered?

The answers to these questions take some time to develop, but one thing is clear from the outset. Students who have had no civics classes or who never studied the subject know less about all aspects of government; they are also less able to interpret written and graphic material about political matters. On every one of the NAEP test items, fewer students answered correctly who had taken no civics classes than students with a half-year or more of civics. Indeed, when the latter group is broken down more finely, the group with no civics classes usually lags behind them at every level of course work, even those with only a half-year of work.

Let us begin a more detailed analysis in the most obvious way, by making use of the amount of civics work that students said they had completed. The first part of table 4.4 shows the average percentage of correct answers for the overall scale of political knowledge for each amount of course work. The results do not immediately support the contention that civics course are valuable. True, the 13 percent of the student population

Table 4.4 Overall Political Knowledge, by Amount of Civics Course Work and by Amount and Recency of Courses

Civics Course Work	Mean Percentage Correct
Amount	
None	57
Less than a half-year	65
A half-year	69
A half-year to one year	68
One year	66
More than one year	67
Raw N = 4,257 Weighted N = 523,694	
Amount and Recency	
Never studied it	51
No course work	57
Grades 9–11 latest[a]	65
Grade 12 latest[a]	68
Raw N = 4,205 Weighted N = 517,317	

[a]One or more courses.

with no course work or with less than a half-year of civics are less knowledgeable than those with more formal training. But knowledge does not grow systematically as more civics course work is added. There is no discernible systematic difference in overall knowledge between those with one semester and those with more than a year of course work. It is the lack of any meaningful relationship among this 90 percent of the students that results in the ambivalent stance taken in *The Report Card*. Were we to look no further, we would be forced to conclude that civics course work, while making some difference in its initial stages, quickly loses its value for enhancing student knowledge about government and politics.[6]

This way of evaluating civics courses, however, treats all such courses as equivalent. In practice, we can distinguish among those that were taken at each grade level. This can be important for at least three reasons. First, there may simply be a recency effect, in that memory of facts about civics and government has a short half-life. Seniors may remember what they learned the week or even the semester before but not what they learned in previous years. Second, civics material for seniors may be more informative; it is more often contained in stand-alone courses than embedded in history and other classes. The nature of the material taught to seniors may also differ and be more aligned with the NAEP test. Third, the interests and perspectives of seventeen-year-olds may be sufficiently different from those of younger students that they are more likely to understand and remember government-related topics.

To test this reasoning, we constructed a measure of amount and recency of civics course work, separating students into those who had never

studied civics (2 percent), those who had taken no civics courses (7 percent), those whose most recent course(s) was in the ninth, tenth or eleventh grade (31 percent), and those whose most recent course(s) was in the
twelfth grade (60 percent).[7] The students who claim to have never studied
civics in addition to never having had a specific course in American government represent only a tiny fraction of the whole—just 2 percent of the
seniors—but they provide an additional comparison group.[8]

The second part of table 4.4 shows that grouping by both the amount
and recency of civics course work does indeed differentiate between students in their overall knowledge of politics. Students who took civics in
the twelfth grade were somewhat more knowledgeable than those whose
latest civics course was in the eleventh grade or earlier. These groups were
well ahead of students who had no course work, while those who claimed
to have never studied civics fell even farther behind. Although the difference at the top end is only 3 percentage points, the overall pattern nonetheless suggests that it is the amount *and recency* of civics course work
that makes the difference. We shall return to the question of how much
importance to attach to a difference of this size, but for now it seems clear
that there is at least some degree of differentiation.[9]

We can carry our analysis a step farther by looking at differences for
each of the ten specific categories of political knowledge by the amount
and recency variable. In table 4.5, the average percentage of correct answers for each of the categories is shown by the amount and recency measure. The results are consistent with the findings in the previous table in
that the amount and recency of civics course work makes a difference in
student knowledge of all ten dimensions. The differences are typically
greatest at the bottom end—between those who have never studied civics
or have had no courses and those who have had some formal schooling in
civics and government. In addition, the smallest differences at the top end
(latest class in ninth–eleventh grades versus twelfth grade) are in the subject areas in which most students do well. This may be because of the immediate relevance of these subjects for high school seniors and because of
their considerable prominence in the media.

Finally, we compare students with differing amounts and recency of
civics on the open-ended question asking about presidential responsibilities. The results, shown in table 4.6, mirror those for the 150 multiple-
choice items. The effects of amount and recency are greatest as students
move from no civics or very little to any amount. Yet small differences
exist as well between those with civics in the ninth–eleventh grades only
and those with civics in twelfth grade. The magnitude of the differences
here cannot be compared directly to differences observed for the multiple-

Table 4.5   Ten Types of Political Knowledge, by Amount and Recency of Civics Courses

Type of Knowledge	Amount and Recency of Civics Courses			
	Never Studied It	No Course	Grades 9–11	Grade 12
	(Mean Percentage Correct)			
Criminal and civil justice	62	68	78	80
General rights of citizens	68	70	79	81
State and local government	53	58	65	68
Political parties	40	51	57	58
Lobbying	43	55	61	65
Women and minorities	56	58	67	71
Structure and functioning of U.S. government	43	50	58	63
Inferences from text, tables, charts	49	59	68	70
Comparative perspective	54	61	71	73
Theoretical perspective	45	46	45	50
Raw N = 4,205 Weighted N = 517,317				

Table 4.6   Performance on the Presidential Responsibilities Essay, by Amount and Recency of Civics Courses

Understanding of Presidential Responsibilities	Amount and Recency of Civics Courses			
	Never Studied It	No Course	Grades 9–11	Grade 12
	(Percentage)			
Unacceptable	19	13	7	6
Minimal	47	33	39	32
Adequate	27	42	36	42
Elaborated	7	13	18	20
Raw N = 1,772 Weighted N = 218,914				

choice items. But reducing by two-thirds the proportion with an "unacceptable" understanding and nearly tripling the proportion with an "elaborated" understanding clearly signals an important effect.

The findings thus far from the 1988 NAEP data offer a sharp contrast to the widely shared view among political scientists that American government or civics courses have little effect on high school students. This may be the case with respect to limited areas of study or for some students, but the evidence so far suggests that civics courses do have an effect on student knowledge, an effect that is wide-ranging in terms of content and, as best we can tell from limited testing, that also appears to raise students' capacity for reasoning and exposition about civic matters.

Civics Course Work and Trust in Government

The conclusion that civics courses have little effect on student knowledge has been extended, with some qualifications, to attitudes. Corbett, for example, concludes that "schools are successful in transmitting . . . loyalty to the country, compliance with laws and authority, and partial support for democracy and democratic principles [i.e., general principles but not specific applications]" (1991: 213) but that civics or government courses as such "are not very effective in transmitting either political knowledge or political attitudes" (215). Corbett relies heavily on the Langton and Jennings (1968) study, but other results suggest the same conclusion. In the 1950s, for example, data from the Purdue Opinion Polls showed only small differences between the political attitudes of high school students who had had a civics course and those who had not; in many comparisons, students who had had civic instruction expressed antidemocratic views more frequently than those who had not (Remmers and Radler, 1957: 211–17; see also Patrick, 1977: 215–16).

The lack of effects on attitudes may be attributed, in part, to the fact that schools at both the elementary and secondary levels seek to avoid controversial subjects, including such topics as civil liberties and political tolerance (Remy, 1981; Wirt, 1986; Carroll et al., 1987; Patrick and Hoge, 1991: 429–30). It may also be that the circumstances in which classes reshape attitudes are limited (Litt, 1963; Morrison and McIntyre, 1971: 162–63). These explanations are supported by the fact that courses or treatments in which students are consciously engaged in purposeful discussions of values have frequently had the effect of altering students' views (Morrison and McIntyre, 1971: 162; Goldenson, 1978; Avery et al., 1992; Brody, 1994). Nonetheless, course effects on attitudes appear not to be widespread.

The attitudes considered in the two items in the NAEP survey are similar to what political scientists call political efficacy and political trust or cynicism. With respect to these specific attitudes, Langton and Jennings (1968) reported that the curriculum had relatively little effect. Moreover, to the extent that there was any relationship between course work and trust, it appeared to be curvilinear. That is, students with little course work were less cynical about politics than those who had none, but those who had additional course work were more cynical (858). Such a pattern makes sense when one considers that cynicism grows with age, presumably as one gains experience with the political system (Jennings and Niemi, 1981: 173–75); it may also increase with further education (Abramson, 1983: 232–33; Morin, 1996: A-6). Thus, to the extent that civics classes influence students' attitudes about the government, it may be to make students more, rather than less cynical; fewer of them might believe that the government is responsive.

As we turn from knowledge to attitudes, we also need to address the question of the causal sequences underlying any associations that are uncovered. In many circumstances, attitudes may affect behavior instead of, or in addition to, the other way around. At the college level, such a possibility exists with respect to curricular choice. For example, students who feel that the government is completely unresponsive to its citizens are not likely to elect courses in politics. At the high school level, however, it is unlikely that attitudes about government are a major factor in course selection. Unlike students in college, high school students have relatively little choice in the courses they take. In addition to state and district requirements, norms for college-bound seniors dictate many other course choices. Insofar as course choice is determined by such factors as student ability and college intentions, the multivariate analysis in chapter 6 will provide effective controls.

Turning to the attitudinal items in the NAEP survey, we find that the evidence points strongly in the direction of course effects and that course work propels students toward more, not less, faith in government responsiveness and toward a greater belief in the efficacy of elections in that process. Table 4.7 shows the relationship between students' attitudes about government responsiveness and the amount and recency of civics course work. As with political knowledge, the effects are greatest as students move from no civics or very little to any amount, with small differences on each item between those with civics in the ninth–eleventh versus the twelfth grade.

The magnitude of the differences is substantial. For each question, the number responding "not much" to the question of how much attention government pays to people is cut in half, and the number answering "a good deal" increases by roughly 10–15 percentage points. Of course, with only two questions, any conclusions about the influence of civics classes are necessarily tentative. And we still have to see whether the results stand up to multivariate analysis. But the initial evidence speaks to positive, substantial effects of civics courses on at least these aspects of students' political attitudes.

Subject Matter Coverage and Knowledge

If civics courses increase student knowledge levels, they presumably do so through some aspect of the course content. In the NAEP study it was

Table 4.7 Government Responsiveness, by Amount and Recency of Civics Course Work

Attitude	Amount and Recency of Civics Courses			
	Never Studied It	No Course	Grades 9–11	Grade 12
		(Percentage)		
Amount of attention government pays to people				
Not much	44	32	24	21
Some	45	55	61	61
A good deal	11	12	15	19
Elections make government accountable				
Not much	22	16	11	9
Some	45	49	49	45
A good deal	33	36	41	46
Raw N = 4,150 Weighted N = 510,931				

impossible to gather detailed information on the content of the highly varied and large number of specific courses taken by students in more than three hundred schools. Nonetheless, the designers of the study felt that the nature and breadth of course content was of sufficient importance that some information should be gathered. As with course enrollments, they turned to the students themselves.

Students were asked how much they had studied various topics in American government or civics "since the beginning of ninth grade." Table 4.8 displays the data (along with reports from eighth graders; see below). For the most part, the categories are broad, making it difficult to draw any conclusions about the precise content of high school civic lessons. It is hardly surprising, for example, that students report studying the "U.S. Constitution and Bill of Rights" more than such topics as "Congress," the "president and the Cabinet," and the "rights and responsibilities of citizens," since study of the Constitution encompasses much of what one would learn about the others. And the fact that more than half the seniors reported studying the Constitution "a lot" (as opposed to "some" or "none") tells us little about what was actually covered. Still, three insights can be gleaned from these data.

First, the student observations appear to reinforce the scholarly notion, based on studies of textbooks, that civics teaching tends toward "dry institutional descriptions" (Katz, 1986: 91). For example, included in the list of topics studied were both "Congress" and "How laws are made." Reported coverage of these subjects was nearly identical (45 percent and 43 percent, respectively, reported a lot of coverage in high school), suggesting that the two were virtually synonymous in the eyes of students. That Con-

Table 4.8 Civics Topics Studied in Grades 5–8 and 9–12,
as Reported by Eighth- and Twelfth-Grade Students

Topics	Coverage		
	A Lot	Some (Percentage)	None
U.S. Constitution and Bill of Rights			
Grades 5–8	56	40	4
Grades 9–12	55	43	3
Congress			
Grades 5–8	42	50	8
Grades 9–12	45	51	4
How laws are made			
Grades 5–8	38	52	10
Grades 9–12	43	53	5
President and the Cabinet			
Grades 5–8	39	49	12
Grades 9–12	40	56	5
Court system			
Grades 5–8	30	53	17
Grades 9–12	39	55	6
State and local government			
Grades 5–8	30	55	15
Grades 9–12	36	57	6
Political parties, elections, and voting			
Grades 5–8	44	47	8
Grades 9–12	45	51	4
Rights and responsibilities of citizens			
Grades 5–8	43	45	13
Grades 9–12	45	51	5
Principles of democratic government			
Grades 5–8	21	52	28
Grades 9–12	32	59	9
Other forms of government			
Grades 5–8	21	50	20
Grades 9–12	26	66	8
Raw N = 4,251 Weighted N = 523,048			

Note: Reports from eighth graders are taken from Anderson et al. (1990: 81).

gress and law-making are equated does not necessarily mean that the description of either was dry, but along with the content of the test items
about Congress, it strongly suggests that unadorned institutional structures are at the heart of teaching about the second branch of government.
Similarly, the fact that "principles of democratic government" and "other
forms of government" were the least frequently studied topics suggests by
way of omission the concentration on the structures of U.S. government.

A second conclusion from student reports of topical coverage is that
the relative emphasis changes little from grade to grade or from minimal
to maximal course work. Although some of the uniformity no doubt
comes from the generality of the labels, the degree of similarity across

grades and numbers of civics courses is noteworthy. Consider, for example, the various levels of coverage reported by students in grades 5–8 and 9–12. Eighth graders report similar levels of attention to the Constitution, Congress, how laws are made, parties and elections, and the rights and responsibilities of citizens, and only slightly less attention than twelfth graders to the courts and to state and local government. Students in grades 9–12 do note receiving more instruction on the principles underlying democratic government and on other forms of government, although these topics remain the least studied of any of the listed categories. Overall, the data suggest a good deal of repetition and little sense of a progression of topics across the grades.

Accounts of coverage by students with varying amounts of high school course work tell a similar story. Table 4.9 shows the relationship between amount of civics course work and the extent to which the ten topics are covered. Shown in this table is the percentage of students who claimed that they studied each of the ten topics "a lot" according to the amount of civics course work. Those with more course work report more coverage of each topic. But the *relative* emphasis is very similar in all cases. The Constitution receives the most attention. Trailing behind is the cluster of rights and responsibilities, parties and elections, and Congress, followed by the cluster of the president, the courts, and state and local government. Least coverage at all levels is afforded to other forms of government and to democratic principles. There is some suggestion in the reports that parties, elections, and voting are covered more heavily when students receive more training, a dim reflection, perhaps, of the considerable emphasis on this topic in political science research and teaching at the college level. Otherwise, more course work seems to mean more coverage of the same topics, with no change in broad subject matter. The charge, made by textbook reviewers (see Carroll et al., 1987), that there is no clear sequence of topics and ideas in the civics curriculum finds support in student reports of what they studied.

A third point can be made if we try, in a general way, to relate what students say they have studied to what they know. Because of the overlap in topics—especially "U.S. Constitution," which covers several of the other categories—it is difficult to make this connection. Nevertheless, there appears to be only a weak link between what students study and what they know. On the one hand, we saw in chapter 2 that students were best informed about individual rights, and we observe that "rights and responsibilities of citizens" was one of the most frequently studied topics. Similarly, knowledge of the justice system as such was somewhat lower, which parallels the reduced curricular emphasis on the court system.

Table 4.9 Civics Topics Studied "a Lot" in Grades 9–12,
by Amount of Civics Course Work

	Amount of Civics Course Work			
	Up to a Half-Year	Between a Half-Year and One Year (Percentage of Students)	One Year	More Than One Year
U.S. Constitution and Bill of Rights	44	56	53	63
Congress	36	46	42	53
How laws are made	30	45	41	52
The president and the Cabinet	30	38	38	48
Court system	28	40	38	47
State and local government	27	33	36	44
Political parties, elections, and voting	34	43	41	55
Rights and responsibilities of citizens	39	46	42	53
Principles of democratic government	25	32	28	32
Other forms of government	20	23	26	33
Raw N = 4,244 Weighted N = 522,406				

And overall, there was a connection between breadth and depth of topical coverage and student knowledge (Anderson et al., 1990: 82). On the other hand, student reports indicate that parties, elections, and voting were among the most-studied topics, yet questions about parties were infrequently asked and poorly answered. Likewise, students reported less coverage of state and local governments than of any one branch of the national government, yet they were able to answer a number of questions about the lower levels. And despite considerable emphasis on the specific question of how laws are made, many students could not read a simple chart about how a bill makes its way through Congress.

Without more details, observations about topical coverage and knowledge must remain tentative. When students reported studying parties and elections, they may have had in mind time spent learning the sequence of presidential administrations; if so, then despite reporting heavy coverage, they may have had little instruction related to the test questions. As for the correlation between overall coverage and knowledge, it may be spurious on two grounds. First, overall coverage is related to the amount of course work taken. Second, students with greater interest in civics (and correspondingly more knowledge; see chapter 5) report considerably more coverage of every topic. Questions of spuriousness may be resolved to a degree by multivariate analysis of the sort we undertake in chapter 6, and we defer further discussion until then. For the moment, the tenuousness of the connection between coverage and knowledge is important because it provides additional preliminary insight into the question of the effectiveness of civics course work. In this instance, unlike the results concerning numbers of courses, these results do not clearly contradict the findings of earlier studies concerning the general ineffectiveness of high school civics course work. Based on students' own reports of what they studied, we cannot yet claim that students benefited from their civics courses.

Instructional Approaches and Knowledge

In an effort to learn about instructional approaches, the NAEP survey once again turned to the students. They were asked: "How often has your American government or civics teacher asked you to do the following things for class?" and given a list. The tasks included such things as "reading material from your textbook," "writ[ing] a report of three or more pages," "tak[ing] a test or quiz," and so on. Here, too, the responses are subject to various sorts of reporting biases and cannot be taken as definitive evidence of classroom techniques. Moreover, techniques used by different teachers in the same school can vary widely, so students who had more than one course may have been exposed to quite different classroom styles. Nevertheless, in the absence of direct observations, these reports provide an overall sense of the pedagogical approaches used in teaching high school civics and enable us to get some sense of whether varying techniques are related to student knowledge.

The results, shown in table 4.10, generally confirm the findings of earlier studies, including studies that used trained observers (for a review, see Cuban, 1991: 199–203). Widespread activities included reading from a textbook and discussing or analyzing the material, which are both at least weekly practices in most classrooms. At the other extreme, group projects and writing reports of three or more pages were relatively infrequent —as one would expect given the amount of effort these activities require of both students and teachers. Between these extremes were such activities as test-taking, writing short answers to questions, and working with material not in a textbook. Perhaps the most significant finding is the frequency with which current events were said to have been discussed; 80 percent of the students reported discussing current events daily or once or twice a week.

Given the similarity of classroom practices described by the students in the NAEP survey and in other studies, it is perhaps unsurprising that curricular approaches vary little by the amount of exposure to civics classes. This is important because it offers additional evidence that there is little progression from beginning work to more advanced work in civics. Consider the following: among students who had up to half a year

Table 4.10 Methods of Instruction in Civics Classes,
Grades 9–12, as Reported by Students

	Almost Every Day	Once or Twice a Week	Once or Twice a Month	A Few Times a Year	Never
			(Percentages)		
Read material from your textbook	47	40	8	3	3
Discuss and analyze the material you have read	55	29	10	4	3
Discuss current events	43	37	12	5	3
Take a test or quiz	14	64	20	1	1
Write short answers to questions (a paragraph or less)	23	45	20	6	6
Give talks about what you are studying	34	18	15	16	18
Memorize the material you have read	17	28	22	16	18
Read extra material not in your regular textbook	11	33	27	16	13
Work on a group project	5	13	31	28	24
Write a report of three or more pages	5	8	31	36	21
Raw N = 3,218 Weighted N = 392,075					

of civics course work, 77 percent said they discussed current events at least weekly; among students who had more than a year of such work, 82 percent reported similar attention to current events. Comparable numbers for the students asked to read material other than their textbook were 43 and 46 percent, respectively. Of those asked to write a report of three or more pages (at least monthly), the figures were 41 and 47 percent.

In fact, there is relatively little variation in classroom procedures between eighth and twelfth grades. Movement is in the direction one might expect—more discussion of current events, more reading of material not in the text, more work on group projects, and more writing of reports. But the differences are generally small. Even the biggest difference—for discussing current events—is only 12.5 percentage points (67.5 percent of the eighth graders and 80 percent of the twelfth graders report at least weekly discussions; Anderson et al., 1990: 84). Just as more course work seems to mean more coverage of the same topics, it also appears to mean more of the same kinds of teaching styles.

Ultimately, our concern is not teaching methods per se but whether various teaching techniques result in greater learning of civics material. At first glance, the results seem disappointing. There seems to be no consistent relationship between more frequent use of the various classroom techniques and student knowledge, and *The Report Card* is silent on the matter. Moreover, inference is rendered difficult by the presence of an obvious reporting bias. Students who are more interested in civics report more frequent use of every kind of activity in their classrooms, suggesting that any positive relationship between use of a particular method and level of knowledge might well be spurious.

Yet close inspection of the results, along with a control for the reporting bias, reveal several important patterns. Two techniques appear to promote learning of civics material, and—equally important—two seem to hinder it. Let us begin with the latter. Given the nature of the NAEP test, it might seem that the best way to raise scores would be for students to memorize facts about the Constitution and be drilled repeatedly about those facts. This approach works only if students remember the facts drilled into them. But the results of the test suggest that this strategy often backfires. Similarly, one might think that frequent tests or quizzes would force students seeking high grades to learn constitutional provisions. But again the results suggest the opposite.

We can see these results in the top part of table 4.11, in which we seek to control for the bias in reporting classroom techniques by showing student scores separately for each level of interest in civics. Under the heading "Memorize material you have read," note how the numbers generally decline as one moves from the bottom to the top of each column. That is, the *more* students say they are asked to memorize what they have read, the *lower* their overall scores on the NAEP test. Similarly, under "Take a test or quiz," note that those tested monthly have higher scores than those tested weekly, and those tested weekly have higher scores than those tested daily. Here the differences are substantial. One might, of course, reject frequent memorization and testing because they are among the least interesting ways of teaching about government and politics. But beyond that, it appears as if they work to the detriment of student knowledge— even on a test that is largely based on recollection of factual information.

Contrasting results occur with two very different approaches. In some classrooms, according to student reports, teachers emphasized discussion and analysis of reading material rather than memorization. This approach appears to considerably enhance student learning. In table 4.11, note how the values rise as one moves from the bottom to the top. Of course, this result will come as no surprise to many educators. Understanding what one has read is not only a "higher-level" skill than memorization; it makes it easier to remember facts as well. Although there may be some instances in which straightforward memorization works—if the material is nonintuitive and if it is necessary to call it to mind every day—this is not the case with civics material. Students who are taught to think about and analyze what they are learning about politics are, among other things, better able to remember the facts involved in those lessons.

Similar contrasting results occur in classrooms in which current events are frequently used. As with discussion and analysis, the differences are quite substantial among students whose favorite subject is not

Table 4.11   Overall Political Knowledge, by Methods of Instruction

Method	Interest in Government/Civics		
	Favorite Subject	Interesting	Like Others Better
	(Mean Percentage Correct)		
Memorize material you have read			
Daily	69	68	63
Weekly	75	69	62
Monthly	79	69	65
Yearly	—	74	65
Never	—	72	63
Take a test or quiz			
Daily	69	68	57
Weekly	77	70	65
Monthly	—	72	67
Yearly	—	—	—
Never	—	—	—
Discuss/analyze material			
Daily	78	71	67
Weekly	77	68	63
Monthly	—	69	62
Yearly	—	—	54
Never	—	—	53
Discuss current events			
Daily	78	70	67
Weekly	76	70	64
Monthly	—	69	60
Yearly	—	—	57
Never	—	—	53
Raw N = 3,193 Weighted N = 389,288			

Note: Dashes indicate too few cases for a reliable estimate.

civics (see table 4.11). The mechanism underlying this relationship may be twofold. First, discussion of current events probably helps students understand what politics and government are all about, and the increased level of understanding may be what increases knowledge. Second, the introduction of current events may enliven learning, both because current events typically involve an element of controversy and because they make students aware of the relationship between textbook lessons and life outside the classroom. In any event, the frequent introduction of current events is another classroom technique associated with greater student knowledge.

These findings, based on the multiple-choice items, are given further support when we examine the essays on presidential responsibilities. Because a smaller number of students responded to this item, we collapsed the frequency of various teaching techniques into two categories, "daily or

4.12 Performance on the Presidential Responsibilities Essay, by Methods of Instruction

Method	Interest in Government/Civics		
	Favorite Subject	Interesting (Mean Score)	Like Others Better
Memorize material you have read			
Daily or weekly	2.8	2.8	2.7
Monthly or less	3.0	3.0	2.8
Take a test or quiz			
Daily or weekly	2.8	2.9	2.7
Monthly or less	—	3.1	3.0
Discuss/analyze material			
Daily or weekly	2.9	2.9	2.8
Monthly or less	2.9	2.9	2.8
Discuss current events			
Daily or weekly	2.9	2.9	2.8
Monthly or less	—	3.1	2.8
Raw N = 3,193 Weighted N = 389,288			

Note: Dashes indicate too few cases for a reliable estimate.

weekly" and "monthly or less." The results, shown in table 4.12, are not as consistent as those for the multiple-choice items, though frequent use of memorization and test taking are clearly associated with lower scores. Frequent analysis of material and discussions of current events appear to have little effect here.

Our preliminary evidence, then, suggests that certain kinds of teaching methods (as well as student interest levels) can significantly add to or detract from learning about government and politics. In some classrooms, the charge that civics classes are repetitious and boring is probably correct. In others, political life comes alive. The important point is that we have research findings from a nationwide study that indicate, at least in part, what approaches can change the former into the latter. It is essential to further test this result, as we do in chapter 6, when we incorporate method of instruction (and level of interest) into a multivariate model in order to test the durability of our conclusions in the face of other factors related to enhanced learning. But tentatively, we can say that what the teacher brings to the classroom by way of methods and material—in ways that are understandable and theoretically plausible—seems to be an important factor in what students take away from their classes.

Teaching techniques do not seem to alter students' attitudes toward government responsiveness. Nevertheless, one possibility needs to be considered. Do analysis and discussion of current events—the very activities that seem to promote factual knowledge—make students more cynical about government? Memorizing government structures and taking tests about them may not alter one's views. But analyzing the activities of candidates and of government leaders, or discussing what Congress and the president have (or have not) accomplished, could lead students to think less highly of government.

As it turns out, none of the teaching styles bears a consistent relationship to students' feelings about trust in government (not shown). After controlling for how much students like to study civics (which is necessary here as it was for knowledge levels), fewer students who reported frequent analysis and discussion believe that government is responsive. But the evidence is the same for memorization and test-taking. Thus, insofar as we can tell, manner of presentation has no effect on students' evaluations of government responsiveness. To the extent that one might be concerned that certain activities would increase cynicism, this nonfinding is reassuring.

The Consistency of Opportunities to Learn

We have characterized exposure to learning about government and politics in high school by the extent of civics course work, breadth and depth of subject matter coverage, and instructional approaches used. Having found that at least two of these characteristics are related to levels of student knowledge, the question needs to be addressed of whether exposure to learning varies systematically by school type, material and teaching resources, and demographic composition. If exposure differs according to these or similar factors, differences in learning may be attributable, in part, to the type of school that students attend—a characteristic that is largely beyond their control—and our interpretation of variations in student scores would necessarily change substantially.

One of the major debates in current educational practice is whether public school systems can provide the kinds of opportunities that are available in private and religious schools. Therefore, we begin by investigating whether public, private, and Catholic schools (the only denomination of religious school with sufficient numbers for investigation) provide comparable levels of exposure to civic learning. We consider differences by type of community and region at the same time because school type varies substantially across areas of the country. Related to the question of school type is whether schools with more material resources and smaller teacher-to-student ratios are able to provide students with greater opportunities in terms of the characteristics noted, and we take that up next.

Although different types of schools vary widely in some important respects, such as in the control they exercise over the selection of students,
they should not differ greatly in basic opportunities to learn civic material. It is unlikely, for example, that schools vary a great deal in their of-
fering of the most basic civics curriculum. American history classes, in
which some civics teaching takes place, are available in virtually every
high school. A single semester of civics is also likely to be widely offered.
It may be, however, that schools vary in the extent to which they offer
more than the minimal amount of civic instruction. In addition, the nature of the instruction in economically disadvantaged schools may differ
from that in wealthier districts—not because school policies differ but
because class sizes, facilities and resources (such as library and computer
facilities), and teacher background and training differ. If schools are
crowded, few resources are available, or teachers are less experienced or
feel overburdened, these problems may show up as less imaginative and
stimulating civics (and other) classes. This, in turn, could explain some of
the differences in achievement levels that we have observed. However, if
the data show little or no difference in the opportunities to learn according to resources, we shall need to look elsewhere for explanations.

Finally, we investigate whether schools that are relatively homogeneous in their racial make up systematically present students with different opportunities to learn about government and politics. Although we
have no reason to believe that teachers consciously differ in how they
teach minority students, differences may occur because of factors that are
correlated with the racial composition of the schools. Inner-city schools,
in particular, are likely to have more minority students and fewer economic resources. If instructional dollars make a difference in classroom
approaches, we would expect these differences to show up when we contrast schools whose students are either largely white or largely minority.
Even if dollars spent make no difference in learning, however, it is possible that differences in the students themselves matter. Studies show,
for example, that African-American adults tend to be Democratic and
relatively homogeneous in their attitudes on many social issues (Gurin,
Hatchett, and Jackson, 1989: 87–96). Such similarities among students
could lead to unintended consequences—for example, by minimizing the
extent to which current events are discussed.

Nonetheless, here we are driven as much by group differences that we
shall uncover in later chapters as by political or educational theory. In
chapters 5–6 we report persistent racial and ethnic differences in student
knowledge levels. It is important to know whether we can explain some of
these differences by the nature of the schools these students attend. We

would still have to search for the factors underlying those school-related explanations, but they would provide us with a beginning point in understanding individual differences in knowledge.

Type of School, Community, and Region

Table 4.13 shows the opportunities to learn about civics by type of school, type of community, and region. As measured by amount of course work, the public schools do a slightly better job of providing at least minimal civic training for all students. Students in private and Catholic schools are slightly more likely to report less than a half-year of civics course work (although even in private and sectarian schools the "coverage" rate in this sense is about 85 percent). Note, however, that public schools do as good a job or better of getting students to take as much as a year of civics classes. As to coverage of different civics topics, students in Catholic schools report a somewhat narrower range; on the other hand, these students report as much discussion of current events as students in public schools. Overall, the image we get is of relatively small, inconsistent differences across type of school.

Geographic differences are somewhat more consistent, though not entirely so, and they are not large. Students in rural and small-town schools are least likely to have had no or minimal civics course work (10 percent versus 13 percent in larger areas with less than half a year) and most likely to have had a year or more of work. Likewise, small-town and rural students report wide (but not the widest) topical coverage and the most frequent discussions of current events. Students in the northeast are most likely to have minimal course work (16 percent versus 11 percent elsewhere with less than half a year), although students in the same region report the second highest frequency of a year or more of work. Students in the northeast also report both the lowest coverage of topics and the least frequent discussions of current events. Although relatively consistent, the differences are modest, and to some extent they can be explained by the distribution of private and Catholic schools (fewer in rural areas, more in the northeast). Thus, the opportunity to learn civic material in all types of schools still seems relatively uniform.

Instructional Dollars per Pupil

We were particularly interested in data that revealed characteristics indicating the overall resources available to the school. In preliminary analyses, we considered several such indicators, such as the percentage of

Table 4.13 Opportunities to Learn Civics, by Type of School,
Type of Community, and Region

	Sample	Had One or More Years of Civics Courses	Studied Six to Ten Topics in Civics Courses	Discussed Current Events Almost Daily
		(Percentages)		
Type of school				
Public	85	63	35	43
Private, not Catholic	4	49	37	37
Catholic	11	61	33	43
Type of Community				
Rural/small town	26	69	36	44
Urban areas	55	60	37	43
Medium sized town	19	61	29	38
Region				
Northeast	25	68	30	39
Southeast	23	70	35	44
Central	25	58	37	45
West	27	56	39	42
Raw N = 3,237 Weighted N = 394,613				

Table 4.14 Opportunities to Learn Civics, by Instructional Dollars per Pupil

Instructional Dollars per Pupil	Sample[a]	Had One or More Years of Civics Courses	Studied Six to Ten Topics in Civics Courses	Discussed Current Events Almost Daily
		(Percentages)		
25–35	4	53	41	48
35–45	12	64	37	48
45–55	19	69	34	43
55–65	17	70	34	42
65–75	11	52	40	41
75–150	35	60	34	41
150+	2	62	30	47
Raw N = 2,842 Weighted N = 333,857				

[a]Thirteen percent of the sample was unclassified by IDP.

students who participated in a subsidized school lunch and nutrition program and the location of the school (big city, urban fringe). These seemed
to make little difference to the amount and nature of civics teaching. We
then looked at an estimate of one measure of the amount of money spent
on instruction per pupil believing that dollars spent would serve as a
proxy for determining the general availability of high-quality personnel
and instructional support.

Table 4.14 shows the relationship between the measure of instructional dollars per pupil and our three measures of civic instruction.[10] We
found that there was little connection between opportunities to learn and

instructional dollars per pupil. For the extent of civic training, students whose schools spent in the middle range of instructional dollars reported most frequently that they had taken a year or more of civics course work. This connection is not entirely trustworthy, however, as the students who reported least frequently taking a year or more civics were also in the middle range of schools.

There is, if anything, a slightly negative relationship between spending per student and coverage of a variety of topics in civics classes. Although we might have anticipated that high-spending schools would be the places where teachers and students discussed the widest variety of topics and schools with less money the places where they discussed the smallest variety, the actual connection is reversed, although the two groups do not differ that greatly. This difference only occurs at the top end; among the bulk of the schools, there is virtually no difference in variety of topics covered. Finally, there is no discernible relationship between money spent per student and the extent to which civics teachers discuss current events. The final column in the table shows that between 40 and 50 percent of all students, regardless of the financial resources of their schools, discuss current events on a daily basis in their civics classes.

Student-Teacher Ratio

The student-teacher ratio, as a more specific measure of the time teachers can devote to individual students and classes, might be related to characteristics of civics teaching even though data on instructional dollars are not. Although lower student-teacher ratios might not mean that students will take more civics courses, one might expect that teachers would be better able to provide creative and interactive learning opportunities in each class, which would manifest themselves in the study of more topics (or perhaps less study of standard topics) and in more frequent discussions. In this sense, the smaller the ratio, the greater the opportunities one might expect for students to learn about government and politics.

The data in table 4.15 do not support such expectations. Intriguingly, there is a limited connection between having small classes and taking more civics courses—the connection we considered the least probable. However, it is only when the student-teacher ratio is very small (10 to 1 or less) that the amount of course taking stands out. Such a low ratio applied to only 5 percent of the student population. The number of topics studied has almost no relationship to class size. It is not true that students in

Table 4.15 Opportunities to Learn Civics, by Student-Teacher Ratio

Student-Teacher Ratio	Sample	Had One or More Years of Civics Courses	Studied Six to Ten Topics in Civics Courses	Discussed Current Events Almost Daily
		(Percentages)		
5–10:1	5	72	38	38
11–15:1	25	64	34	41
16–20:1	43	62	37	44
21–25:1	22	59	31	43
26–29:1	3	58	38	37
30–43:1	3	65	42	47
Raw N = 3,227 Weighted N = 392,891				

schools with more teachers cover more topics. Finally, there is ragged relationship between the student-teacher ratio and the discussion of current events in civics classes. Notably, even where the student-teacher ratio is very small, students report no more frequent discussion of current events than in large classes.

Racial Homogeneity and Minority Population Concentration

We noted a variety of reasons why students in racially homogeneous schools—especially those with high concentrations of minorities—might have differing opportunities to learn about civics. To find out whether the relationship in fact existed, we contrast schools that are almost exclusively white with schools that are largely African-American, Hispanic, or Asian. For the first two groups, these are schools where more than half the students are of the given group; in the case of Asians, these are schools where more than 10 percent of students are of this background. The results are shown in table 4.16.

The data show some potentially interesting but ultimately ambiguous patterns. Students in heavily Hispanic schools took the fewest civics

Table 4.16 Opportunities to Learn Civics, by Minority Student Concentration

Minority Population Concentration	Sample	Had One or More Years of Civics Courses	Studied Six to Ten Topics in Civics Courses	Discussed Current Events Almost Daily
		(Percentages)		
50 percent and more African-American	6	63	42	41
50 percent and more Hispanic	4	55	33	48
10 percent and more Asian	4	60	48	52
98 percent and more white	18	64	40	43
Raw N = 3,237 Weighted N = 394,613				

classes and tended to cover a smaller range of topics in those classes. However, these students reported discussing current events more often than those in heavily white or African-American schools. Students in heavily African-American schools reported discussing current events least often, as we hypothesized, but they took more civics courses than students in the other heavily minority schools, and they discussed a variety of topics more often than students in the heavily Hispanic and white schools. Students in schools with a large proportion of Asians fall either at the top of the list or the bottom, according to category. Thus, the overall message is that students who attend schools with a relatively high proportion of minority students do not appear to be systematically disadvantaged, compared to students from virtually all-white schools, in terms of their opportunity to learn civic material.

At the outset of this chapter we outlined a number of reasons why civics course work might not have its intended effect and why high school students might gain much of their political knowledge and attitudes outside of the school. Earlier, in chapter 1, we noted that a number of research studies seemed to confirm this reasoning by finding little or no effect of civics courses on students' knowledge and attitudes. Against that background, the findings of our work here are especially striking in that they are highly supportive of school efforts. We must temper our conclusions somewhat until we see the results of the multivariate analysis in chapter 6, but the findings in this chapter strongly suggest that civics course work can and does have an impact on student learning.

Why do we find positive effects when others have not? We are tempted to say that we simply have better data, thanks to the extensive nature of the NAEP test. And, indeed, this is probably part of the answer. But there is more to it than that. One of the things we have learned is that there appears to be a difference between the effect of civics classes taken in the early grades of high school and those taken in the senior year. Methodologically, this means that simply dividing students into two groups — those who have had civics course work and those who have not, or those who have had minimal work and those who have had more — is insufficient. If our results are correct, they suggest that students learn more about government and politics when it becomes meaningful to them, when they have reached or are about to reach adulthood. Efforts to find course effects must take this factor into account.

Of course this conclusion carries with it more than a methodological point for researchers. It means that if we want students to learn more about civics and government, one option is to insist that they take relevant course work in their senior year. As it stands, we found that about 60 percent of the students reported having a twelfth-grade course in civics. That leaves considerable room for advancement. Implementing a change to more twelfth-grade courses might be an easy matter if all civics work came about in free-standing courses. But in many instances, states do not require a separate course, and operationally, it is likely that a considerable amount of course work in civics is contained in history classes, which are often taught in the eleventh grade. Thus, a "simple" finding that twelfth grade is a more appropriate time for civic education carries with it quite substantial implications for many school systems.

Another of our findings also has methodological and substantive connotations. We found initial evidence (that also needs verification in our multivariate model) that students learn more when teachers use certain classroom techniques over others. On the one hand, this means that in looking for school effects, researchers need to take into account more than amount of classroom exposure. This point has been widely recognized when attitudes were the subject of study. What we have added is that knowledge itself about politics and government is increased when teachers use more analytical approaches that focus on contemporary concerns.

Classroom practices are already weighted in the direction of the techniques that bolster civic learning. More than half of the students reported discussing or analyzing what they have read almost every day, and just under half reported that current events were nearly a daily item in civics classes. At the other extreme, few said that analysis was infrequent and that current events were rarely considered. But many students also report that daily or weekly memorization was a part of their civics course work, and the vast majority say that they were given a test or quiz at least once a week. We have no way of knowing, of course, the nature of such assignments and tests; no doubt some kinds of memorization and testing are better than others. Yet it appears that too much civics teaching is still devoted to memorizing constitutional provisions and government-organization charts without comprehension of what these things mean. Nor can we be sure that memorization and testing per se are the problem. It may be that less experienced teachers, or teachers who are less interested in civics and themselves less knowledgeable about government use memorization and frequent tests to mask their indifference or lack of ability. Nevertheless, our results carry the strong suggestion that efforts at rote learning of constitutional provisions are not the best way to learn even the facts.

Because of the nature of the NAEP test, our focus was on knowledge, not attitudes. Nevertheless, our results for the two attitudinal items were reassuring. The concern that students might become more cynical by frequent discussion of current events or by analyzing what they read was not borne out. And course work per se seemed to bolster students' feelings about the responsiveness of the government. So here, too, our findings can be viewed positively.

The one more negative finding was the absence of any progression of topical coverage across the grades and as students moved from less to more course work. It appears that at each level civics courses are centered around U.S. Constitutional provisions and therefore involve a great deal of repetition. It is noteworthy, in light of this, that course work overall is as strongly related to knowledge as it is. Here, then, is another way in which civics teaching could be improved. A progressive element might be introduced in many ways. Teaching more about other forms of democratic government, like any comparative view, would lead naturally into questions of the theoretical foundations of democratic systems—both topics that students reported as receiving relatively little coverage. But the point is not the specific way civics is taught but that some way be devised of creating what is regarded as advancement rather than repetition.

That point aside, the results of both chapter 2 and our preliminary look here at educational effects convey an upbeat message. In contrast to sweeping condemnations of student ignorance, our topic-by-topic examination showed that students do know a lot about some aspects of American government and politics. In addition, there was at least some indication that their lesser knowledge of other aspects could be traced to absence of coverage in high school classes. Now we find that school factors are of considerable importance in determining what young people know, and we have gone a step farther by identifying some of the specific factors that are relevant. Educational effects do not have to be attributed to selection effects or to some impenetrable black box. What takes place in the civics curriculum—the amount, content, and approach—makes a difference.

CHAPTER FIVE

Selection and Retention

In this chapter we deal with what we referred to in chapter 3 as individual characteristics—those features of individual students that help regulate the selection of information for retention. Teachers have always known that exposure to information is not enough to guarantee that students will learn. In saying this, we are not adopting a cynical view of students, for researchers have long known that for a variety of reasons, people may fail to understand, consciously ignore, or simply forget information they have been exposed to. An obvious example in the realm of public affairs is that people often cannot recollect, without prompting, stories they saw on evening news programs even when interviewed a few hours after the broadcast (see Neuman, 1986).

We shall examine only a subset of the relevant factors identified in chapter 3. In the home environment, we identified two factors that are potentially significant. One of these, parents' education, has been frequently related to young people's knowledge levels, as we noted, and we can set it aside for the multivariate analysis in the next chapter. In this chapter, we shall consider in detail the amount of television that students watch, for the strength of and reasons for the connection between television viewing and civic knowledge is less clear-cut. Then we shall turn to individual achievement factors. Again, it can safely be assumed that one of them— plans to attend a four-year college—is strongly related to civic knowledge; this factor can therefore be carried over to chapter 6 with no further analysis at this point. The other two—interest in studying government and participation in such activities as student councils—will be considered here.

Finally, we shall look at the relationship between race or ethnicity and knowledge and that between gender and knowledge. These characteristics are somewhat different, in that we presume that they are not themselves the causal factors underlying any observed associations. Thus, for example, we assume that if girls score lower than boys, it is because of lesser interest or some other correlated factor and not because of their sex as such. If our knowledge were unlimited, it would make sense to control directly for the causal factors at work. Even then, however, we might want to know whether there were racial and gender differences because of the great interest in these groups at the present time.

In each case, we shall look at scores on all knowledge questions combined, as well as at scores for each of the categories defined in chapter 2; at responses on the open-ended question about presidential responsibilities; and at the two items about government responsiveness.

Home Environment: Television Viewing

Just as the amount of civic training is an obvious school characteristic to relate to high school seniors' knowledge of politics and government, so the amount of television viewing is an important characteristic of the home environment. Of the various features of the home environment, television viewing stands out because of the many hours Americans devote to it. High school seniors are no exception. In 1988, almost 30 percent of the seniors in the NAEP survey reported watching television for four or more hours, and 72 percent watched for two or more hours, *per day*. In addition, the amount of exposure students have to television is important because it is relatively controllable, although it is regulated by students and parents, not teachers. If television viewing is found to be detrimental to learning, reducing its intake represents a virtually cost-free (but by no means easy) way to improve knowledge.

It would be surprising if this amount of attention to television were not related to civic as well as other types of academic knowledge, at least among those watching the most frequently. Most obvious, time spent watching television is time spent *not* doing homework. But time spent watching television may also mean less time spent reading newspapers, and perhaps less time devoted to school clubs, student councils, and other activities that could teach students about government. In addition, those who watch a great deal of television may coincidentally care a good deal less about school-related concerns and have lower expectations for

Table 5.1 Overall Political Knowledge, by Amount of Television Viewing

Hours per Day Watching Television	Percentage of Sample	Civic Knowledge (Mean Percentage Correct)
Up to one	28	69
Two to three	44	68
Four to five	21	63
Six or more	7	55
Raw *N* = 4,261 Weighted *N* = 523,908		

the future, so their incentive to learn about any school subject is also reduced.

Looking at the responses to all the knowledge items combined confirms these expectations for the most part. Table 5.1 shows the distribution of the television-viewing measure and the mean percentage of correct answers in overall political knowledge. First, note that up to three hours a day of television viewing does not make much difference in civic knowledge. Those who watch two to three hours of television per day have almost the same score on the overall political-knowledge test as those who watch less than one. Admittedly, the results are not as complete as we would like; there are too few students who watch no television to make a meaningful comparison between viewers and complete abstainers. Still, as far as we can tell, a moderate (by today's standards) amount of viewing does not detract from students' knowledge levels. The explanation may be that students who watch limited amounts of television combine viewing with other activities. As students would say, perhaps they *can* do their homework with the television on.

More viewing, however, clearly coincides with lower levels of civic knowledge. Yet here, too, the differences are not great. Even those who claim to watch television six or more hours a day score "only" 14 percentage points below those who watch the least frequently. It is worthwhile in this connection to recall the results for those with different amounts of civics course work. There, as here, the greatest differences are at the "low" extreme in terms of knowledge. Students with no civics courses and students who watch television more than six hours a day— both, coincidentally, representing about 7 percent of the population— were the most distinctive group. Having some course work, or watching less television, left one less knowledgeable than the top group, but not by a large margin. Thus, by itself, neither course work nor television viewing fully differentiates the knowledgeable from the uninformed. Yet precisely because this is the case, these results move us a step farther toward an understanding of the role of the multiple factors that help create politically knowledgeable high school seniors. We shall return to this point as we move through the various factors in this chapter.

It is important, however, that we also take a look at television usage and the various categories of political knowledge delineated in chapter 2. One can imagine that at least some genuine civic lessons are derived from television programs. Indeed, studies of adults often test for the positive effects of television on political knowledge, though the results are mixed (Neuman, Just, and Crigler, 1992: chap. 5; Young and Patterson, 1994; Delli Carpini and Keeter, 1996: 185). With respect to the specific items in NAEP, we pointed out in chapter 2 that television is one possible reason for the relatively high levels of knowledge about criminal rights and procedures.

Considered by category, there are small differences consistent with the hypothesis that some learning derives from television. Table 5.2 displays the mean percentage of correct answers for the ten types of political knowledge by amount of television viewing. For the first two categories, the differences between least- and most-frequent television viewers are 12 and 13 percent, respectively. For most of the other categories, the differences are 14 percent or more, with the biggest difference being found in the ability to make inferences from tables, text, charts (19 percent), and knowledge of lobbying (24 percent). Even so, there are many individual items pertaining to criminal rights that do not fit the pattern. Setting aside the relative sizes of the differences, high-frequency television viewers are less knowledgeable than low-frequency viewers for all but a handful of the 150 items. Moreover, despite the larger differences in most of the categories, there are two (Political Parties and Women and Minorities) in which the differences between the extremes of television viewing are no larger than those for the "rights" categories. Thus, one cannot reasonably sustain the argument that television is a contributor to civic knowledge even in those subjects where it is most plausible.

Television viewing is also related to the quality of responses on the presidential responsibilities question. Table 5.3 shows the performance on this item by the amount of television viewing. The pattern is slightly different here from that for the multiple-choice items: the largest difference occurs at the low end of the viewing scale. Even a modest amount of television viewing (one hour or less) is associated with a drop of 4 percentage points in the ability to provide an elaborated answer. It is also worth noting that here, in contrast to overall knowledge, the overall relationship—as judged by the differences between the extremes—is less extensive than that for taking civics courses.

In short, while television may provide some facts relevant to civics

Table 5.2 Ten Types of Political Knowledge, by Amount of Television Viewing

	Hours per Day Watching Television			
Type of Knowledge	Up to One	Two to Three	Four to Five	Six or More
		(Mean Percentage Correct)		
Criminal and civil justice	80	81	76	68
General rights of citizens	82	81	78	69
State and local government	69	67	63	55
Political parties	59	59	52	46
Lobbying	67	66	57	43
Women and minorities	72	70	65	62
Structure and function of U.S. government	63	62	56	48
Inferences from text, tables, charts	71	70	64	52
Comparative perspective	74	74	64	59
Theoretical perspective	51	49	41	37
Raw N = 4,261 Weighted N = 523,908				

Table 5.3 Performance on the Presidential Responsibilities Essay, by Amount of Television Viewing

	Hours per Day Watching Television			
Understanding of Presidential Responsibilities	Up to One	Two to Three	Four to Five	Six or More
		(Percentage)		
Unacceptable	10	5	7	13
Minimal	29	35	39	40
Adequate	38	41	41	36
Elaborated	23	19	15	12
Raw N = 1,789 Weighted N = 221,491				

and government, the message is that high rates of television viewing detract from political knowledge. Students who watch many hours of television a day are less able to answer questions about the structure and functioning of their government, to make reasonable inferences from relevant information, and to describe what the president does. The differences are not as large as one might have expected—they are of about the same magnitude as for civics course work (or possibly less)—but frequent viewing of television is a negative factor with respect to civic learning.

Political material on television is often critical of the political process or of bureaucrats, candidates, elected officials, and other representatives of that process. Even though few high school students watch the kind of news and public-affairs programs that contain a great deal of information about politics, by watching television, they are likely to be exposed to such critical views. In addition, because students who are less interested in civics and less involved in school activities are the ones who watch more television, there may be a relationship between amount of television

Table 5.4   Government Responsiveness, by Amount of Television Viewing

Attitude	Hours per Day Watching Television			
	Up to One	Two to Three	Four to Five	Six or More
		(Percentage of Students)		
Amount of attention government pays to people				
Not much	20	21	27	40
Some	62	61	60	46
A good deal	19	18	13	14
Elections make government accountable				
Not much	10	8	11	23
Some	45	47	48	42
A good deal	45	45	41	36
Raw $N = 4,202$ Weighted $N = 517,245$				

watched and cynicism toward government, even if the connection is not causal.

The results for the two available questions leave us with a certain amount of ambiguity. Table 5.4 shows the relationship between the two measures of attitudes about politics—the amount of attention government pays to people and the extent to which elections make government accountable—by amount of television viewing. Students who watch a great deal of television think that the government is less responsive to the people, but there is a smaller connection between television viewing and judgments about the role of elections in making the government accountable (though in both cases the relationship is similar to that for civics course work). Thus we are left with uncertainty about the possible effects of television on attitudes about political responsiveness. What we can say is that the evidence does not support a sweeping conclusion about the negative effects of television viewing on political attitudes.

Individual Achievement

Participation in Mock Elections, Councils, Trials

It is widely hypothesized that student involvement in extracurricular activities influences civic participation—or at least individuals' evaluations of participation (Beck and Jennings, 1982; Miller, 1985; Holland and Andre, 1987; Ferguson, 1991). The reason is that individuals are believed to learn both an ethic of participation and the skills involved in understanding and influencing group decision making. Later in life, this ethic and these skills encourage them to take more of a part in group activities than others. Less likely, but still possible, is the idea that participation influences students' knowledge levels. Students who internalize the procedures for collective decision making may better remember facts about the role of different parts and levels of government, about checks and balances, and so on. Or it may simply be the case that those who participate in these activities feel impelled to pay more attention in their civics classes.

The NAEP survey collected only one piece of evidence about student involvement that might include activities outside the classroom. Students were asked: "How often have you participated in mock or imitation elections, governmental bodies (like a council, legislature, or Congress), or trials?" We cannot know for certain whether students answered most often in terms of student councils and other school-wide activities or in terms of classroom experiences. And although we interpret this measure as school-related, it may be that some nonschool activities were on their minds as well.

In spite of this ambiguity, we need to consider the possible effects of such participation. On the one hand, we wish to tap into as many school-related elements as possible in order to capture the full effects of high schools on students' civic knowledge. This factor, insofar as it is exclusively school related, is useful because it is under the control of students more than other school factors; students are not required to participate in student councils, for example. On the other hand, we wish to control for possible nonclassroom effects in order to avoid overestimating the effects of civic classes per se. Again, this variable serves the purpose to the extent that it measures students' involvement outside normal classes. Yet another reason for considering this variable is that, perhaps more than any other school factor, it might more strongly affect students' feelings about government responsiveness than their factual knowledge. Simulated participation, more than most reading from texts or even classroom discussions, may guide students' thinking about how likely it is that government leaders will respond to public opinion.

The data in tables 5.5 and 5.6 show that student participation in mock elections, councils, and trials is related to both political knowledge and attitudes. A little less than half of all high school seniors took part in mock elections, councils, and trials, and those who participated were better able to answer factual questions as well as to explain the president's responsibilities. The differences on the multiple-choice items are of about the same magnitude as those for civics courses and for television viewing. In addition, students who participated were also more likely to believe that the government is responsive to citizens and, more than was the case with television viewing, to believe that elections help make it that way.

Table 5.5 Overall Political Knowledge and Presidential Responsibilities Essay, by Participation in Mock Elections, Councils, Trials

Frequency of Participation	Percentage of Sample	Mean Percentage Correct	Understanding of Responsibilities of the President			
			Unacceptable	Minimal	Adequate	Elaborated
			(Percentage of Students)			
Never	52	63	8	37	40	14
Once or twice	36	69	6	30	41	23
Several times	12	74	6	34	34	26
Raw N = 1,784	Weighted N = 221,103					

Table 5.6 Government Responsiveness, by Participation in Mock Elections, Council, Trials

	Frequency of Participation		
Attitude	Never	Once or Twice	Several Times
	(Percentage of Students)		
Amount of attention government pays to people			
Not much	26	22	16
Some	60	60	60
A good deal	15	18	24
Elections make government accountable			
Not much	12	9	6
Some	48	47	37
A good deal	40	44	57
Raw N = 4,204 Weighted N = 517,574			

Given these results, it is important to carry over this variable to the multivariate analysis of chapter 6. Note, however, that even if the measure of student participation survives that analysis, its impact is muted by the fact that fully half of the students indicated that they had never participated in this kind of activity. Further, in light of the ambiguities of the question itself, we would be uncertain of just what activities to encourage even if we believed in their effect. But the results deserve further consideration.

Interest in American Government

However much course work students have had, and whatever their backgrounds, an important correlate of civic knowledge is likely to be their interest in the topic. Certainly this has proved to be the case in studies of political knowledge among adults (Luskin, 1990; Young and Patterson, 1994: 11; Delli Carpini and Keeter, 1996: 182–84). At the teenage level, such a connection may come about, in part, because students who are interested in a subject pay more attention to teachers and texts and make an active effort to remember information related to the topic. Indeed, students who regarded civics as one of their favorite subjects reported spending considerably more time on homework and achieved markedly better grades in civics classes than those who did not. As we noted in chapter 4, they also reported more frequent exposure to each kind of teaching activity in their classrooms, which may be an indication of how much attention they were paying to what was taking place.

In addition to possible direct causation through course work, interest is also likely to affect students' behavior both inside and outside the school in ways that lead to greater knowledge. For example, students who were more interested in civics participated more frequently in mock elections and the like. It is also likely that highly interested students read and listened to reports of the news more frequently than others and more often engaged in politically relevant conversations. In any event, students who are interested in a subject are likely to try to remember more of what they hear about it.

Analysis of the NAEP items tentatively confirms this link between student interest and acquisition of civic knowledge. Overall (table 5.7), and within each of the ten categories (table 5.8), students who liked other subjects better were the least knowledgeable, while those who regarded civics as their favorite subject were the most knowledgeable. The average differences are smallest in the areas of criminal justice and rights of citizens, in which all students scored higher, but even here the gap is large enough that it is relatively consistent across the individual items within the categories.

Significantly, interest in civics makes a difference even on questions that do not require memorization of facts about government and politics and on topics that are underemphasized in civics classes. Consider, for example, the question that required students to read a table showing that the more education people have, the more politically active they are. All the information needed to answer this question is contained in the item itself (see chapter 2), so students with more knowledge about political behavior would not seem to have an advantage. Relatively little time seems to be spent on this kind of exercise in civics classes, so the fact that interested students are more attentive during class time would not seem to benefit them either. Nonetheless, there is a fifteen-point gap in the percentage of students answering this question correctly, from 56 percent among those who liked other subjects better to 61 percent among those who found civics interesting to 71 percent among those who said civics was their fa-

Table 5.7   Overall Political Knowledge, by Interest in American Government/Civics

Interest in American Government/Civics	Percentage of Sample	Civic Knowledge (Mean Percentage Correct)
Favorite subject	10	74
Interesting	41	69
Like others better	47	63
Raw N = 4,244 Weighted N = 522,291		

Table 5.8   Ten Types of Political Knowledge, by Interest in American Government/Civics

	Interest in American Government/Civics		
Type of Knowledge	Like Others Better	Interesting	Favorite Subject
	(Mean Percentage Correct)		
Criminal and civil justice	76	81	84
General rights of citizens	77	82	85
State and local government	63	69	73
Political parties	53	59	65
Lobbying	58	66	73
Women and minorities	65	73	74
Structure and function of U.S. government	56	63	71
Inferences from text, tables, charts	65	70	76
Comparative perspective	68	73	81
Theoretical perspective	43	50	58
Raw N = 4,244 Weighted N = 522,291			

vorite subject. Similar gaps appear on seven of the eight items calling for inferences from text, tables, and charts. Differences of a similar magnitude appear in such categories as Political Parties and Lobbying, which are also underemphasized in civics courses.

The results offer interesting comparisons to our findings showing knowledge levels among those with varying amounts of civics course work and television viewing. In contrast to those results, the differences here are equally large as we move from the "high" to the "low" end: those for whom civics was their favorite subject and the much larger group of students who found it "interesting" or liked other subjects better. In another crucial respect, however, the results are similar. The difference between the extreme categories—at 11 percentage points—is identical to that for participation in mock elections and somewhat less than that for television viewing and civics course work. Here as well, then, a factor that offers a clear distinction between more and less knowledgeable students shows a meaningful but not overwhelming gap between the top and bottom groups.

Table 5.9 Students' Performance on the Presidential Responsibilities Essay, by Interest in American Government/Civics

Understanding of Presidential Responsibilities	Interest in American Government/Civics		
	Like Others Better	Interesting (Percentage)	Favorite Subject
Unacceptable	9	5	7
Minimal	37	32	29
Adequate	39	42	36
Elaborated	15	21	28
Raw N = 1,786 Weighted N = 221,158			

Similar conclusions carry over to the question about presidential responsibilities. That is, the difference is greatest between students for whom civics was their favorite subject and the remaining students, and the size of the gap is about the same as for varying amounts of civics course work and television viewing (table 5.9).

In short, although there may be a number of causal connections, many of which involve the school but some of which do not, there is no doubt that a significant relationship exists between level of interest in civics and knowledge of it. That this result simply confirms a commonsense expectation makes it no less important, and it is noteworthy that the result holds for such a wide range of items and for variations at both higher and lower levels of interest. There is no magic potion that makes students enjoy studying civics, and there is no single way of teaching them to do so. But these results suggest, as one would expect, that any success in making politics and government more interesting for students will pay off in increased civic knowledge.

From the perspective of our investigation into school effects, there are two major implications. The first is that in our multivariate analysis we have to control for interest levels (as well as participation in mock elections) in order not to overestimate the effects of civics courses per se. The second implication is, in a sense, the reverse of this point. That is, any residual effects of the interest factor in the multivariate model may to some degree be attributable to what occurs in the school, including what happens when civic material is being studied. We need to remember both these points when we interpret the results of the analysis.

It seems likely that students who are interested in civics will be more inclined than others to believe that the government is responsive to citizens and that elections help make it that way. Two mechanisms may be at work. First, interested students may absorb lessons about government responsiveness and about how elections constrain political leaders. They

Table 5.10   Government Responsiveness, by Interest
in American Government/Civics

| Attitude | Interest in American Government/Civics | | |
	Like Others Better	Interesting (Percentage)	Favorite Subject
Amount of attention government pays to people			
Not much	26	21	17
Some	61	61	57
A good deal	14	19	26
Elections make government accountable			
Not much	12	8	7
Some	50	45	37
A good deal	38	48	56
Raw N = 4,199 Weighted N = 516,913			

may be more sensitive to historical examples of leaders who were especially good and bad in this regard. Second, there may be an element of cognitive consistency involved. That is, students who are interested in politics might not want to believe that the government is uninterested in them or that the primary mechanism of control doesn't work.

Whatever the reasons, students who are more interested in government are considerably more optimistic about its attentiveness to citizens and about the role of elections in making responsiveness the norm. Table 5.10 shows the relationship between the items concerning government responsiveness and students' interest in civics. This result, along with our earlier finding that civics course work strongly inclined students to perceive more responsiveness, suggests that greater attention to civics and government while in high school may help to retard the cynicism that seems inevitably to come with adulthood. At the very least, course work in civics and government, along with high levels of interest in the subject, do not contribute to declining trust or hasten the arrival of adult levels of cynicism.

Gender, Race, and Ethnicity

It is conventional in analyses of both political knowledge and attitudes to consider their relationship to background characteristics like gender and race and ethnicity. Indeed, such is the interest in these characteristics that they are standard reporting categories for the NAEP assessments. It should be obvious that gender and race and ethnicity differ from the other factors determining exposure to and retention of civic material. Those factors are clearly hypothesized to be causal in nature. We assume, for purposes of testing, that students learn about politics and government *because of* what happens in their civics courses. We assume that television viewing has a detrimental effect on learning *because* it is time spent away from homework, reading, and adult conversations. With respect to attitudes, as well, we assume that students think differently about government responsiveness *because of* their participation in student councils, *because of* their experience with different teaching styles, and so on.

This is not to deny that some part of the relationship between these factors and civic knowledge and attitudes is indirect or even spurious, owing its existence to still other correlated factors. We noted, for example, that parental education is a major determinant of where students live and therefore of the kinds of friends students associate with. Thus, when we observe the relationship between parents' levels of education and student knowledge, part of that connection may be due to what friends think and say.[1]

When we turn to gender and race and ethnicity, however, the balance shifts heavily toward the presumption that these are not direct causal factors. We presume that neither girls nor boys are inherently smarter or have inherently different political views and that any differences between African-Americans, Hispanics, and non-Hispanic whites (hereafter identified as whites) are not due to their race and ethnicity per se. We remain interested in gender and racial differences, however, even while believing that, generally, those factors do not in and of themselves cause the observed differences.[2] Many of us interpret our democratic values as meaning that such differences should be minimized or eliminated altogether and wish to see how far we are from that goal. Both the tabular (bivariate) results in this chapter and the differences after controls are imposed in the next chapter offer important insights on this point. If these differences were the focus of our research, we would want to decompose them much more than we do with the model in chapter 6. But because our emphasis is on the contribution of school factors to student learning, we shall be content to see what gender or racial and ethnic differences exist in the first instance (here) and what differences remain after we take into account the variety of other factors in our model (chapter 6). We shall, in addition, consider how race and ethnicity interact with school factors.

We begin by looking at whether male-female and African-American–white–Hispanic differences exist, how large they are, and whether they vary by subject matter.[3]

Gender

Over the years, a standard conclusion of studies of political knowledge is that males are more knowledgeable than females, at both the preadult and adult levels (Hess and Torney, 1967: 176; Jennings and Niemi, 1981: 281). Until recently, there was nothing surprising about such results. When scientific surveys began in the 1940s, and indeed until quite recently, the attitude that politics is a man's work was widespread. That there were relatively few women in elective and appointive political office reflected and reinforced that attitude. The fact is, however, that gender differences in political knowledge have persisted right up to the present time. In extensive adult surveys in 1988 and 1989, for example, Delli Carpini and Keeter (1996) found that the median percentage able to answer a series of questions covering a wide range of local, national, and international issues, events, and personalities was 15 points lower for women than for men (see also Verba, Schlozman, and Brady, 1995: 349). Over-time comparisons are harder to find, but Delli Carpini and Keeter (161–72) suggest strongly that the knowledge levels of women, in both absolute terms and relative to men, "are about the same today as they were in the 1950s and 1960s" (163).

The NAEP data, which by definition exclude older generations of men and women, offer an opportunity to reconsider this matter and to examine the specific types of knowledge on which young men and women differ. If changing attitudes and opportunity structures are altering the relative knowledge levels of males and females, it is likely to be most apparent in the younger generation. People coming of age in the 1990s may show no gender differences even if those differences existed among schoolchildren in years past and even if adult cross sections, which include many who grew up before the women's movement of the 1970s, show continuing gaps.

In addition, structural explanations for gender differences are inapplicable to a sample of high school seniors. In earlier generations, women had less formal education than men, a factor that is virtually always related to amount of knowledge. Women worked less outside the home and are even now likely to work in less political environments or occupations (Verba et al., 1995: 318–19). Child-care responsibilities still fall heavily upon mothers, who are therefore less likely to have political conversations or to be in situations where politics play a part. Among high school seniors, however, these sorts of gender differences are far less significant.

At the same time, however, attitudinal differences remain. Adult women still express less interest in politics than do men (Verba et al., 1995: 349).

Correspondingly, high school girls in the NAEP study were less interested in civics classes than were boys. And differences in policy preferences and in such things as the way males and females approach problems have not disappeared and may affect the kinds of subject matter in which students are interested and knowledgeable (Schumaker and Burns, 1988; Delli Carpini and Keeter, 1996: 206–7). Thus, we should not expect male-female differences to have disappeared among new generations of students, though they may be small.

The overall results from the NAEP test indicate exactly this: among high school seniors in the late 1980s, male-female differences in knowledge of government and politics remained, but they were small. Over all 150 multiple-choice items, boys scored 67 percent correct while girls scored 64 percent, a difference of only 3 percentage points. At about the same time, girls scored about 4.5 percentage points lower on the 1986 NAEP history test (Ravitch and Finn, 1989: 130), and as recently as 1994, twelfth-grade girls scored slightly below boys in history, although gender differences were nonexistent at the fourth- and eighth-grade levels (Paul Williams et al., 1995: 9, 22). The story is the same if we consider the various categories of political knowledge. Males usually outscored females, but the differences were never more than 5 percentage points; in a few categories the sexes were tied (General Rights of Citizens, Women and Minorities); and in one area (Structure and Function of Government), girls scored a percentage point above boys. Indeed, there was not a single item out of the 150 on which the difference was as high as 15 percent.

Still, some differences persist. Tables 5.11 through 5.13 document the differences in the abilities of boys and girls to answer individual political knowledge items correctly. Most notable, boys were consistently better at answering questions about political parties (table 5.11). Similarly, questions that were related to elections were consistently answered better by boys than by girls (table 5.12), even though these came mostly from the "structure and function" category, on which girls scored a percentage point higher than boys. (The first two items in the table are exceptions, but this is not surprising when questions are answered by nearly everybody.) Boys were typically more likely to answer correctly even on such straightforward items as the length of a senator's term. Boys were also more knowledgeable about lobbying (table 5.11). And from the category of citizens' rights, two items that touched on protest activity—whether hunger strikes and boycotts are legal—were more often answered correctly by boys than by girls (2 percent and 14 percent, respectively). Perhaps boys are more interested and attentive when the subject involves aspects of participation. Even in these cases we should emphasize that the

Table 5.11   Students Responding Correctly to Items
about Political Parties and Lobbying, by Gender

Item	Girls	Boys
	\(Percentage\)	
Political Parties		
Multiple countries have political parties	79	85
The Constitution does not define the activities of political parties	77	77
Parties choose candidates in primaries	73	75
Soviet Union has only one political party	59	64
The United States has more than two political parties	55	62
National convention selects presidential candidate	53	61
Only registered voters with a party affiliation may vote in a closed primary	43	46
The procedure for nominating presidential candidates is established by parties	38	41
How presidential candidates are nominated	32	45
Average	57	62
Lobbying		
Lobbying is a legal way to change laws	83	85
Lobbying is legal	71	77
Lobbyists are known as the Third House	63	71
National Rifle Association activity is known as lobbying	59	64
The Supreme Court is least influenced by lobbying	53	61
PACs are set up by special interests to raise money for candidates	36	34
Average	61	65
Raw N = 1,711 Weighted N = 218,880		

differences are considerably lower than for the typical information question among adults.

It was also the case that items dealing with war and foreign affairs were more often answered correctly by boys (table 5.12), although the single item about the United Nations, which is perhaps seen in idealistic, conflict-resolving terms by high school seniors, was more often answered correctly by girls (64 percent versus 60 percent). Once again, these modest differences might result from differential interests. But it is again noteworthy that the differences extended to such structural items as whether treaties must be approved by the Senate. A little bit of interest appears to go a long way.

For their part, girls are as knowledgeable as boys on questions about criminal and civil justice and about citizens' rights. One might have thought that issues related to crime would attract much more attention among boys; whether that is so we cannot tell, but in terms of knowledge, there is no difference across the items in this category (not shown). With respect to the rights of citizens, girls scored the same as boys, on average. In both cases, girls were more knowledgeable not only on the largely consensual items but on some less well-known matters as well. For example,

Table 5.12 Students Responding Correctly to Items about Elections and War and Foreign Affairs, by Gender

Item	Girls	Boys
	(Percentage)	
Elections[a]		
Presidential election held every four years	94	94
Payment of a poll tax is not required to vote in national elections	92	90
Many countries have elected national leaders	83	86
Senators are elected[b]	75	80
Senators are elected[b]	72	78
The most recent amendment lowered the voting age to 18	65	63
The Electoral College permits a candidate who did not win a majority of popular votes to be declared president	62	66
At one time, laws prevented some people from voting	56	60
Chart shows steps to become president	43	46
Senator's term is six years	34	40
Candidate gets 100 percent of the electoral votes in a state	24	34
Average	64	67
War and Foreign Affairs[c]		
Federal government regulates international trade	85	85
National defense is not a responsibility of local government	84	81
Treason is making war against the United States or giving "aid and comfort" to the enemy	80	84
Local government does not regulate military	80	82
U.S. courts cannot declare war	76	80
A declaration of war must be approved by Congress	66	78
Main purpose of the United Nations	64	60
The Supreme Court can declare a war unconstitutional	63	69
Treaties must be ratified by the Senate	43	48
The Department of State deals with foreign affairs	32	40
Average	67	71
Raw N = 1,781 Weighted N = 220,578		

[a]Items are from several categories used in chapter 2. See tables 2.5–2.7.
[b]There were two different questions on this subject.
[c]Items are from several categories used in chapter 2. See tables 2.3 and 2.6.

girls were more often aware that a landlord could bring a lawsuit against tenants (78 percent versus 66 percent); and they more often knew that the right to religious freedom is found in the amendments to the Constitution (55 percent versus 48 percent).

Girls and boys were equally knowledgeable on questions about women. On the civics test there were only two, so we draw primarily on the history test (Hammack et al., 1990: 108–10). Nearly 90 percent of both sexes knew that the courts can decide matters of sex discrimination; boys outscored girls on one question about women's right to vote, but the reverse was true on another. When asked to identify various historical figures, girls outscored boys in several instances. On the other hand, boys were slightly more often able to identify both Sandra Day O'Connor and leaders of the women's movement of the 1970s. Overall, the near equality of re-

Table 5.13 Students Responding Correctly to Items Requiring Inferences from Text, Tables, or Charts, by Gender

Item	Girls	Boys
	(Percentage)	
Bill must pass both House and Senate (chart)	92	85
Supreme Court can protect individual rights (text)	82	78
Community must consider pros and cons of a proposed project (text)	80	77
Conflict between maintaining order, freedom of speech (text)	76	70
Bill goes first to House committee (chart)	72	68
Madison believed in informed citizens (text)	70	68
More educated people are more politically active (table)	61	64
Kind of question for which one would conduct a public opinion poll	48	50
Average	73	70
Raw N = 1,771 Weighted N = 219,535		

Table 5.14 Students' Performance on the Presidential Responsibilities Essay, by Gender

Understanding of Presidential Responsibilities	Girls	Boys
	(Percentage)	
Unacceptable	5	10
Minimal	35	33
Adequate	38	41
Elaborated	22	16
Raw N = 1,793 Weighted N = 221,901		

sponses, when compared with the overall higher scores of boys (especially on the history test) suggests a slight increase in girl's (relative) knowledge when the subject matter is women.

Finally, it would seem that girls are more able than boys at making inferences from textual and other material. On all four of the questions requiring students to read and interpret text, girls outscored boys (table 5.13). The same is true of the two questions calling for an interpretation of charts. However, on the lone question involving a table, boys answered correctly slightly more often than girls. Boys were also more often correct on the item asking about the best question for a public opinion poll. Girls performed better on the essay about "presidential responsibilities," (table 5.14) with 22 percent of girls versus 16 percent of boys giving an elaborated answer.

Viewed in their entirety, the NAEP tests suggest that while some explainable gender differences exist in political knowledge, the larger message is that seventeen-year-old boys and girls have absorbed approximately the same amount of material about government and civics and about the same content. In earlier decades and for previous generations,

explanations of gender differences in knowledge might have been attributed to socialization into "women's ways" or "women's interests." The
legacy of that kind of socialization still lingers in the existence of male-
female differences among older adults. But in the 1980s and 1990s, at
least, it would appear that political knowledge has to a large extent been
equalized for male and female students leaving high school. Differences
may exist among high school dropouts or may develop later, but these differences cannot necessarily be attributed to civic instruction.

Gender differences in feelings about government responsiveness among
high school seniors are small and somewhat inconsistent. On the whole,
at the adult level, fewer women have felt that the government is responsive, but the margin of difference between men and women has usually
been small (Miller, Miller, and Schneider, 1980: 284). At the preadult
level, Hess and Torney (1967: 180–81) found that elementary school girls
in the mid-1960s more often thought that the president would be responsive to them but that boys more often thought that the Supreme Court
would be responsive. Thus, it was unclear what to expect in the NAEP results other than that the differences would probably not be large. At the
same time, the lower levels of knowledge about parties and elections
found among girls suggested that there might be greater differences when
students were asked whether elections make government pay attention to
people.

Table 5.15 shows the distribution of responses to the government-
responsiveness questions. Differences are relatively small on both items,
with a slightly larger difference on the question about elections. The results suggest that gender differences remain for attitudes as well as for
knowledge related to politics and government, but that they are small and
may disappear (among young people) in the near future.

Table 5.15 Government Responsiveness, by Gender

Attitude	Girls	Boys
	(Percentage)	
Amount of attention government pays to people		
Not much	23	23
Some	62	58
A good deal	15	19
Elections make government accountable		
Not much	9	11
Some	51	42
A good deal	40	47
Raw N = 4,206 Weighted N = 517,722		

Race and Ethnicity

Differences between whites and African-Americans on matters related to politics are an everyday observation. As with gender, however, some portion of the generally observed differences stems from factors that are inapplicable when the comparison is limited to high school seniors (see, e.g., Delli Carpini and Keeter, 1996: 203). In particular, the nominal education level, which is strongly related to most forms of political knowledge, is held constant in the NAEP assessment. Moreover, as we discussed in chapter 3, at least some learning about political matters occurs outside the classroom. Therefore, one might expect reduced differences for civic knowledge compared to other areas of study, where curricular choices and the quality of schools would play a larger role. Finally, to the extent that civics classes have an impact on students, one might recall Langton and Jennings's (1968) finding that African-Americans were more positively affected by such course work than were whites.

With respect to Hispanics, there is little previous information on which to form expectations, but given the recent-immigrant status of some Hispanics and the fact that for many English is a second language, we might also expect lower scores for this group as a whole. As with African-Americans, however, differences may be less strong because we are considering groups with equal levels of education. Likewise, arguments about extracurricular learning and the effects of civics classes are not specific to African-Americans, so differences specifically in the area of civics may be less clear. Finally, when the groups are compared to each other, there is little reason to expect much difference in minority groups' overall levels of knowledge.

Considering the equal education levels and other issues just alluded to, the breadth and depth of the racial and ethnic differences are somewhat surprising. On average, whites scored 11 percentage points higher than Hispanics and 13 points higher than African-Americans (table 5.16).[4] Whites outscored Hispanics on nearly every one of the 150 items, blacks on 144 of the 150. The white–African-American differences among high school seniors are smaller, however, than those found at about the same time in adult cross sections: 13 points versus a median difference of 27 points on a fifty-item test given to adults.[5] The differences are not strictly comparable inasmuch as they are a function of the specific questions asked. But the point remains true if one observes individual, almost identical questions (Delli Carpini and Keeter, 1996: 158–60). On an item concerning the length of a presidential term, the white–African-American differences are 8 percent for adults and 4 percent for high school students;

Table 5.16 Overall Political Knowledge, by Race or Ethnicity

Race or Ethnicity	Percentage of Sample	Civic Knowledge (Mean Percentage Correct)
Whites	79	69
Hispanics	9	58
African-Americans	12	56
Raw *N* = 4,125 Weighted *N* = 503,357		

Note: Students identifying themselves as Asian or Pacific Islander or as American Indian are too few in number for reliable estimates and have been excluded.

Table 5.17 Ten Types of Political Knowledge, by Race or Ethnicity

Type of Knowledge	Whites	Hispanics	African-Americans
	(Mean Percentage Correct)		
Criminal and civil justice	81	70	70
General rights of citizens	81	72	73
State and local government	68	59	55
Political parties	60	48	44
Lobbying	66	50	48
Women and minorities	71	60	62
Structure and function of U.S. government	63	52	50
Inferences from text, tables, charts	71	62	54
Comparative perspective	73	68	59
Theoretical perspective	49	40	38
Raw *N* = 4,125 Weighted *N* = 503,357			

on an item about appointing judges, the differences are 30 percent for adults, 12 percent for students.

From an analytical perspective, what is more important than the overall comparisons is that the differences across the subject matter categories tell us a bit more about the reasons for and probable sources of students' knowledge. Table 5.17 shows the mean percentage of correct answers for the ten types of political knowledge. Here we see that African-Americans were relatively knowledgeable when the questions turned to matters directly relevant to racial matters. This point is hard to establish from the civics test alone because of the paucity of such items. On the history test, however, African-American students were relatively more knowledgeable on racial matters from recent political history as well as on questions related to the nineteenth century. Regarding a statement that the civil rights movement of the 1960s focused on equality for minorities, for example, African-American students were only 3 percentage points below whites, and on a question about the chronology of the movement, African-Americans scored 4 points higher. Martin Luther King, Jr., was better known to African-Americans. Far more were able to say that King first gained national prominence in the Montgomery bus boycott of 1955 (71 percent for African-Americans, 43 percent for whites). More associated King with nonviolence (79 versus 68 percent). And on the literature test, 5 percent more African-Americans identified King as the author of the "I have a dream" speech (Ravitch and Finn, 1987: 270). Ironically, African-Americans were consistently less aware, sometimes by wide margins, of the significance of the Supreme Court's decision in *Brown v. Board of Education*—scoring lower than whites by 12 percent and 6 percent, respectively, on items in the civics test and by 17 and 11 percent on questions on the history assessment.

Only one question on either test was related to the contemporary Hispanic experience, a question calling for recognition of the heavy immigration from Southeast Asia and Latin America during the 1970s and 1980s. Hispanics did relatively well on this item, tying the percentage of whites who were correct. Note also that on the few comparative items, the difference between Hispanics and whites is relatively low, suggesting that at least some Hispanics are more attentive to or more aware of government forms in other countries.

The gaps in ability to make inferences from text, tables, and charts might be due to differences in reading ability, especially among Hispanics, for whom English may be their second language. But although reading levels may be part of the explanation, the text items show smaller differences in ability than do those requiring students to interpret visual cues. In fact, Hispanics scored less than 6 percentage points below white students on the textual items, whereas they scored 20 points lower in interpreting charts. For African-Americans, the differences are on the order of 10 and 20 points, respectively. On the one item in which students were asked to interpret a table, the differences are also large—12 and 20 points, respectively, for Hispanics and African-Americans. Although there are too few questions of each subtype for us to draw any firm conclusions, it is clear that minority students have considerable difficulty overall in putting to active use the discrete bits of information they have acquired just prior to adulthood.

Note, in regard to sources of student learning, that the differences on the "structure and function" category fall in the middle range with respect to majority-minority differences. This is significant because these are probably the items most likely to be learned in civics classes and not elsewhere. If civics classes were a much greater influence on minority students than on whites, one might expect the differences in this category to be smaller than average. Yet they are not. Thus, although we shall not examine the effects of civics courses on racial groups until chapter 6, the evidence here suggests that minority students are relatively *less,* not more, likely to absorb what is being taught in the schools.

The areas in which African-American and Hispanic students are closest to whites (apart from issues related to minorities per se) are those that are probably the most ubiquitous in the lives of students outside the classroom. As we noted in chapter 2, the justice system and the rights of citizens are frequent subjects of television and newspaper stories and are often a major component in them. It is in these categories that African-American students (and to some extent, Hispanic students) display knowledge levels that are closest to those of whites.

Finally, with respect to the various categories, we note that the large differences in knowledge about lobbying are, insofar as we can tell, a function of the specific questions asked and do not reflect any special ignorance on the part of minorities about this aspect of governance. For example, the three groups were within 5 percentage points of one another in their recognition that PACs raise money for candidates, and on an item asking whether lobbying is legal, blacks scored closer to whites than average, while on a similar item, Hispanics scored quite close to whites.

The differences across the racial and ethnic groups are, if anything, even sharper on the item about presidential responsibilities (table 5.18). Hispanics scored lower than whites, and African-Americans scored lower than Hispanics on both of the top two categories. The poorer quality of the answers provided by minority students may stem, in part, from language differences or from a difficulty in expressing themselves in writing. Nonetheless, this single item, by being very general and by allowing students to fashion their own responses, is important not only for its own sake but in making it more difficult to dismiss the differences on the multiple-choice part of the test as being due to the particular selection of items or the particular form of the test. Unfortunately, from a social point of view, minority groups fall behind whites with respect to a wide array of civic knowledge, using more than one type of assessment.

Table 5.18 Performance on the Presidential Responsibilities Essay, by Race or Ethnicity

Understanding of Presidential Responsibilities	Whites	Hispanics (Percentage)	African-Americans
Unacceptable	6	7	12
Minimal	31	40	49
Adequate	42	38	30
Elaborated	20	15	10
Raw N = 1,727 Weighted N = 212,541			

Table 5.19   Government Responsiveness, by Race or Ethnicity

Attitude	Whites	Hispanics (Percentage)	African-Americans
Amount of attention government pays to people			
Not much	21	26	34
Some	61	58	53
A good deal	18	15	9
Elections make government accountable			
Not much	9	13	12
Some	47	43	46
A good deal	44	45	42
Raw *N* = 4,061 Weighted *N* = 496,305			

In contrast to the findings concerning knowledge about civics and government, race and ethnicity have a variable correlation with the items about government responsiveness (table 5.19). When asked about the role of elections in making government accountable, the three groups answered in almost identical fashion. Perhaps the attention given to voting rights as part of the civil rights movement, along with emphasis in civics classes on the importance of participation, have combined to make minority students as likely as whites to think that elections influence government. Nonetheless, Hispanic and, especially, African-American students are considerably more likely than whites to say that the government does not pay much attention to people. How much of this difference is accounted for by lower interest in civics and other such factors will be an important consideration in chapter 6.

Our findings in this chapter are more traditional than those in chapter 4 but no less important for that. Television viewing, especially when carried to an extreme, is detrimental to learning. Students who are more interested in a topic learn more about it. Boys still have a slight edge over girls in what they know about civics, and white students score higher than African-American and Hispanic students. And these same variables have a connection, though a less consistent one, to political attitudes about government responsiveness. Only the finding that students who participate more in mock elections and the like are more knowledgeable about government could possibly be called unanticipated.

The findings are important for several reasons. From the perspective of current American society, the racial-ethnic differences may be the most significant. The fact that young African-American and Hispanic children score lower on all types of political knowledge questions is serious, among other reasons, because gaps in political knowledge make it harder

for students to participate in ways that will overcome existing imbal-
ances. Likewise, a feeling that government is unresponsive can feed upon
itself, causing students not to participate and thereby strengthening the
feeling of unresponsiveness. And these results are for young people who
have achieved nominally equal educational levels—that is, without taking into account any possible effects of college and university education.

African-American students were nearly as knowledgeable and sometimes more so than whites when the topic shifted to black history. But
these results cut two ways. On the one hand, it is encouraging to see di-
minished racial differences on at least some items. These results also support the notion that civic learning should be more relevant to minority
groups by focusing to some extent on their history. More generally, this is
consonant with our message in chapter 2 that students learn more when
they can see the relevance of the material to their own lives.

At the same time, it is disconcerting that white students do not know
more about these topics, perhaps because they regard the history of
African-Americans as irrelevant to them. That less than half of the white
students knew that Martin Luther King, Jr., gained national prominence in
the Montgomery bus boycott of 1955, that a third of them did not know
the significance of the *Brown* desegregation decision, that a quarter did
not even know that the goal of the civil rights movement of the 1960s was
political and social equality for minorities (Ravitch and Finn, 1987:
264–65) all show a lack of historical awareness of the racial history of this
country among young generations of whites.

Our findings in this chapter are important from a very different perspective as well. The factors examined here are variously under the control of students and parents, the school, and society in general. Among
other things, this suggests how much students and parents can do on their
own. It is not necessary for families to look elsewhere—to impoverished
schools, bad teachers, difficult social circumstances, and so on—when a
prominent reason for less-than-stellar performances is almost literally
right under their noses. Simply turning off the television would be a good
beginning.

Of course, it is not really this easy. The infrequent television users in
the NAEP sample almost certainly differ from the frequent users in ways
other than their television habits. There is no guarantee that current high-
volume users would use their time as productively as these students if
they turned off their sets. Nevertheless, our results suggest that television
has a large impact when compared with the effects of other factors, so that
lowering one's television viewing time is likely to increase one's intake
and retention of civic material.

Another way of making much the same point is to say that home and social environments place heavy constraints on what schools can accomplish. Schools can offer more and better courses, as well as other school experiences, and they might in this way alter students' interests as well as lessen gender and racial-ethnic differences. But schools have no direct control over such home factors as television viewing, and they surely cannot alone solve the problems of racial and ethnic differences. This is hardly a new point, but it deserves emphasizing nonetheless, along with the reassurance that it applies to civics no less than to other kinds of learning.

Finally, finding that a number of individual and background factors influence student achievement outlines the task of the multivariate analysis of the next chapter. The individual analyses in this chapter and the previous one have provided presumptive evidence of effects, helped us determine appropriate measurements (especially of the variable measuring "amount and recency" of course work), and allowed us to establish some more refined effects (of gender and race on specific kinds of information, for example). We must now determine whether these apparent effects remain when we look at all the factors we have discussed, and more, simultaneously. In light of political scientists' considerable skepticism about the effects of civics course work, along with the moderate size of the various group differences we have seen so far, there are no guaranteed results. But that will make the quest all the more interesting.

CHAPTER SIX

What Makes Students Learn

In previous chapters we considered singly a variety of factors that appear to contribute to high school seniors' knowledge of government and politics. There appear to be many such factors, ranging in scope from the individual to the home to the school, and in locus of control from the student to the school to parents to such immutable characteristics as race and gender. By itself, this wealth of factors suggests multiple causes for both praise and blame concerning observed knowledge levels. It is almost certain that no one factor is responsible for what students know and do not know. Likewise, no single factor can be said to be the key to helping students learn about government.

The problem, as we noted throughout, is that these characteristics are overlapping in their influence. Some may be genuine causes of student learning. We would like to think, especially, that students learn more because of the various school factors. Some, however, may be only spuriously related to what students know. We may think, for example, that if we took their relative interests into account (that is, *controlled for* interest), girls would be no less knowledgeable about government and politics than boys—suggesting that the observed difference is due only to their varying interests and not to anything more intrinsic about gender. Of course, it may be that schools are ineffective and that we cannot explain away gender differences. In order to sort out, as best we can, which factors contribute to student learning and which are only spuriously related to what students know, we need to bring them all together in a multivariate analysis. This is the task we set for ourselves in this chapter.

In the analysis that follows, we begin by focusing on civic knowledge overall rather than exploring specific dimensions of knowledge. There are two reasons for this emphasis. The first is theoretical. We believe that for the most part, similar factors contribute to gains in each of the substantive areas of knowledge. Having more civics course work or watching less television, for example, should contribute to most kinds of political knowledge. Similarly, coming from a home in which there are many learning resources, or having parents who are well educated, should also contribute to all kinds of civic learning. Indeed, the results in chapters 4 and 5 strongly support this perspective. Although there were some differences in magnitude between knowledge of citizen rights, federalism, political parties, and so on, each of the factors in the exposure-selection model was related in relatively similar fashion to knowledge in each area. A partial exception was gender; but there were only minor differences between male and female students, making it easier for inconsistencies in direction to occur.

A second reason for focusing initially on civic knowledge as a whole has to do with limitations in the data. Recall that NAEP uses a "spiral" design in the administration of the assessment, so that students were asked only a subset (roughly 50–75) of the overall set of 150 knowledge questions. If we now tried to create summary variables for each of the subjects used in previous chapters, we would find that some students received a very small set of questions on any given topic. For example, even though there are seventeen questions about the general rights of citizens, some students were asked only five items in this category, making measurement of their knowledge of the area less reliable. Trying to examine the contribution of multiple factors to each area of knowledge would thus result in fewer items per category (less reliable measurement) or the use of many fewer students for each analysis (increased sampling variability).[1]

We begin, therefore, by estimating the exposure-selection model for overall civic knowledge. First we consider the student population at large. We then turn to the impact that the various factors in the model have on relevant groups of students. In particular, we analyze which characteristics of the school and civics curriculum, the home environment, and individual achievement and motivation influence overall civic knowledge among African-American, Hispanic, and white students separately, and follow this with a separate analysis by gender.

We then turn our attention to the possibility that some explanatory factors may contribute in different ways to certain dimensions of political knowledge. Mindful of the limitations of the data, we combine specific dimensions of political knowledge to make several broad categories, analyzing the relevance of the exposure-selection model to each of these groupings.[2] The findings about these more specific types of civic knowledge contain important lessons about the relative emphases of high school civics teaching and about civic learning.

Finally, we add as a brief postscript the application of the exposure-selection model to knowledge of U.S. history as measured by the 1988 NAEP History Assessment. This excursion beyond the Civic Assessment adds confidence in our findings about the contribution of school and curriculum factors to students' understanding of civics.

Overall Knowledge of Civics and American Government

We begin the multivariate analysis by estimating the effect of exposure and selection characteristics—those structural factors representing exposure to political information and those individual characteristics signifying the selection of information—on the overall measure of knowledge of civics and American government. Knowledge is measured as the percentage of questions answered correctly by each student across all of the questions he or she was given. For all students, the mean score on the overall knowledge measure is 65 percent correct.

The explanatory variables included in this model were for the most part introduced in previous chapters. In chapter 3 we outlined the characteristics of the civics curriculum, home environment, individual achievement, and student background that contribute to the civic knowledge of high school seniors, and in chapters 4 and 5 we explored in detail the relationship between many of these variables and overall knowledge.[3] The actual survey questions on which the variables are based are given in Appendix D; operational definitions and marginal distributions are provided in Appendix E. Factors not previously considered in detail, such as parents' education, are relatively straightforward. All of the measures were coded with zero for the "low" or baseline category, and, with the exception of race or ethnicity and amount of television viewing, all were expected to have positive coefficients.

With overall civic knowledge as the dependent variable, our first analysis is a regression that includes the full array of explanatory variables representing both structural (exposure) and individual (selection) characteristics, estimated with a method of ordinary least squares. The results of this estimation are detailed in table 6.1.[4] All coefficients are in the direction consistent with the expectations of the exposure-selection

Table 6.1 Effects of Structural and Individual Characteristics on
Twelfth Graders' Knowledge of American Government/Civics

Variable	Civic Knowledge
Constant	34.1**
	(1.8)
School and civics curriculum	
Amount and recency of course work (0–2)	2.0**
	(0.5)
Variety of topics studied (0–2)	1.3**
	(0.4)
Discussed current events in class (0–4)	1.0**
	(0.3)
Individual achievement	
Participated in mock elections or government (0–2)	2.6**
	(0.4)
Likes to study government (0–3)	3.7**
	(0.4)
Four-year college planned (0–1)	10.2**
	(0.7)
Home environment	
Reading and reference materials at home (0–4)	1.9**
	(0.4)
Only English spoken at home (0–1)	2.7**
	(0.9)
Two-parent household (0–1)	2.6**
	(0.7)
Educational level of parents (0–3)	1.7**
	(0.4)
Amount of television viewing (0–6)	−0.7**
	(0.2)
Background/demographics	
Male (0–1)	2.6**
	(0.7)
Hispanic (0–1)	−5.6**
	(1.2)
African-American (0–1)	−9.4**
	(0.9)
Adjusted R^2	.31
Raw N = 4,275 Weighted N = 525,723	

Note: Standard errors are in parentheses.
**$p<.01$; *$p<.05$.

model, and all are statistically significant. Because the dependent variable is scaled as a percentage from 0 to 100, the results are easily interpreted. For example, the estimate of the constant of 34.1 indicates that a student in the lowest categories on all of the other characteristics (no civics course work, little or no variety in the topics studied, no discussion of current events in class, no reading or reference materials at home, and so on) is expected to answer about 34 percent of the questions correctly. At the high end of the scale, someone with characteristics yielding the maximum value on each feature could be expected to score more than 90 percent correct.

School and Curriculum

The results indicate that each of the three curriculum factors is significantly and positively related to overall political knowledge. School and curriculum—in the form of amount and recency of civics course work, the variety of substantive topics studied in American government and civics courses, and the extent to which teachers incorporate discussions of current events into the curriculum—matter. These findings persist even after accounting for the positive and powerful influence of individual achievement measures, such as whether a student plans on attending a four-year college after graduation and how much interest the student has in American government, as well as for the home environment and the respondent's gender and racial or ethnic background.

The estimated coefficient for the amount and recency of civics course work is of special interest. It indicates that, net of all the other influences, having had a civics or American government course in twelfth grade gives a student a 2 percentage–point edge over someone whose last course was earlier, and an additional 2 points over students who have had no civics courses.[5] This effect is independent of the impact of the other characteristics of civic instruction in the model, including the variety of civics topics studied and the extent to which current events were discussed in class. The positive and significant coefficient on the measure of the amount and recency of civics course work represents the advance in political knowledge that comes from having had a formal civics course, although it does not measure the entire effect of civics teaching in the schools. Gains coming from civic instruction in history classes, for example, would add to the effects of course work as measured here.

The impact of formal civics courses—persisting as it does in a context in which other structural and individual characteristics are accounted for—is uncommonly meaningful. It suggests an altogether different conclusion from one of the enduring findings in the field of political socialization—the (apparent) utter absence of effect of civics courses on the level of political knowledge of high school seniors. As noted in chapter 1, what was heretofore the major analysis by political scientists of the high school curriculum, that reported thirty years ago by Langton and Jennings (1968), concluded that "the magnitude[s] of the relationships [between civics courses and a number of dependent variables] are extremely weak, in most instances bordering on the trivial" (858), so trivial, indeed, that high school government courses were thought to contribute almost nothing to what students know about American government and politics. Our analysis and interpretation of the 1988 NAEP civics data are in sharp contrast to that conclusion. An effect of 4 percentage points in overall political knowledge—when it resists efforts to be overwhelmed by other powerful predictors and when it rivals the impact of other important variables—is anything but trivial. Just how significant an impact of this magnitude is needs to be discussed after we have evaluated all the coefficients of the exposure-selection model as well as the additional models introduced below. Yet even at this point, before further interpretation, our results demonstrating the significant and positive impact of civics course work on student knowledge run directly counter to the conclusion that civics classes are worth little.

Beyond the effect of the amount and recency of civics courses, the estimated effects of two additional characteristics of the school and civics curriculum demonstrate that other aspects of the educational context also influence student knowledge. When students reported having studied a wide variety of topics, their likelihood of successfully answering the questions increased considerably—by more than 2.5 percent at the extremes. Precisely what lies behind such effects cannot be determined from the NAEP data. It may be, for example, that students reporting greater depth of coverage received civics material in many different courses, or it may simply be that they had better teachers and better classes. Whatever the underlying mechanism, curricular *content,* as well as amount of course work, plays a significant role in civic learning.

Frequent discussions of current events are another curricular factor that improves student test scores, by as much as 4 percent if one contrasts having no discussion at all to having nearly daily discussion. Again, the mechanisms at work here remain hidden in the NAEP data. As we noted in chapter 4, it may be that current events are sufficiently stimulating to students that they pay more attention to the content of their civics courses or that the context of current events gives meaning to learning in such a way that it enables students to retain more of what they study. Both processes would increase the exposure of students to civics material and aid in the identification of political content as interesting, relevant, and worth retaining. Whatever the explanation, the impact of classroom attention to current events is all the more impressive because the NAEP assessment did not specifically call for knowledge of contemporary politics. What goes on inside the civics classroom thus appears to leave an appreciable mark on levels of knowledge among students.

Combined, these three aspects of the school and civics curriculum—

amount and recency of course work, variety of topics studied, and discussion of current events—have a combined effect of nearly 11 percentage points on overall political knowledge.

Individual achievement

School-related structural factors, which to a large extent regulate student exposure to civics content, are clearly important predictors of student knowledge of government and politics. But so, too, are the individual factors that help determine what students select to retain from the material available to them in the school. The three characteristics of individual achievement included in the model—participation in mock elections and the like, interest in American government, and plans to attend college—represent individual processes of selection in the exposure-selection model of knowledge acquisition and retention. The results in table 6.1 indicate that all three measures of individual achievement contribute strongly and positively to civic knowledge, with interest in studying American government and postsecondary school college plans having the largest effects. In addition, participation in student government also contributes to overall knowledge.

Important in their own right as measures of individual achievement, two of these variables serve another purpose as well. Whether a student plans to attend a four-year college after graduation is important as a measure of the student's general abilities, and its inclusion here helps to avoid attributing the effects of those qualities to curricular factors. Considering the entire effects of this variable noncurricular represents a conservative interpretation; insofar as the school plays a role in students' decisions about higher education, it may influence students' decisions concerning how much attention to give their class work and therefore how much they get out of course work. In any event, by helping control for student ability and achievement, this variable adds greatly to our confidence in our interpretation above of course work and other curricular effects.

Whether the student enjoys studying government and civics is also in the nature of a control variable that is included to avoid spurious attribution of course and other school effects. It is especially important to include this control when we consider the effects of participation in mock elections and government. Insofar as such participation is extracurricular and voluntary, those who like to study government are most likely to participate. Including interest in our model might well have erased entirely the bivariate relationship between participation and civic knowledge. Instead, participation clearly seems to enhance student knowledge. Student councils, of course, are not part of civics course work as such, and they may be some of what the participation variable is tapping. Yet, regardless of whether interest is strictly *course*-related, it is another *school*-related factor that helps raise student scores on the civics test.

Thus, the strong effects of being a student of high overall achievement as well as being interested in government do not overwhelm the significance of the relationship between the formal curriculum and civic knowledge. Specifying these characteristics as separate effects in the model keeps the variation in civic knowledge that is explained by curricular factors from being confounded by the effect of general ability. Together, the exposure and selection characteristics that are directly related to school— both course work and otherwise—contribute strongly to the development of knowledge about American politics and government among high school seniors.

Home Environment

Characteristics of the home environment of students also play a role in differentiating which are more or less knowledgeable. The results in table 6.1 detail the impact of both structural and individual characteristics in the home environment that affect exposure to American government and politics as well as selection of that knowledge for retention. Having more reading and reference materials at home, higher levels of educational attainment among parents, speaking English at home, and living in a two-parent household are strong, positive contributors to student knowledge. Conversely, knowledge declines as the amount of time spent watching television increases. Collectively, there is an expected gap of more than 20 percentage points in overall knowledge of politics between students at the bottom on each of these variables and students at the top on each of them.[6]

Students in homes where there are few or no reading materials, where a language other than English is spoken, where only one parent is present, where the parent has only a grade-school education, and where the student spends many hours a day watching television can be expected to score well below their classmates, even with similar levels of interest in American government and civics and comparable amounts and types of curricular work. It is important to note that the number of students who live in home environments at the low end on these measures is often quite small. For example, there are very few homes without some reading and reference materials, and few students watch television for five or more hours a day. Likewise, parents with only a grade-school education are few in number (see Appendix E). Nevertheless, those who would argue that the home is the key to increasing student civic knowledge have some evidence to support their view.

It should also be noted that no single factor in the home environment is of overwhelming importance. The greatest estimated effect is for the measure of reading and reference materials at home; although a simple and convenient item, this variable no doubt captures more than the mere presence or absence of books and magazines. Next in line is the educational level of parents, a standard reporting category for NAEP because of its consistent and strong relationship to student knowledge in all subjects. Though significant, parental education accounts for an expected gain of "only" 5 percentage points as one moves from the lowest level (grade-school education) to the highest level (completed college).

Of the characteristics of the home environment, the one that might cause some misunderstanding or controversy is the one concerning whether a language other than English is spoken in the home. The importance of this factor probably stems less from the use of some other language than from the fact that households where other languages are spoken are more likely to include immigrant parents, who themselves probably have lower levels of knowledge about U.S. government and politics and therefore are less likely to pass along such material.[7] It seems likely that the language measure may capture some of the effect of the recency of immigration, where newly immigrant families are both less likely to use English exclusively and less likely to help students learn civics material about the United States through their daily conversations and activities. But no further information about immigration status and generation of students was collected in the 1988 NAEP study.

Combined, characteristics of the home environment contribute significantly to student knowledge. In trying to teach civics to students, schools have a lot to build on when home conditions are positive, as well as a lot to overcome when the home environment does not encourage student learning. Yet there is no quick fix for low student scores in the home realm alone; even if one could magically increase education among parents, or turn off all the televisions, as long as nothing else about schools and individual achievement changed, levels of student knowledge would be less than one might expect. We shall return to this point below, as we interpret the influence of the various contributions on student learning.

Race or Ethnicity and Gender

Finally, the regression results sustain and amplify our conclusions in previous chapters about the effects of background factors including race or ethnicity and gender. Males and females differ relatively little in their knowledge of politics and government, but the average difference of 3 percentage points reported in chapter 5 survives almost exactly in the multivariate analysis. Even after taking into account students' self-reported interest and participation in high school government, as well as course work, high school girls still know slightly less than boys about politics on the overall scale.

For Hispanic students, the multivariate results, while confirming the existence of lower knowledge levels, show cause for guarded optimism. Not accounting for other factors, the percentage of items answered correctly by Hispanics was 11 points less than for whites (see table 5.16), but the difference is halved in the multivariate model.[8] Moreover, it is possible that if we were able to account for the amount of time spent in the United States and for such other factors as the student's English-language ability, this difference would be reduced still farther. Simply taking account of these differences does not change the fact, however, that Hispanic parents have lower educational levels, that Hispanic students less often plan to attend four-year colleges, and so on, all of which contribute to lower levels of overall political knowledge. But as these factors change, it seems likely that Hispanics will become more knowledgeable about U.S. government and politics.

More disconcerting, both because of the larger overall size and because of a smaller reduction in the magnitude of the difference after taking other factors into account, is the persistent difference between white and African-American students. The simple bivariate difference in overall knowledge between the two groups was 13 percentage points, slightly more than the difference between white and Hispanic students. Having accounted for the same factors of curriculum, home environment, and individual achievement, however, African-American students still lag behind whites by 9.4 points on the overall scale of political knowledge. Although change is occurring, for example, in educational levels for African-American parents, it cannot be expected to be as rapid or dramatic as for Hispanics, where deficits associated with recent immigration are more quickly overcome. For African-American students there is no reason to expect rapid, wholesale changes. In light of the size and persistence of the gap between African-American and white students, we now turn to a more extensive analysis of civic knowledge by race or ethnicity.[9]

Political Knowledge and Race or Ethnicity

Having documented the considerable, persistent significance of race or ethnicity to overall knowledge of American government and civics, we shall examine the effects of schooling, individual achievement, and home environment on knowledge levels of students grouped by race or ethnicity in order to see the extent to which the curriculum or other school factors either lessens or increases this margin. Minority students consistently score significantly lower on the scale of overall knowledge of American government and politics, even after accounting for possible deficits in other explanatory factors. The differences might stem from a variety of causes, each with significantly different interpretations and each potentially suggesting different strategies for reducing or overcoming them.

There are at least three possible explanations for the lower scores of minority students. First, the differences in knowledge may be attributable to differences in structural and individual characteristics that serve either as sources to encourage political learning or as mechanisms that limit exposure or incentives for selection. Minority students more frequently come from homes with less highly educated parents than do whites, and many grow up in a home environment in which a language other than English is spoken. It is also possible that minority students are less likely to study civics in school, although the results in chapter 4 about the distribution of courses by race and ethnicity indicate that this is not the case. To the extent that differences in knowledge can be traced to majority-minority differences in the independent variables, the key to increasing scores for minority students lies, at least in part, in those factors. Altering the distribution of such characteristics in order to increase knowledge among minority students may not be easy, however. One might be able to remedy a shortage of civics courses fairly simply, but if the differences are largely due to the home environment, the solution is far from straightforward.

A second possible explanation for the lower scores of minority students relative to whites is that there are differential effects of structural and individual characteristics. For example, studying civics or watching television may have a greater or smaller effect on minorities than on whites. For most variables it is not obvious why such a difference would exist. Yet as we noted in chapter 1, there is evidence in political-science research that civics courses have more of an effect on African-American students. Confirmation of differential effects, insofar as they affect school-related variables, would be useful in that it might suggest ways courses could be made more effective for students who are not well served by the present format.

The third possible explanation for the lower scores of minority students is that whites and minorities know more and less about different specific topics. If a scale of overall knowledge is heavily dependent on the items for which minority students systematically know less, then their score on the set of general items might be artificially depressed. There are hints that this explanation has merit with respect to African-American students, whose knowledge of questions regarding blacks and Martin Luther King, Jr., for example, were at par or above that for white students. Whether this is a broader phenomenon is now the concern. If it is, the results would demand a very different interpretation.

Each of these explanations for the divergent levels of civic knowledge between students of different racial and ethnic backgrounds can be assessed with the NAEP data. We shall now examine results from similar regression analyses of the exposure-selection model predicting overall political knowledge, but for separate samples of students in each of the three categories: whites, Hispanics, and African-Americans. We begin, however, by considering the impact of differences by race or ethnicity in the structural and individual achievement characteristics that affect overall political knowledge.

White, African-American, and Hispanic students differ sharply with respect to many of the factors related to political knowledge. First, there are significant differences in terms of characteristics that help determine *exposure* to information about politics.[10] With respect to the home environment, the differences all seem to favor greater knowledge among white students. That is, white students are far more likely to have a large amount of reading and reference materials in the home than are either African-American or Hispanic students. The majority of white and Hispanic students come from two-parent households, whereas half of the African-American students come from single-parent households. In addition, the majority of Hispanic students live in households where a language other than English is spoken. With respect to the school setting, in contrast, differences in exposure are somewhat more mixed in terms of who is likely to be advantaged. Hispanics, for example, are more likely to have taken civics courses in twelfth grade, while African-American students report the most diversity in the topics covered in their civics courses. At the same time, African-American students least frequently report that they discuss current events in civics classes.

There are also big differences among students of different racial and ethnic groups in terms of characteristics related to *selection* and retention of information. Parents of white students have considerably more education than African-American parents; parents of Hispanic students are especially likely to have only grade-school education. However, most striking are differences in the amount of television students watch. A quarter (23 percent) of the white students watch television for four or more hours a day, but more than twice as many African-American students, 56 percent, watch that much. Hispanic students, at 30 percent, fall in between white and African-American students, though their viewing habits are more similar to those of whites than of blacks. School factors related to selection are again mixed. White students most often participate in mock elections and government. In terms of their future plans, almost as many African-Americans students as whites intended to attend a four-year college, but Hispanics were much less likely to do so. Finally, there is no difference among the three groups in terms of the proportion of students who say government is their favorite subject in school.

These descriptive data, combined with the results of the regression analysis in the previous section, make two major points about the lower knowledge levels of minority student populations. First, exposure and selection attributes of African-American and Hispanic students help explain their lower scores on political knowledge. In particular, less reading material at home, less frequent two-parent households (among African-Americans), the lower educational levels of parents, the greater amount of television viewing (among African-Americans), and infrequent plans to go to a four-year college (among Hispanics) all work in a negative direction, pushing down scores on the overall scale of political knowledge among minority students. The effects of these variables are lessened but not overcome by the slightly more frequent amount of civics course work among Hispanics and the greater variety of topics studied by African-Americans.

Second, although these factors are important, they clearly do not account for all the differences in knowledge levels among the three groups. As we noted earlier, Hispanic students are almost 6 percentage points lower than whites in correct answers, even after controlling for this array of factors. The observed difference between whites and Hispanics is 11 percent, and the exposure-selection model explains about half of that difference. For blacks, the factors in the model account for less. Of the original 13 point discrepancy, only about a quarter is explained, leaving the average score of African-Americans 9.4 percentage points lower than that of whites, even after taking into account all the factors in the exposure-selection model. Clearly, differences in the distribution of resources—those structural and individual factors that promote and inhibit political learning—are only a partial explanation of why minority students score lower.

The model of structural and individual effects summarized in table
6.1, though accounting for differences by race or ethnicity, nevertheless
assumes that the variables affect whites, African-Americans, and Hispanics in the same way. Thus, for example, civics course work or living in a
two-parent household increases civic knowledge to the same degree in all
three groups. This may not be the case. To test for the possibility that
some of the factors have differential effects on the various groups, we estimated the exposure-selection model separately for each group. The results are reported in table 6.2. For white students, with respect to characteristics of the home environment, these findings mirror almost perfectly
those discussed above for all students in the sample. This is almost necessarily the case given the percentage of whites in the population. Still, it
is useful for later comparisons to be able to say specifically that *among
white students,* those who come from homes with more reading material,
in which only English is spoken, and so on, do better than other white
students on the government and politics test. The results for other factors
for whites vary in small ways. The impacts of civics course work and participation in mock elections or government are slightly greater for whites
than for students as a whole, while whether current events are discussed
in class has a slightly smaller effect for whites. Overall, the impression remains that school factors are important.

The results for the same model estimated for African-American students tell a different story. What is most striking about these results is the
lack of significance of two of the school and curriculum factors and one of
the individual achievement factors closely related to the curriculum. The
coefficient for the amount and recency of civics course work is substantially smaller in magnitude than in the model estimated for whites and is
not significant; that for the variety of topics studied is negative and insignificant; and that for participation in mock elections or government is
smaller and insignificant. The only school and curriculum factor that is
substantially more important for blacks than for whites is whether current
events—things happening outside the school—are discussed. And even
here one should note that African-American students reported discussing
current events substantially less often than whites, mitigating the larger
effect of the measure. It appears that the focus on classroom material is of
less consequence for African-American students than for white students,
a finding that stands in stark contrast to the conclusion reached in the
1960s that civics courses affected only African-Americans in a significant
way. Langton and Jennings (1968) interpreted those results as indicating
that African-American students were "more likely to encounter new and
conflicting perspectives or content" (866) in civics courses. White stu-

Table 6.2 Effects of Structural and Individual Characteristics on Twelfth Graders' Knowledge of American Government/Civics, by Race or Ethnicity

Variable	White	African-American	Hispanic
Constant	34.5**	25.8**	28.3**
	(2.5)	(4.6)	(3.8)
School and civics curriculum			
Amount and recency of course work (0–2)	2.2**	0.5	2.3
	(0.6)	(1.3)	(2.1)
Variety of topics studied (0–2)	1.4**	-0.2	2.5*
	(0.4)	(1.1)	(1.1)
Discussed current events in class (0–4)	0.7*	1.7**	1.8*
	(0.3)	(0.7)	(0.7)
Individual achievement			
Participated in mock elections or government (0–2)	2.9**	1.8	1.1
	(0.5)	(1.2)	(1.2)
Likes to study government (0–3)	3.6**	3.5**	4.5**
	(0.5)	(1.1)	(1.7)
Four-year college planned (0–1)	10.3**	9.6**	6.2**
	(0.8)	(2.0)	(2.0)
Home environment			
Reading and reference materials at home (0–4)	1.9**	1.9*	1.2
	(0.6)	(0.8)	(0.7)
Only English spoken at home (0–1)	2.2*	3.9*	3.6
	(1.1)	(1.9)	(2.4)
Two-parent household (0–1)	2.7**	-0.1	5.6*
	(0.8)	(1.2)	(2.6)
Educational level of parents (0–3)	1.8**	1.9*	1.1
	(0.4)	(0.8)	(0.7)
Amount of television viewing (0–6)	-0.7**	-0.3	-0.9
	(0.2)	(0.4)	(0.8)
Background/demographics			
Male (0–1)	2.9**	3.5	0.5
	(0.7)	(2.0)	(2.8)
Adjusted R^2	.28	.21	.22
Raw N	2,960	678	487
Weighted N	397,201	62,247	43,906

Note: Standard errors are in parentheses.
**p<.01; *p<.05.

dents, having already seen the material either in school or elsewhere, had "reached a saturation or quota level which is impervious to change by the civics curriculum" (860). We cannot say what information students encountered previously, but neither inference is supported here. White students did learn from their civics courses; African-American students learned less, especially if the classes failed to emphasize what was happening outside of school.[11]

It does not appear that the reduced effect of curriculum on African-Americans as compared to whites is due to widespread student indifference about politics or about school more generally. If anything, African-

American students are slightly more interested in government than are whites. Moreover, the results in table 6.2 show that preference for the study of government increases student knowledge by the same amount for white and African-American students. Likewise, planning to attend college has similar effects on knowledge. At the same time, however, African-American students participate in mock elections and student government less often than do white students, and the effect of taking part for those who are involved is lower than the effect on knowledge for white students. We can only speculate that civics courses themselves seem less relevant to African-American students. We shall return to this point later in the chapter, when we consider more specific dimensions of political knowledge.

In contrast to the relatively modest effect of school and curricular factors, several characteristics of the home environment appear to have a large effect on African-American students. Having a number of reading and reference materials in the home is important for blacks, as is the level of parental education, with coefficients of almost identical magnitude to those for white students. The fact that black parents more often have less education and less reading material in the home than do white parents, adds to the disparity in civic knowledge that can be attributed to these variables. Coming from a home in which a language other than English is spoken—which is true for about a fifth of the African-American students—also contributes substantially to lower levels of knowledge of American government. But being raised in a household with two parents does not enhance learning for African-American students. And although the effect of watching more television is negative, it is not statistically significant. Finally, the gender coefficient is slightly larger than for whites, suggesting that male-female differences are somewhat more evident among African-Americans than among whites.

The pattern of political learning for Hispanic students is somewhat more complex than for African-Americans. On first glance at table 6.2, it appears that the home environment is less relevant for Hispanics, since only the measure of living in a two-parent household is a statistically significant predictor of knowledge. Even the language spoken at home does not reach significance at the conventional level. Cautious interpretation of substantive significance is important, nonetheless, because the lack of statistical significance of many of the coefficients stems in part from the relatively small number of Hispanic students in the sample. The pattern of the results for the variables measuring home environment suggests that speaking only English in the home strongly contributes to overall knowledge, much more so than for white students. Likewise, the effect of living in a two-parent household is also strongly positive. Educational level of parents and having reading and reference materials in the home are less important for Hispanic students, while watching television has a similar though slightly stronger negative effect on overall knowledge than it does for white students.

Most relevant for our inquiry, however, is the impact of characteristics of the school and civics curriculum and of individual achievement at school. The results for these variables are quite strong. The amount and recency of civics courses has no statistically significant impact on knowledge, though the estimated effect is almost identical to that for whites. But what happens in courses—the variety of topics studied and whether current events are discussed—appears to be very important, as these coefficients are statistically significant and large. Whether students like studying government and whether they plan to attend college are also important. Overall, if we judge by the size of the coefficients and not by their statistical significance alone, knowledge scores for Hispanic students are about as dependent on school-related factors as for whites. Finally, the coefficient for gender suggests that Hispanic boys and girls have essentially the same levels of knowledge after accounting for all other factors in the exposure-selection model.

Overall, the results support the conclusion that characteristics of the school and civics curriculum have the largest and most consistent impact on white and Hispanic students and a smaller impact on African-American students. Both African-American and Hispanic students report more often than whites that they like to study government, yet African-Americans are less affected by their civics courses. Perhaps the traditional coverage of such courses seems less relevant to minority students. Such an interpretation is consistent with the strong and positive coefficients on the variables measuring the variety of topics studied and, especially, the frequency of discussions of current events in civics classes. It is also consistent with our interpretation in chapter 2 of why students know much more about some subjects, such as rights of citizens, than about others. Even if students express general interest in a subject, they are not likely to absorb it if it has little connection to their daily lives. We shall return to this point later, when we examine the extent to which students from different racial and ethnic backgrounds differ by specific dimensions of political knowledge.

Gender and Political Knowledge

Unlike those of race, differences in overall political knowledge between female and male students were small. Moreover, we have fewer theoreti-

Table 6.3 Effects of Structural and Individual Characteristics on Twelfth Graders' Knowledge of American Government/Civics, by Gender

Variable	Girls	Boys
Constant	39.5**	31.9**
	(2.4)	(2.6)
School and civics curriculum		
Amount and recency of course work (0–2)	1.5*	2.6**
	(0.6)	(0.9)
Variety of topics studied (0–2)	1.2*	1.5**
	(0.5)	(0.5)
Discussed current events in class (0–4)	0.7*	1.3**
	(0.3)	(0.4)
Individual achievement		
Particpated in mock elections or government (0–2)	2.8**	2.3**
	(0.6)	(0.7)
Likes to study government (0–3)	3.3**	3.9**
	(0.6)	(0.5)
Four-year college planned (0–1)	11.3**	9.1**
	(0.9)	(1.0)
Home environment		
Reading and reference materials at home (0–4)	1.9**	1.6*
	(0.5)	(0.7)
Only English spoken at home (0–1)	0.9	4.4**
	(1.1)	(1.1)
Two-parent household (0–1)	0.7	4.6**
	(0.8)	(1.3)
Educational level of parents (0–3)	1.1**	2.5**
	(0.3)	(0.6)
Amount of television viewing (0–6)	−0.5*	−1.0**
	(0.2)	(0.3)
Background/demographics		
Hispanic (0–1)	−6.1**	−5.2*
	(1.5)	(2.1)
African-American (0–1)	−10.8**	−8.3**
	(1.5)	(1.5)
Adjusted R^2	.32	.32
Raw *N*	2,226	2,049
Weighted *N*	271,531	254,192

Note: Standard errors are in parentheses.
**p<.01; *p<.05.

cal reasons to offer as to how the civics curriculum in particular, and school factors in general, might differentially influence the knowledge boys and girls have about American politics and government. Nevertheless, it is worth considering briefly whether exposure and selection factors have a similar impact on what male and female students know about the topic. Similar to the analyses of overall knowledge for white, African-American, and Hispanic students, we estimated the exposure-selection model separately for male and female students. The results are reported in table 6.3.

For every curricular factor and every factor in the home environment except the presence of reading and reference materials, the estimated effects are larger for male students. Amount and recency of civics course work, variety of topics studied, and discussing current events in class have more of an impact on boys than on girls, with large differences for the amount and recency and current events measures. With regard to the home environment, the most dramatic differences between males and females are in the measures of language spoken at home and two-parent households. Living in a household where only English is spoken has a much stronger, positive impact on boys than on girls, as does having both parents living at home. In sum, structural differences of exposure in the civics curriculum and the home environment have a much stronger impact on males than females.

The pattern of results for the individual-achievement characteristics is the opposite. In fact, the estimated effects of two out of the three measures are stronger for girls than for boys. In these data, it appears that characteristics of individual motivation are more important for females, and civics knowledge is less dependent on and unresponsive to structural factors in their environments. If girls participate in civics-related exercises, which we take to be at least partly self-initiated, they learn more from the effort than do boys. If female students plan to go on with their education beyond high school, they are more affected than are males. But girls are inhibited to a lesser extent than boys by such factors as low parental education, and they benefit to a lesser extent by strong curricular efforts. Males appear to react more to their environments in absorbing civic knowledge. Given our focus, the larger point is the importance of school-related factors for females and males alike.

Differential Effects by Dimensions of Knowledge

Up to this point in our multivariate analysis, we have treated political knowledge as a unitary concept. It is appropriate now to reintroduce different dimensions of knowledge. We do so for three reasons. First, analyses of various subject areas can provide additional insight into the question of racial and ethnic differences. In fact, we shall see that the area in which school factors have the most influence is the area in which African-Americans score lowest in comparison with white students, suggesting that the relative influence of school versus non-school factors helps explain variations in the knowledge gap between white and African-American students. Second, analyses of specific political-knowledge dimensions can yield additional support for the importance of structural and individual characteristics. To the degree that school factors affect all areas of knowledge—or have variable effects that are consistent with the theoretical expectations—this increases confidence that our the model of student learning is a reasonably accurate portrayal of how high school students develop knowledge of American government and politics. Finally, we can further our inquiry into whether the differences in knowledge across subject areas are related to the school curriculum—whether certain kinds of subject matter are more likely to be traceable to the effects of civics course work and other school factors.

As we explained at the beginning of this chapter, the design of the NAEP study makes it necessary to combine certain of the categories defined in chapter 2 in order to establish subject-area measures reliably. We have thus created four larger, more general categories of political knowledge: citizens' rights, state and local government, structures and functions, and a miscellaneous category. The category of citizens' rights includes the questions on criminal and civil justice along with the items on the noncriminal rights of citizens. The second general category, state and local government, is comprised of the same set of measures originally discussed under that heading in chapter 2, as is the third general category of structures and functions. The fourth general category includes the questions on political parties, lobbying, women and minorities, inferences from text, tables, and charts, comparative perspectives, and theoretical perspectives. This miscellaneous category contains a mixture of disparate topics; however, they hang together in a way that will become clear shortly.

Though perhaps not obvious at first, these four general categories can be placed on a kind of continuum that permits a novel test of the effects of school-related factors. The structures and functions category tests for knowledge of facts about government structures that are unlikely to be the substance of daily conversations. As a result, we hypothesize that this knowledge is relatively likely to be influenced by school-related factors. Similarly, participation in school councils and the like, and greater interest in the study of government are most likely to contribute to knowledge of those areas that are least frequently a part of ordinary student discussions. At the other extreme is the category about citizens' rights. As we have seen repeatedly, knowledge of this area is high compared to other types of political knowledge, and sources outside the school are more likely to be important.

The other two categories probably fit somewhere in the middle with respect to school and curricular influence. As we noted in chapter 2, the state and local government category contains some items that many students would know from personal knowledge (that state governments regulate automobile licensing and that local governments control the schools but not the military), but it also contains items that are more likely to be learned in the classroom (which part of the government is executive, which is legislative). The residual miscellaneous category contains topics that are unlikely to be the main subjects of discussion and study in civics courses or in such contexts as high school student councils (political parties, women's issues). Yet they are also unlikely to be the subject of interaction outside the classroom. Thus, along with the state and local government category, knowledge of this category is somewhat less likely to be influenced by the curriculum and school-related individual factors than are government structures and functions but more likely to be influenced by such factors than are questions about citizens' rights.

We next reestimated the exposure-selection model for each of the four dimensions. The results are shown in table 6.4. As expected, school and curriculum characteristics are most influential for knowledge of government structures and functions; all three characteristics have strong, positive coefficients, with a particularly strong effect from amount and recency of civics course work. In general, the school and civics curriculum factors, apart from discussion of current events, tend to be more important as one moves from citizens' rights to the state and local government and miscellaneous categories (with some reversals within these two sets) to structures and functions. Even more consistent results are observed for the three measures of individual achievement; each has the strongest effect on knowledge of structures and functions and the least on knowledge of citizens' rights. That the major exception to the expected pattern is discussion of current events also makes sense. Current events can involve any of the subjects; if there is a surprise here, it is that such discussions appear to contribute as much to knowledge of structures and functions as to other kinds of political knowledge.

In contrast to school-related characteristics, features of the home environment have a more ambiguous connection to the varieties of civics subject matter. The presence of reading and reference materials has the opposite effect from that of school-related factors; this variable makes the most difference in knowledge of citizens' rights and the least in knowledge of structures and functions. This reflects the fact that political information that students receive at home is likely to be more relevant to the substance of everyday politics, including citizens' rights, and less relevant to knowledge of structures and functions. That the language spoken at home has a relatively large coefficient for the miscellaneous category is not surprising when one notes the presence of comparative items

Table 6.4 Effects of Structural and Individual Characteristics on Twelfth Graders' Knowledge of Four Areas of American Government/Civics

Variable	Citizens' Rights	State and Local Government	Miscel-laneous	Structures and Functions
Constant	57.8**	35.6**	32.2**	25.0**
	(2.4)	(2.8)	(2.3)	(2.4)
School and civics curriculum				
Amount and recency of course work (0–2)	1.7*	1.9**	1.5**	2.8**
	(0.7)	(0.7)	(0.6)	(0.7)
Variety of topics studied (0–2)	0.9*	1.2**	1.8**	1.3*
	(0.4)	(0.4)	(0.5)	(0.5)
Discussed current events in class (0–4)	1.1**	0.6*	1.0**	1.1**
	(0.3)	(0.4)	(0.3)	(0.3)
Individual achievement				
Participated in mock elections or government (0–2)	1.5**	2.7**	2.8**	3.2**
	(0.5)	(0.7)	(0.5)	(0.6)
Likes to study government (0–3)	2.9**	3.2**	3.4**	4.6**
	(0.4)	(0.5)	(0.4)	(0.6)
Four-year college planned (0–1)	7.5**	9.4**	11.6**	12.3**
	(0.7)	(0.8)	(0.8)	(0.8)
Home environment				
Reading and reference materials at home (0–4)	2.1**	1.7**	1.8**	1.2*
	(0.6)	(0.5)	(0.5)	(0.6)
Only English spoken at home (0–1)	2.9**	3.2**	3.5**	2.2*
	(0.8)	(0.8)	(1.1)	(1.1)
Two-parent household (0–1)	1.6	3.6**	3.0**	2.2**
	(0.9)	(1.0)	(0.9)	(0.8)
Educational level of parents (0–3)	1.4**	1.6**	2.4**	2.1**
	(0.4)	(0.4)	(0.5)	(0.4)
Amount of television viewing (0–6)	−0.7**	−0.7**	−1.0**	−0.6**
	(0.2)	(0.3)	(0.2)	(0.2)
Background/demographics				
Male (0–1)	−0.1	3.6**	2.1**	4.4**
	(0.7)	(0.8)	(0.8)	(0.9)
Hispanic (0–1)	−5.1**	−5.0**	−3.8*	−6.9**
	(1.4)	(1.3)	(1.6)	(1.5)
African-American (0–1)	−6.3**	−9.6**	−10.8**	−10.1**
	(1.0)	(1.1)	(1.0)	(1.3)
Adjusted R²	.18	.19	.25	.28
Raw *N*	4,262	4,261	4,262	4,265
Weighted *N*	523,986	523,905	523,986	524,658

Note: Standard errors are in parentheses.
**p<.01; *p<.05.

in that group. Nor is it surprising that both the education level of parents and television viewing have the highest coefficients (positive and negative, respectively) for the same category, inasmuch as this group includes inferential skill items like reading tables, along with a few theoretical questions.

The results in this analysis provide an insight into differences between minority and white students and allow us to revisit the three explanations for the divergence in political knowledge by race and ethnicity. The data in table 6.4 demonstrate that differences between African-American and white students are clearly the smallest for the category of citizens' rights—exactly the kind of knowledge most likely to be affected by non-school experiences. In contrast, the greatest differences between African-American and white students lie in the miscellaneous and structure and functions categories, the latter of which is information most likely to be learned through exposure to relevant material in school and in the civics curriculum. Differences in both structural and individual characteristics, especially of the home environment, must be considered a significant part of the explanation for the typically lower scores of African-Americans. Minority students come from different, and typically less advantaged, backgrounds than majority students, and these differences surely contribute to lower knowledge levels. One might ideally think that schools can and should make up for these differences in backgrounds. But instead of gaining more from school efforts, African-American students appear to be less influenced by school and by the civics curriculum. The effect of school and curriculum on knowledge is greatest where the subject matter is not likely to be part of the day-to-day lives of teenagers. This, as far as we can tell, is true for all students, but the overall reduced impact on African-Americans helps identify the locus of the greatest differences between African-American and white students.

In noting these differences according to varieties of subject matter, we should not lose sight of the fact that school-related factors are important for all four dimensions of political knowledge. Even for citizens' rights, all curricular and individual-achievement factors had positive and significant effects. To some degree, certain kinds of knowledge evidently can be picked up outside of the school, but even for topics that lend themselves to learning outside of school, the civics curriculum does make a difference. This conclusion is not without its downside, however. The larger effects of school factors on knowledge of structures and functions combined with the more modest effects of school and civics curriculum effects for minority students means that for this type of knowledge, African-

American students (and to some extent Hispanics) are even farther behind whites than the initial results revealed.

Civic Knowledge and Trust in Government

What effect do the school and civics curricula have on political attitudes toward government? In particular, does the civics curriculum affect the extent to which students believe that government pays attention to citizens, or whether they think that elections make political leaders responsive? We attempt to provide some insight into these questions by estimating the effect of characteristics in the exposure-selection model of political learning on the two political attitudes measured in the 1988 Civics Assessment.

When we turned our attention in chapters 4 and 5 to students' expressions of trust in the government and the role of elections in encouraging that trust, our expectations for finding structural and individual correlates were lower and our findings less strong. Nevertheless, it is important to see whether school and other characteristics are associated with political trust in a multivariate context. The results of the estimation of the exposure-selection model for these two attitudinal measures are detailed in table 6.5. As expected, the overall explanatory power of the model for both political attitudes is relatively small compared with the model predicting overall political knowledge. This is consistent with the earlier bivariate results showing a weaker relation between school and curriculum factors and the trust measures (as well as with the lower reliability generally expected of single-item measures).

Of the school and civics curriculum measures, the amount and recency of civics course work and the variety of items covered have a positive effect on both attitudes. The importance of the curriculum shows some effect, and the effect remains strong in the presence of the home and background characteristics. Individual characteristics appear to be the most substantial predictors of these two political attitudes, at least in an immediate sense. Enjoying the study of government and participating in mock elections or government are related to both attitudinal measures. Indeed, one could argue that thinking of the government as responsive to citizens is a prerequisite to, rather than a consequence of, participation in the process. The effects of home and background variables are generally in accord with our expectations. Although none of the effects are large, students with better-educated parents more often feel that elections are an important factor, and those who watch a lot of television are more often cynical about government. Males are more likely than females to agree

Table 6.5 Effects of Structural and Individual Characteristics on Twelfth Graders' Attitudes about Government Responsiveness

Variable	Amount of Attention Government Pays to People	Elections make Government Accountable
Constant	1.70**	1.86**
	(.08)	(.07)
School and civics curriculum		
Amount and recency of course work (0–2)	.05*	.02
	(.02)	(.02)
Variety of topics studied (0–2)	.03	.06**
	(.01)	(.01)
Discussed current events in class (0–4)	.00	.01
	(.01)	(.01)
Individual achievement		
Participated in mock elections or government (0–2)	.04**	.05**
	(.01)	(.02)
Likes to study government (0–3)	.07**	.08**
	(.02)	(.02)
Four-year college planned (0–1)	.08**	.07**
	(.02)	(.02)
Home environment		
Reading and reference materials at home (0–4)	.03	.03*
	(.02)	(.01)
Only English spoken at home (0–1)	−.03	.03
	(.03)	(.03)
Two-parent household (0–1)	−.04	−.04
	(.03)	(.03)
Educational level of parents (0–3)	−.00	.04**
	(.01)	(.01)
Amount of television viewing (0–6)	−.03*	−.02*
	(.01)	(.01)
Background/demographics		
Male (0–1)	.04*	.03
	(.02)	(.02)
Hispanic (0–1)	−.08*	.03
	(.04)	(.04)
African-American (0–1)	−.15**	−.02
	(.04)	(.04)
Adjusted R^2	.05	.05
Raw *N*	4,206	4,212
Weighted *N*	517,719	518,705

Note: Standard errors are in parentheses.
**p <.01; *p <.05.

that government pays attention to people and that elections create incentives to do so. Further, minority students are more skeptical than whites about the motives of government by a substantial margin.

The results of the estimation of these effects are less meaningful than the findings for political knowledge, but they nonetheless highlight the finding that school factors have a *positive* effect on these two political attitudes. To the extent that the school influences students, the evidence suggests that it encourages them to be more trusting of the government, not more cynical. Even the null finding with respect to current events is important here. As we noted in chapter 4, real politics often fails to match ideals, so frequent discussion of current events might actually make students more cynical about government. The result here gives us more confidence that this is not the case and, combined with the positive effect of current events on student knowledge, supports discussing them in the classroom.

Postscript: American History Curriculum and Knowledge

If the school and civics curriculum make a difference to knowledge of American government and politics, are there similar patterns of influence for other subjects? In particular, do students in American history courses reap similar benefits from exposure to material in their classes? We take a brief look at this question of educational context by analyzing additional data from the 1988 NAEP. Here, we repeat the regression analysis and estimate the exposure-selection model to predict knowledge of American history with data from the 1988 NAEP History Assessment.[12]

The results of this analysis, displayed in table 6.6, show strikingly parallel findings to the civics data. Structural characteristics of the school environment, including amount and recency of American history course work, studying a variety of topics, and discussing and analyzing material presented in those classes, have a significant and positive impact on knowledge of history. Moreover, amount and recency of history course work has a virtually identical impact on knowledge of American history as does civics course work on civics knowledge. The variety of topics studied in history classes contributes to student knowledge in a similar fashion, while discussing and analyzing material in class has a much stronger effect on history knowledge than do discussions of current events on civics knowledge. The individual-achievement characteristics display a similar pattern in the history data as in the civics data, as do characteristics of the home environment and race and gender. These findings from the history data lend credence to the validity of the exposure-selection model of political learning. In addition, the fact that the sample of students from whom these data were gathered is distinct from the sample of students in the civics assessment adds further support for the validity of our results.

In all the analyses in this chapter, one finding is clear and consistent: school and curriculum have an enduring impact on the development of

Table 6.6   Effects of Structural and Individual Characteristics
on Twelfth Graders' Knowledge of American History

Variable	History Knowledge
Constant	19.5**
	(2.6)
School and history curriculum	
Amount and recency of course work (0–2)	2.1*
	(0.9)
Variety of topics studied (0–2)	1.9**
	(0.4)
Discussed material in class (0–4)	2.4**
	(0.3)
Individual achievement	
Likes to study American history (0–3)	5.6**
	(0.5)
Four-year college planned (0–1)	9.2**
	(0.7)
Home environment	
Reading and reference materials at home (0–4)	1.8**
	(0.3)
Only English spoken at home (0–1)	2.1**
	(0.6)
Two-parent household (0–1)	1.5*
	(0.7)
Educational level of parents (0–3)	2.1**
	(0.4)
Amount of television viewing (0–6)	−0.5**
	(0.2)
Background/demographics	
Male (0–1)	2.1**
	(0.7)
Hispanic (0–1)	−6.8**
	(1.2)
African-American (0–1)	−10.4**
	(1.0)
Adjusted R^2	.33
Raw *N*	4,268
Weighted *N*	524,674

Note: Standard errors are in parentheses.
**p <.01; *p <.05.

civic knowledge in high school students. By *enduring,* we mean that their
effects are positive, statistically significant, and of meaningful size in
comparison to and in the presence of other competing explanations of
civic knowledge, including individual abilities and interests and home
environment. Despite variations across specific dimensions of political
knowledge, as well as by race or ethnicity and gender, aspects of the civics
curriculum and school characteristics were consistently important deter-
minants of civic knowledge.

Our findings stand in sharp relief to the conventional wisdom about the development of political knowledge in the study of political socialization, best exemplified by the work of Langton and Jennings (1968). They also offer a contrast to exaggerated criticism by educators and others of overall education effects as applied to this realm. Because our results challenge what has for thirty years been the conventional wisdom of a professional discipline, it is important to put our findings from the 1988 NAEP data into context and to examine the reasons why our conclusions differ so substantially. It is not enough to say that our results are different, or that our data base is superior because of its large number of items, or even that different times yield different results. We can, however, offer a number of well-founded explanations, all of which suggest that the conventional belief is not merely inappropriate today but that it was misleading as a picture of school effects in the mid-1960s.

First of all, Langton and Jennings (1968) did find some differences in knowledge based on exposure to civics course work. Indeed, their conclusion about the absence of effects was based on an analysis that was heavily weighted with attitudinal items. As we reported in chapter 1 and found in our analysis here (see table 6.5), the effects of school factors on students' attitudes have generally been weaker than their effects on knowledge. True, the magnitude of the differences that Langton and Jennings reported was not great, even for knowledge—a point we shall take up in chapter 7. Yet they reported that the biggest effect of their civics variable (in a multivariate model) was for political knowledge (858). And on a cognitive item about ideological differences between the Republican and Democratic parties they reported a 4 point margin between those who had and those who had not taken a civics course (derived from table on page 860); assuming this finding also held up to multivariate controls, it is in line with the differences reported for course work in this chapter.

A second reason to cast doubt on the earlier finding is that Langton and Jennings's measure of having taken civics courses did not account for the grade in which students took such classes. As we have argued, supported by analysis in chapter 4, it is not enough to tabulate the number of courses a student takes. There is good reason to believe that civics material taught in the senior year may be more informative or more likely to be remembered by students in the twelfth grade, for students are then are old enough to have a better understanding of politics and society and close enough to formal adulthood that civics lessons have a degree of meaningfulness lacking in earlier years. Our variable, by including recency, took this factor into account.

Third, we included in our model additional measures of class and school effects. Especially noteworthy, in light of Langton and Jennings's emphasis on redundancy, is our inclusion of the current-events variable. By the twelfth grade, students may well have encountered much of the material that they are given in civics classes, as our own discussion of the similarity in subject-matter coverage in the eighth and twelfth grades suggested. But current events are, by definition, new. Neither previous classes nor even "cues from other information sources" (859) will have duplicated the lessons to be learned from discussion of current political developments.

Finally, there are more technical matters. The Langton and Jennings analysis of political knowledge rested on six factual questions. As it turns out, only two of the questions—one asking about the length of the term of a U.S. senator and the other asking for the number of members on the U.S. Supreme Court—were of the "structures and functions" type that we found to be most affected by school-related factors. Three of the others fell into our miscellaneous category (what country Marshall Tito led, the World War II nation that had many concentration camps, and whether Franklin Roosevelt was a Republican or a Democrat), and the last fell into our state and local government category (the name of the governor of their state). In addition, two of the six items were well known, allowing little room for variation because of course taking or any other factor. Had the items been different, with a greater selection from the kinds of facts that are most likely to be emphasized in civics classes as well as a smaller proportion of "common knowledge" items, their results would almost certainly have shown a greater difference between those who had taken civics courses and those who had not.[13]

In light of these factors, it is unsurprising that our interpretation offers such a striking contrast to the conventional wisdom on the utility of the civics curriculum in promoting knowledge about American government and politics. While Langton and Jennings suggested that their results did not support the "thinking of those who look to the civics curriculum in American high school as even a minor source of political socialization" (865), we argue that our analysis demonstrates that the civics curriculum has an impact of a size and resilience that makes it a significant part of political learning. While they thought that "the increments [in political knowledge] are so minuscule as to raise serious questions about the utility of investing in government courses in the senior high school " (858), we emphasize the likelihood that civics courses can be made more engaging, relevant, and effective if curriculum designers take into account their differential effects on various kinds of political knowledge, their relative effectiveness or ineffectiveness for different types of students, and the qualities that give them more or less of an impact.

Finally, with respect to our contrasting findings about the impact of civics courses on African-Americans, we are inclined to accept the explanation of time dependence. In the early to mid-1960s, it may well have been the case that African-Americans were so excluded from the mainstream of American politics that civics courses introduced them to new information. One indication of this in the 1965 socialization study is that, after correcting for guessing, the percentage of African-American students estimated to have known which party was more conservative was not simply low, it was zero (860). In such a context, supplying any new information can result in large gains.[14]

In addition, it is clear that a major change occurred in African-Americans' attitudes toward the political system just after the data were collected for the Langton-Jennings work. Abramson (1983: 213), after analyzing more than three dozen studies of preadults, concluded that early studies showed that African-Americans and whites had similar feelings of political trust but that "black preadults are less trusting than whites in most surveys conducted during and after the summer of 1967." Given such a turnabout, it would not be surprising if African-American students reacted differently now from the way they did in the mid-1960s to lessons about government and politics—especially to lessons that stress a civic model of government benefiting everyone. That African-American students today appear to learn less from civics classes may be due to perceived irrelevance of the classes or to an active level of disbelief in government beneficence that was not present in the earlier period.

Recalling the reduced impact of the civics curriculum for African-Americans serves to remind us that schools are not the only relevant factor in the development of political knowledge. Our emphasis on school and civics curriculum stems from the fact that their contributions have often been neglected or downplayed. But in focusing on the school, we hasten to add that scholars and policymakers should not overlook the roles of individual achievement and the home environment, for our results show strong effects from these variables as well. Schools, even if greatly improved, still operate in the environment that surrounds them, and changes in the schools must be matched by changes in the home and in society at large if we are to significantly upgrade students' knowledge levels. Schools alone cannot do it, but neither can we do it without them.

CHAPTER SEVEN

The Future of Civic Education

The most important message to come out of our study of the political knowledge of high school seniors is that the school civics curriculum does indeed enhance what and how much they know about American government and politics. Furthermore, these educational effects on civic knowledge persist even after accounting for other powerful predictors of knowledge. This may seem to be obvious; after all, schools, their curricula, and specific course material exist precisely to promote learning. Yet the message implicit or explicit in a good deal of educational literature in the 1980s and 1990s has been that students are learning far too little about their academic subjects and that the blame for this state of affairs can be laid squarely, if not entirely, on the nation's schools. In addition, research in political science has sent a more narrow but explicit message: civics courses have virtually no effect on the political knowledge or values of high school students. Against this backdrop, what would otherwise appear to be a mundane finding becomes central.

We might, therefore, rest our case with the findings from the data analysis. But because the 1988 NAEP data clearly demonstrate that schools and the civics curriculum are significant locations of student learning, the implications of our findings require further reflection. We begin this chapter by assessing the relative magnitudes of the impact of various characteristics of exposure and selection on student political knowledge, noting, in particular, that we should not overemphasize the impact of simply taking civics courses. Rather, the magnitude of this effect must be considered in the context of the other factors—both inside and outside the educational setting—that also enhance student knowledge. Schools are not the only locus of political learning; simply requiring that students take more civics classes will not be an adequate solution for their deficiencies in political knowledge. We next consider the implications of our findings for reforming civics curricula and conclude with reflections on some lessons that educators, political scientists, and policymakers can take from our study. In so doing, we suggest how much and in what way we can continue to explore the contribution of school to civic learning. That the courses themselves, as well as what goes on inside the classroom, make a difference raises a series of challenges to all concerned to transform textbook and classroom civics into a more relevant discipline for the real political lives of students.

The Magnitude of School Effects

One might argue that the total estimated effect in the exposure-selection model of a 4 percent increase in overall political knowledge attributable to the amount and recency of civics course work is a contribution of insufficient magnitude to warrant much attention or fuss. In contrast, we claim that there are several reasons why this is a substantial magnitude that should be interpreted as highly relevant. First, while simply taking civics courses has a total impact of 4 percent on overall political knowledge, the combination of this with more specific aspects of the civics curriculum adds up to much more. The two additional measures of what happens inside those civics classes—studying a wide variety of topics and incorporating discussions of current events in class—contribute an additional 7 percent to overall political knowledge.[1] This combined effect is far from trivial; schools and civics curricula influence civic knowledge to a substantial degree above and beyond individual motivation and family-socialization influences.

Moreover, the 4 percent effect exists in an educational environment in which more than 90 percent of all high school seniors in the United States report having some civics course work. When nearly everyone is doing some civics, the effect of the course work is underestimated; in the absence of civic training at the high school level, the effects would probably be much larger than 4 percent.[2] In addition, not all of the effects of the school and curriculum are captured in the overall political knowledge measure; civics classes may have unobserved effects as well. For example, course work may lead students to ask questions of their parents, to pay attention to and perhaps understand better what they hear and see about politics in the media. Finally, the school and civics curriculum may also be important for more than increasing political knowledge. In particular, our analysis suggests that these school characteristics have a positive impact on democratic political attitudes.[3]

But even if we were to consider only the 4 percent estimated influence on political knowledge that comes from simply taking a civics course, the magnitude of the effect is still significant compared to that of other exposure and selection characteristics that enhance student learning. Only the individual selection measures of interest and future plans (a proxy for achievement) are consistently stronger predictors of overall knowledge than civics course work. Indeed, level of parental education, typically regarded as of singular importance to student achievement, has an effect that is just slightly larger than that for course work. Civic knowledge clearly has many sources, of which the civics curriculum is among the most important; it remains significant and of substantial magnitude against some tough competitors.

Finally, when evaluating the significance of the various contributors to political knowledge, it is important to take into account what can and cannot be altered in an effort to increase the level of political knowledge in young people. Our analysis of the 1988 data, for example, indicates that having two parents in the home who are relatively well educated or watching fewer hours of television would certainly enhance political knowledge, but such changes are not matters of direct educational policy. Indeed, many of the important influences on civic knowledge among students are outside the purview of public policies. In contrast, changing the amount and nature of civic instruction to enhance student knowledge is not only feasible, it is a normal function of the school system.

In short, the school and civics curriculum are major positive influences on student knowledge about politics and are a major factor in explaining why high school seniors know as much—or as little—as they do. However much we might wish for still greater knowledge and understanding, students' levels of civic knowledge would almost certainly fall below current levels in the absence of civics classes.[4]

Suggestions for Reform

We believe that there is considerable potential for reform in the ways students are encouraged to learn about government and politics. Students do not know as much as they could know, and the civics curriculum could be strengthened to address current weaknesses. How civics is taught in the classroom should be carefully scrutinized and reexamined with the idea of designing curricula that incorporate aspects of real politics as well as integrate teaching methods and techniques that enhance student learning through the development of critical analytic skills. Reform is also necessary in order for differences between students of different racial and ethnic backgrounds as well as between male and female students to be more adequately addressed and mitigated.

We offer first a number of suggestions for changes in curriculum content. In doing so, we draw on what our analysis revealed to be large gaps in student knowledge, typically associated with areas that are underemphasized in the civics curriculum.

Our first recommendation is based on the recognition that American government and politics is a controversial and contested territory. Indeed, the practice of democracy is often characterized by strong differences and contentious debate, and its teaching should reflect this reality. To do so, civics courses must incorporate more about politics in the real world. In particular, the relative absence of such subjects as political parties and interest groups is a distortion rather than an accurate representation of American politics. The reason for these gaps in course coverage may well be the desire to avoid controversy. But although the motivation is understandable, the results are unfortunate. When we say that students have a "textbook" knowledge of how government operates, what we mean is that they have a naive view of it that glosses over the fact that democratic politics is all about disagreement and the attempt to settle quarrels peacefully, satisfactorily, and in an orderly manner. We believe that it is a disservice to students to let them think that government ideally operates without conflict, as if it were possible to enact and administer laws that benefit everyone and harm no one. The cynicism that adults develop about politics may stem, in part, from the Pollyannaish view of politics that is fostered by the avoidance of references to partisan politics and other differences of opinion and to the rough and tumble ways in which those differences are resolved in real political life. If students can be taught to understand that political parties and interest groups form to promote and protect legitimate differences in points of view—sometimes to the benefit of large numbers of people, sometimes to the benefit of narrow interests—they would be in a much better position to understand, appreciate, and participate in the political process.

We also recommend that schools try to treat the role and status of minority Americans and women in politics more prominently and with more awareness of the complexity of the issues involved. We are not simply concerned that students were unable to identify particular women by name or that they were unable to recall certain figures and movements.

Rather, it appears—again, as much by omission of relevant questions as by low proportions of correct answers in the NAEP assessment—that little is taught about the history of gender and race relations in the United States and about the realities of past and present discrimination. The fact that so many students seemed to be unaware that laws had once been used to prevent people from voting indicates the scope of the problem. Instead of a balanced approach, the emphasis in teaching about gender and race appears to be exclusively on the "good things"—the abolition of slavery, the end of legal segregation, the enfranchisement of women, the fall of many barriers to women's participation. As with political parties and interest groups, the emphasis is on formal rules (Constitutional amendments); much less emphasis is given to what led up to those rules or to practices of the distant past like slavery and the disfranchisement of women. Likewise, little seems to be done to examine current perspectives on women and minorities—again, perhaps to avoid controversy.

Third, civics courses could increase their coverage by teaching theoretical and comparative perspectives. Students should know about such concepts as limited and unlimited government, private versus civic life, federalism, and representative government. They could learn about alternative ways of organizing governments, including parliamentary systems, and features of democracy that are found in other countries, such as multiparty systems and coalition governments. Likewise, they should learn about the values and principles underlying the American political system and how these ideas have developed and changed.[5] Students do not need to become experts on political theory or comparative government; rather, civics courses should encourage knowledge of the theoretical foundations of government and the many ways people organize and manage their collective affairs (among other reasons) so that students can achieve a far better understanding and appreciation of the American government. An awareness of the values and principles underlying our system might, in addition, instill a greater commitment to them.

A final area for the expansion of subject-matter coverage is in the teaching of skills relevant to understanding politics—specifically, basic quantitative skills that are involved in reading charts and tables. The graphics and related questions on the Civics Assessment were very simple, yet many students failed to find the correct answers. It is true that there was room for optimism here, for students' abilities appeared good in light of the severely limited attention in civics course work to data presentation and interpretation. With only a modest increase in instruction, considerable advancement could take place.

Styles of teaching, too, are important, and we recommend that interactive and expansive strategies of teaching be further utilized to maintain interest and to develop and enhance students' critical analytic skills. Here, our findings reinforce the message that "rote and ritual" (Torney et al., 1975: 149; Powell and Powell, 1984; Sidelnick, 1989) is detrimental to learning. In particular, drawing directly on our analysis, we suggest that there should be more discussion of politics and political issues, especially as they are revealed in current events. Fortunately, as we noted in chapter 4, classroom practices are already weighted in this direction, and current events appear to be a regular part of many classes. Indeed, this may be precisely why course work was found to enhance learning overall. Introducing or increasing the practice of discussing and analyzing current events where possible is therefore another way to improve current civics teaching.

Our suggestions about subject-matter coverage and classroom style are meant to be mutually reinforcing. Material about political parties, for example, could be introduced through use of only historical examples. The experience of African-Americans could be covered solely through discussions of the nineteenth-century South and a few prominent events in the mid-twentieth century. And so on. But this is not what we have in mind. Rather, it is *current* divisions between the parties, the *contemporary* concerns of African-Americans that we recommend that teachers explore.

Bringing in almost any contemporary issues will simultaneously introduce a degree of real politics. Yet for other reasons it matters what contemporary events are brought into the classroom, and this leads to a further recommendation. We noted in chapter 2 that students learned aspects of civics that were meaningful to them in some immediate sense. Thus, almost all students learned which level of government issues drivers' licenses but many fewer knew which regulates marriages; and although almost all students knew a lot about their individual rights, few understood how the president is nominated. These examples suggest that students would learn more effectively if instruction focused more heavily, perhaps initially, on those aspects of government that they can directly observe and immediately understand. Such matters are most likely to be found in local government and its operations. Issues like street repair, zoning rules, and capital construction may be less grandiose and more mundane than issues like Social Security, international trade, and defense spending, but students can nevertheless relate to local issues in ways that they cannot relate to national and international affairs.

Perhaps the relative ease of associating with local government is especially great if one thinks about government in a broad sense rather than concentrating exclusively on the chief executive. At the national level, the president is highly visible, and students can readily learn who he is and what he does on a day-to-day basis. But Congress, especially as an institution, is more abstract and less well covered in the media. The federal court system, especially beyond the Supreme Court, receives little play. And the bureaucracy is hard to visualize, let alone to understand in detail. At the local level, some of the same factors apply. It is easier, for example, to learn about a mayor or a single county executive than about a city council or zoning board. Yet the findings we have reviewed suggest that students learn more readily about things they can deal with directly, and local institutions—even bureaucracies—can be encountered directly. When learning about their own towns and cities, for example, students can be shown the actual plot of land that the zoning board is ruling on. They often have direct access to local officials and can talk directly to individuals who regulate zoning. And they can certainly observe legislative bodies, including school boards. The idea may seem obvious when posed in this fashion, but what seems to be confirmed by the NAEP results is that students learn about and understand local government more easily than they learn about the federal government. Indeed, it is likely that students could generalize from local situations to those at the state and national levels much more easily than the other way around.

But most civics courses place by far the greatest stress on the federal government, with the centerpiece of most courses the U.S. Constitution. State and local governments are often dealt with as a package, even though local governments typically deal with much smaller geographic areas and, in many instances, with quite manageable numbers of individuals. We do not argue that studying the Constitution is irrelevant or unnecessary; indeed, there are important reasons for its prominence in civic education—namely, that the national level is the only level of government all Americans hold in common, and that federal authority usually prevails over local government. Our argument is not that students should focus on local government to the exclusion of the other levels but rather that students might better understand the Constitution, and American government in general, if they learn about them by first dealing with more parochial issues. Understanding why it can be so difficult to pave one street or zone one piece of land, and examining all the individuals and interests affected, for example, can make it easier for students to understand how politics works at all levels and why there is a need for executive, legislative, and judicial components. In addition, learning about government and decision-making processes in local democracy may require studying local maps, reading municipal laws, and examining town budgets; this would encourage interpretive and inferential skills in which the NAEP assessment showed students lacking.

When Easton and Dennis (1969) studied elementary school children in the 1960s, they identified a "head and tail" effect, in which young people viewed the president and the policeman as the two most visible symbols of government. Yet although the policeman was connected in their minds with authority and government, young children had almost no sense of *local* government (213–14). They quickly learned that the policeman does not make the laws (216–17), but they did not replace that piece of misinformation with any understanding of what local government does and who is most involved. Indeed, "for younger children all government seems to be national in character" (214). Against this backdrop, the emphasis in high school on the Constitution and the national government may simply reinforce the notion that government in general is distant and not closely connected with daily lives. Children do not "automatically" learn about local government, either because it is highly visible (it is not) or because it is in fact close at hand. A conscious effort by civics teachers to relate government and politics to individuals and institutions that are smaller, closer, and more approachable than the national government might well be a way to make civics teaching convey to students a greater theoretical understanding of why governments exist, how and why they are organized in particular ways, and how they might be influenced.

There are clearly difficulties in redirecting a civics curriculum away from a national-level emphasis and toward a stress on local matters. Textbooks about local governments are rare, and given the diversity of local structures, it is hard to imagine how a textbook could be written to cover all their areas.[6] Furthermore, teachers must be more creative and enterprising when adopting such a shift. Nevertheless, teaching civics through the study of local government makes American politics and democracy more tangible to students. Instead of seeing government as distant and defined by a collection of unmemorable rules, with a focus on community democracy, students may learn why governments exist and how they operate.

Finally, in emphasizing comprehension of the real workings of government at the expense of rote learning of abstractions, we are not arguing that students do not need to know basic facts. Clearly, some amount of memorization and testing are necessary to ensure that they do. Yet learning facts need not, and should not, involve only memorization, drilling, and testing. Understanding and factual learning are not mutually exclusive, and the subject-matter coverage, approach, and classroom style we recommend represent an effort to enhance both.

*   *   *

If our message is generally upbeat about the effects of civic instruction on the level of student knowledge about politics and government, it has a downside, in that the conclusion applies less strongly to minority and female students, in particular, to African-Americans. African-American students scored, on average, almost 10 percentage points lower than white students—even after controlling for important individual and home attributes. And although the gap in overall knowledge between white and Hispanic students is not as wide, the differences were nonetheless persistent. In addition, female students also had consistently lower scores on the overall scale of political knowledge than male students. Combined with the persistence of the findings of lower scores for minority and female students is the companion result that school and curricular factors had less of an effect for students in all three groups than on the students in the reference group. In other words, course work is not as important a factor in enhancing civic knowledge for Hispanic, female, and particularly African-American students as it is for white and male students.

It is easier to identify this problem than to explain its origins. With regard to the findings on race, we could rule out at least one important hypothesis, namely, that African-American students learned less because they were uninterested in government and politics; they were not. Beyond that, we are left largely with the explanation that African-American students find political material, at least as it is taught in high schools, less relevant to their lives than whites do. One reason for this conclusion lies in the kind of questions on which African-American students did well relative to whites. On questions about racial matters, African-Americans outscored whites in a number of instances and were only slightly below them in others. If more of the material in high school courses related government and politics to the day-to-day experience of African-Americans, there might well be greater equality in the effect of those courses on student knowledge.

If there is a bright side to our finding about the relationship of course work to race, it is that identifying a problem is sometimes the first step in solving it. And in this instance, identification was not a trivial matter. Research in political science has long supported the notion that civics courses have a greater effect on African-Americans than on whites because for African-Americans the material was thought to be "less redundant." If we have convinced teachers and researchers that this is not the case, or at least that the matter is open to debate, we may have set in motion the means by which African-Americans can derive more from civics courses and, ultimately, by which the imbalance in knowledge levels might be alleviated. And although the evidence does not lead unambiguously to the conclusion that minority and female students learn less from their civics courses because they find the material less relevant to their daily lives, the indicators supporting this conclusion are strong. Altering the civics curriculum so that it speaks more directly to the experiences of a diversity of students may well help reduce the differences in students' levels of civic knowledge.

Messages for Educational Policymakers and Political Scientists

From what we have learned about the extent of student civic knowledge and about the processes by which students become knowledgeable about politics, we derive several important messages for educational policymakers and political scientists alike. We begin with those addressed primarily to educational policymakers.

First, educators should consider carefully at what point to teach civics, for our findings suggest that teaching civics later in high school, specifically during the twelfth grade, has the most impact. Based on work in political socialization concerning when students begin to understand political life (especially see Adelson and O'Neill, 1966) and our own discussion of student interests, there appear to be good reasons for teaching students about politics and government as they reach the age at which they are about to take on adult responsibilities, including the exercise of their most basic citizenship right—voting. Some material about government and politics may be impossible for younger students to comprehend fully, and although it is desirable that students have some kinds of civics course work in earlier grades, the capstone course should not be taken before the senior year. Especially if students are to understand politics, and not merely try to memorize constitutional provisions, they must have reached an age when they are capable of achieving that understanding and are interested in doing so. This strongly suggests the last year of high school.

Second, educators must reconsider the choice of subject matter that is emphasized in civics classes; topics that address questions and problems of real politics should be emphasized. Undertaking these changes will not be easy, for appropriate textbooks are not readily available, and it is the nature of contemporary issues to be constantly changing. Moreover, considerable skill on the part of teachers is needed to discuss topics that necessarily involve controversy—much more skill than is required for discussing safe issues from the past or abstractions so benign that few can disagree with them. Greater support will also be needed from school administrations and boards. Teachers cannot be expected to introduce subjects like political parties if merely mentioning them in any form (other than to point out that they are not mentioned in the Constitution, or that as a formal matter they select presidential nominees) is seen as too controversial.

Finally, how civics is taught—that is, what goes on in the classroom—should be structured to put less emphasis on rote learning and more on analytical and critical understanding of problems of democracy. This, too, will not be easy. Many teachers already teach this way, and those who do not probably find it difficult to do so—perhaps because of perceived opposition and perhaps because textbooks and established practices make memorization and drilling easier. But both national and international studies of civics have found more student learning where there is greater emphasis on discussion and less on drill. Indeed, the important point is that discussion and understanding enhance rather than preclude factual learning.

Our longer message to political scientists is related to their roles both as researchers and college-level teachers. We begin by arguing that political scientists should now be encouraged to engage in more research on students, classes, and teachers. When political scientists were convinced that civics classes taught students little, the decision to avoid research on preadults may have been sensible. But the message of this book is that preadults—especially those emerging adults in their last year of high school—do learn about politics and that part of what they learn comes from civics course work. If we want to understand what adult citizens know and do not know about political life, and how they got that way, the late adolescent years, and the schools, are good places to begin.

The renewed study of preadults need not bring with it the doubts that surround earlier work on political socialization (Niemi and Hepburn, 1995). Studies in the 1960s and 1970s of preadolescent children failed to produce evidence that what young children think about politics is connected to later life, even though in some ways it almost certainly is. The question of the relevance of such studies was one of the reasons for the near-abandonment of socialization work. But it is another matter altogether to study mid- to late teenagers. Young children may think that the mayor puts up swings in the park or that the president comes out to greet you personally when you go to Washington or that the queen of England is perfect, but these are not the beliefs of high school seniors. The study of high school students, especially in their senior year, is not in any way invalidated by questioning the relevance of early childhood beliefs.

As scholars, we should also reengage the study of the origins and development of political attitudes. Civic education is infused with the development of attitudes and values (Butts, 1980; Hursh, 1994), and if we are to understand the full role of civics courses and other aspects of the school, we need to have a more complete picture of their influence over this aspect of learning. Given our greatly revised picture of the role of the school and curriculum in the development of civic knowledge, a broad-ranging study of their effects on attitudes and values is long overdue. Because NAEP cannot undertake the study of political attitudes, political scientists should recognize it as their responsibility to expand our knowledge of this domain.

In addition to their role as researchers, political scientists also have multiple roles as teachers and college administrators. As teachers, political scientists ought to be concerned with precollegiate learning out of self-interest. Yet although the legal profession (see Gallagher, 1987) and, to a lesser extent, the psychology and economics professions (Ernst and Petrossian, 1996; Schug and Walstad, 1991: 412–13) have developed programs of study for the secondary levels and have lobbied hard for their inclusion in the curriculum, political scientists have largely remained aloof.[7] In essence, we have had a hands-off policy toward the high schools, neither suggesting new curricula nor developing new materials for existing courses. Political scientists could play a much larger role in the establishment of voluntary standards, in statewide curricular revisions, in developing evaluation strategies, and in writing better textbooks. On the administrative side, colleges regularly grant credit for Advanced Placement courses in American (and Comparative) Government and Politics, and these courses take place in high schools. Yet there is remarkably little concern among political scientists about what goes on in secondary schools.

As college educators, political scientists should also pay more attention to secondary school teacher training. It is rare, in our experience, for political scientists to think about education for secondary teachers. We do consider the education we provide for those going into law (because that is where so many of our students have traditionally gone), and we certainly think about the education of those whom we want to send on to graduate school (so we can place them well). But we know little about and rarely think about primary or secondary teacher training, whether we mean by this the number or combinations of courses future teachers should have or the content of those courses. Yet if teachers in high schools are to better understand politics so as to better teach about it, political scientists should bear a major part of the responsibility for their training.

Some of this effort should take place at the associational level. Here, political scientists have suggested guidelines for teacher training, recommending certain minimum amounts and types of undergraduate course work (APSA Guidelines, 1994), and they have issued reports from time to time—the last one in 1971 (Committee on Pre-Collegiate Education, 1971) —calling for more interest in and greater cooperation with secondary schools. But we have not worked with teacher groups, state associations, legislators, or others to ensure that teachers of civics will have adequate training to provide the kind of teaching we outlined above. The association directorate has gently pushed us, but at least until recently, the profession has not responded.[8]

A full agenda for work and research in civic education remains for educators and political scientists. Our findings from the 1988 NAEP Civics Assessment have demonstrated that civics course work is an important part of the way high school students learn about American government and politics. While the implications of these results can help invigorate the study of the cognitive and attitudinal development of some of the newest adult citizens in the American polity, we hope that our research also speaks to another important concern—namely, how best to educate "newly emergent" citizens in countries with recently established or re-established democracies. Throughout Latin America, Eastern Europe, and parts of Asia, new (democratic) citizens are not just high school age but all ages, only recently embarked on a new form of governance. How and to what extent these citizens are educated about democratic politics may have a great deal to do with the success and legitimacy of the regimes they elect. We hope that self-scrutiny of the way we educate our own emerging adults will make it possible for us to assist, when called upon, in the global effort to educate citizens around the world in the ways and means of democratic governance.

Design of the 1988 NAEP Civics Assessment

The National Assessment of Educational Progress (NAEP) is an ongoing, congressionally mandated project established in 1969 to obtain comprehensive data on the educational achievement of American students. NAEP is sponsored by the National Center for Education Statistics of the U.S. Department of Education. In 1988, a National Assessment Governing Board (NAGB) was created to formulate policy guidelines and to select the subject areas to be assessed. Fieldwork is currently administered by the Educational Testing Service in Princeton, New Jersey.

NAEP monitors student ability in a wide variety of fields. During 1988, NAEP tested students in reading, writing, U.S. history, geography, and civics. Students were selected from three groups: nine-year-olds (fourth graders), thirteen-year-olds (eighth graders), and seventeen-year-olds (twelfth graders). Two types of civics assessments were conducted. The first was designed to monitor trends in knowledge of citizenship and social studies among thirteen-year-olds (eighth graders) and seventeen-year-olds (twelfth graders). Students' scores were related to those from earlier NAEP studies (see Anderson et al. 1990: part 1).

The primary Civics Assessment, which we shall use, was designed as a cross-sectional survey to evaluate student knowledge and understanding of U.S. government and politics in 1988. Approximately 11,000 fourth graders/nine-year-olds, eighth graders/thirteen-year-olds, and twelfth graders/seventeen-year-olds, in 1,000 private and public schools across the country were tested. In this book, the analysis will be limited to twelfth graders. (The target population for the high school portion of the study was students who were *either* in twelfth grade or were seventeen years old. We use only the twelfth graders.) The number of seniors, before deletions for missing data, is 4,275. They were drawn from 304 schools. For descriptive purposes, it is necessary to weight the cases. We do so, though we report unweighted *N*s as well as a conservative indication of the precision of the estimates.

Questionnaires for twelfth graders included a background section asked of all students and a short "civics questionnaire" concerning courses taken in civics or American government and about the content of those courses. At the heart of the study were 150 multiple-choice questions about a wide range of subjects relating to U.S. government and politics. In addition, students were asked to name the president of the United States and, in fifteen minutes, to write "one or more paragraphs" describing his "most important responsibilities."

In order to avoid fatigue, individual students were given a response booklet containing a subset of the 150 questions and the presidential responsibilities item (question and essay). Most booklets contained about 75 multiple-choice questions; students who wrote the essay about presidential responsibilities answered about 50 multiple-choice questions. Consequently, when we combine items—calculate the percentage of questions answered correctly—the measure is unusual, in that it is not based on an identical set of respondents for each question. This does not present a validity problem, however. Random "spiraling" was used to interleaf the booklets "in regular (systematic) sequence so that each booklet appears an appropriate number of times in the sample," and "the students within an assessment session were assigned booklets in the order in which the booklets were bundled" so that "typically, each student in an assessment session received a different booklet and, even in schools with multiple sessions, only a few students received the same booklet or block of items" (Johnson, Zwick, et al., 1990: 29).

Questionnaires for twelfth graders were administered in randomly chosen "winter" and "spring" sessions (January 4–March 11, 1988, and March 14–May 18, 1988, respectively). The school participation rate (for the twelfth grade/seventeen-year-olds sample) was 82.8 percent. The participation rate among students was 78.5 percent (Anderson et al. 1990: 94).

We make occasional use of the 1988 NAEP History Assessment. A brief description of that study, along with some results, is contained in Hammack et al. (1990). We also draw on a similar study (among seventeen-year-olds only) conducted in 1986, which was sponsored by the National

Endowment for the Humanities as part of its Foundations of Literacy project. The results of that study can be found in Ravitch and Finn (1987). Because for the 1986 study, "the sampling, the test administration, and the wording and selection of individual questions were all ultimately the responsibility of NAEP" (Ravitch and Finn 1987: 3), we do not distinguish between them in the text, referring to them collectively as "the history NAEP."

A complete description of the design and implementation of all parts of the 1988 NAEP study is found in Johnson, Zwick, et al. (1990). A shorter version is given in Anderson et al. (1990).

Technical Note

The Report Card (Anderson et al., 1990) cites 144 as the number of items in the seventeen-year-old/twelfth graders assessment, and it lists 144 items on pages 108–10. In fact, these students were given 150 multiple-choice items plus the presidential responsibilities item (question and essay) noted above, which make a total of 152 items. The following multiple-choice questions do not appear in *The Report Card:*

Many countries have political parties
Many countries have a written constitution
Many countries have elected national leaders
Country with most influence on U.S. way of life
More educated people are more politically active
Authors of a quotation were delegates to the 1848 Seneca Falls
    Convention
The secretary of defense is appointed
The president nominates federal judges (similar to an item reported in
    The Report Card).

Public-Release Questions from the 1988 NAEP Civics Assessment

1. The right to counsel, which is guaranteed to a person arrested for committing a crime, means the right to be
    A represented by a lawyer
    B protected against self-incrimination
    C protected against search and seizure
    D free from being tried twice for the same crime

2. Most of the first ten amendments to the United States Constitution deal with
    A individual rights
    B the method of electing the President
    C the taxing powers of the federal government
    D the powers of the Supreme Court

3. Which of the following best describes the way in which the United States Constitution assigns governmental power?
    A It assigns it entirely to the states.
    B It assigns it entirely to the national government.
    C It divides it between the states and the national government.
    D It divides it between the states and the federal courts.

4. All of the following are requirements for voting in a national election EXCEPT the need to
    A be registered to vote
    B be a United States citizen
    C pay a poll tax
    D meet the age requirement

5. A witness who invokes the Fifth Amendment at a hearing of a United States Senate investigating committee is
  A demanding to have the assistance of a lawyer
  B demanding the right to confront and cross-examine witnesses
  C refusing to answer questions to avoid self-incrimination
  D refusing to answer questions before a nonjudicial body

6. According to the United States Constitution, which of the following has the power to declare war?
  A United States Supreme Court
  B United States Congress
  C United Nations
  D Joint Chiefs of Staff

7. In the United States House of Representatives, the member who is elected to preside is called the
  A whip
  B speaker
  C chair
  D president pro tempore

8. The members of which of the following groups are most likely to vote in the United States presidential elections?
  A Middle-aged professionals
  B College students
  C The unemployed
  D Factory workers

9. How is the Chief Justice of the United States Supreme Court selected?
  A By a national election with approval by a majority of the state governors
  B Through a majority vote by the existing Supreme Court Justices
  C By constitutional amendment and presidential signature
  D Through appointment by the President with the consent of the Senate

10. How many representatives does each state have in the United States House of Representatives?
  A Two
  B Three
  C The number varies according to the area of the state.
  D The number varies according to the population of the state.

11. Which of the following activities is an example of cooperation between state and national governments?
  A Printing money
  B Building interstate highways
  C Collecting and delivering mail
  D Making treaties

12. *Juan*: "I think it's important that governments maintain order. All of these protests are disturbing the peace. People tend to be too critical of the government and that is very disruptive. How can elected officials ever do their work if people are criticizing them all the time?"

Faye: "I think it's important that people let their opinions be known. Protests are okay as long as they aren't violent."
   The conflict expressed in the dialogue above is between
   A the maintenance of order and freedom of speech
   B union protests and student protests
   C a representative government and a true democracy
   D dictatorship and authoritarian rule

13. What is the major criticism of the electoral college system in the United States?
   A Its procedures delay the selection of the winner in presidential elections.
   B Its existence encourages the growth of third parties.
   C It permits a candidate who did not win a majority of popular votes to be declared President.
   D It undermines the power of the national party conventions.

14. The First Amendment to the Constitution guarantees
   A the right of all citizens to vote
   B the right to an education
   C freedom of religion
   D freedom from slavery

15. In the execution of its responsibilities, which of the following is LEAST likely to be influenced by lobbying?
   A The Supreme Court
   B The House of Representatives
   C The Senate
   D A state governor

16. How many senators does each state have in the United States Senate?
   A One
   B Two
   C Three
   D The number varies according to the population of the state.

17. The statement, ". . . Governments are instituted among Men, deriving their just powers from the consent of the governed," reflects which of the following theories?
   A Social contract
   B Federalism
   C Rule of law
   D Absolutism

18. Percentage of People Engaged in Political Activity by Educational Level in Year 19XX

Educational Level	Very Active	Fairly Active	Fairly Inactive	Very Inactive
College Education	28%	30%	30%	12%
High School Education	9	17	40	34
Grade School Education	5	11	33	51

Which of the following best summarizes the information presented in the table above?
  A The more education people have, the more likely they are to be politically active.
  B The more education people have, the less likely they are to be politically active.
  C The kind of education people have is more important than the amount of education in influencing political participation.
  D There is no relationship between educational levels and political activity.

19. Under the United States Constitution, the power to tax belongs to the
  A President
  B Department of the Treasury
  C Supreme Court
  D Congress

20. Which of the following groups may vote in a closed primary election?
  A All eligible voters
  B Only registered voters with a party affiliation
  C Only dues-paying members of a political party
  D Only elected delegates to a party convention

21. The procedure by which a candidate is nominated for President of the United States is established by
  A congressional legislation
  B the United States Constitution
  C the Bill of Rights
  D political parties

22. Judicial review is best described as the
  A right of Congress to reverse decisions made by the Supreme Court
  B assessment by the American Bar Association of the quality of judges' decisions
  C President's right to review and possibly veto the actions of federal judges
  D authority of the courts to decide whether the actions of other branches of government are constitutional

23. "We hold these truths to be self evident, that all men *and women* are created equal, that they are endowed by their Creator with certain unalienable Rights, that among these are Life, Liberty and the pursuit of Happiness . . ."

The authors of this quotation, who revised an important earlier document, were the

    A justices of the Supreme Court in *Marbury v. Madison* in 1803

    B delegates to the Seneca Falls Convention in 1848

    C members of the Free-Soil party in 1856

    D officers of the Whig party of the 1840s

24. Bicameralism is best defined as a

    A government composed of two principal branches

    B multilevel judicial system containing a higher court for appeals

    C system of checks and balances between two branches of government

    D legislative system composed of two houses or chambers

25. Which of the following describes a political action committee (PAC)?

    A An organization made up of members of Congress who combine to support common political ideas

    B An organization set up by a special-interest group to raise money for a candidate

    C A group organized by a political candidate's campaign manager to get favorable media exposure for the candidate

    D A group supported by funds raised through contributions from income tax returns

Standard Errors for Chapters 2, 4, and 5

The 1988 NAEP utilized a complex (stratified and clustered) sampling scheme rather than a simple random sample. Each individual student is therefore assigned a sampling weight reflecting his or her probability of being selected. Analyses of these data must utilize these weights. Computation of standard errors of estimates of descriptive and inferential statistics utilizes a jackknife technique. Statistically inclined readers will want to have these available, so they are provided here for all tables in chapters 2, 4, and 5. Standard errors for the regression results in chapter 6 are provided in the tables in the text.

Tables

2.1 *Knowledge of Criminal and Civil Justice:* .4; .6; .7; .9; .6; 1.0; 1.2; 1.0; 1.0; 1.3; 1.1; 1.3; 1.1; 1.2; 1.8.

2.2 *Knowledge of General Rights of Citizens:* .4; .5; .6; .7; .9; .9; .8; .9; .9; 1.1; 1.2; 1.2; 1.7; 1.3; 1.5; 1.6; 1.6.

2.3 *Knowledge of State and Local Government:* .6; .8; .8; .9; 1.1; 1.2; 1.1; 1.2; 1.3; 1.2; 1.3; 1.4; 1.1; 1.6; 1.4; 1.6; 1.7; 1.7; 1.5; 1.7; 1.6; 1.3.

2.4 *Knowledge of Political Parties and Lobbying:* 1.2; 1.5; 1.3; 1.2; 1.5; 1.3; 1.6; .9; 1.7; 1.4; 1.5; 1.2; 1.4.

2.5 *Knowledge of Issues Relating to Women and Minorities:* .8; 1.1; 1.3; 1.7; 1.4.

2.6 *Knowledge of Basic Structure and Functioning of the U.S. Government:* .6; .9; 1.2; 1.0; 1.3; 1.0; 1.2; 1.1; 1.4; 1.5; 1.5; 1.2; 1.3; 1.4; 1.6; 1.1; 1.4; 1.0; 1.4; 1.1; 1.5; 1.7; 1.6; 1.5; 1.3; 1.7; 1.7; 1.5; 1.2; 1.4; 1.4; 1.3; 1.4; 1.3; 1.5; 1.3; 1.3; 1.3; 1.4; 1.4; 1.4; 1.4; 1.5; 1.7; 1.1; 1.3; 1.0.

2.7 *Ability to Make Inferences from Texts, Tables, or Charts:* 1.1; 1.3; 1.0; 1.4; 1.2; 1.3; 1.4; 1.5.

2.8   Knowledge of Comparative and Theoretical Perspectives: 1.1; 1.1; 1.2; 1.2; 1.4; 1.4; 1.5; 1.6; 1.4.

2.9   Students' Performance on the Presidential Responsibilities Essay: (column 1) .9; .8; .9; 1.8; (column 2) .9; .3; 1.5; .8.

2.10   Government Responsiveness to People and to Elections: (column 1) .7; 1.0; .9; (column 3) .9; .6; .8; (column 4) .9; .9; .5; (column 6) .9; .6; .8.

4.1   American Government/Civics Course Work That Students Report Taking in Grades 9–12: .5; .5; 1.1; .5; 1.0; 1.4.

4.2   American Government/Civics Course Work Taken in Grades 9–12, by Type of School Program: (column 1) 1.9; 1.0; 2.0; 1.6; 2.7; 3.0; (column 2) .9; .5; 1.4; .9; 1.2; 1.5; (column 3) .6; .7; 1.2; .6; 1.4; 1.8.

4.3   Grade in Which the Most Recent American Government/Civics Course Was Taken: .8; 2.0; 2.2.

4.4   Overall Political Knowledge, by Amount of Civics Course Work and by Amount and Recency of Courses: (Amount) 1.2; 2.1; 1.1; 1.1; .8; 1.4; (Amount and recency) 2.0; 1.6; .6; .6.

4.5   Ten Types of Political Knowledge, by Amount and Recency of Civics Courses: (column 1) 2.6; 3.8; 2.3; 4.4; 5.2; 6.5; 2.0; 4.5; 5.0; 5.3; (column 2) 2.5; 1.9; 2.0; 2.5; 2.9; 3.5; 2.0; 3.2; 2.9; 2.6; (column 3) .8; .8; .9; 1.1; 1.3; 1.1; .8; 1.1; 1.1; 2.0; (column 4) .8; .6; .7; .9; 1.0; 1.0; .8; 1.1; .9; 1.3.

4.6   Performance on the Presidential Responsibilities Essay, by Amount and Recency of Civics Courses: (column 1) 9.0; 11.0; 9.0; 5.0; (column 2) 4.0; 6.4; 4.0; 4.0; (column 3) 1.1; 4.0; 1.8; 2.9; (column 4) .8; 4.0; 1.9; 1.9.

4.7   Government Responsiveness, by Amount and Recency of Civics Course Work: (column 1) 8.0; 8.0; 4.0; 5.6; 6.0; 5.3; (column 2) 4.0; 4.0; 2.9; 2.4; 2.9; 3.5; (column 3) 1.5; 1.6; 1.3; 1.0; 1.8; 2.0; (column 4) .8; 1.0; .8; .6; 1.1; 1.0.

4.8   Civics Topics Studied in Grades 5–8 and 9–12, as Reported by Eighth- and Twelfth-Grade Students (standard errors were available only for grades 9–12): (column 1) 1.5; 1.6; 1.3; 1.2; 1.3; 1.2; 1.1; 1.0; 1.1; 1.9; (column 2) 1.4; 1.5; 1.2; 1.1; 1.2; 1.1; 1.2; 1.0; 1.1; .8; (column 3) .3; .5; .5; .5; .5; .5; .3; .4; .6; .5.

4.9   Civics Topics Studied "a Lot" in Grades 9–12, by Amount of Civics Course Work: (column 1) 2.4; 2.4; 1.9; 2.0; 2.3; 1.6; 1.7; 1.7; 1.6; 1.1; (column 2) 2.8; 3.5; 3.3; 2.8; 3.2; 2.8; 2.9; 2.8; 3.1; 2.4; (column 3) 2.6; 2.7; 2.3; 2.0; 1.8; 1.9; 1.9; 1.5; 1.9; 1.8; (column 4) 1.9; 1.8; 1.5; 1.8; 1.9; 1.6; 1.9; 1.6; 1.7; 1.4.

4.10   Methods of Instruction in Civics Classes, Grades 9–12, as Reported by Students: (column 1) 1.5; 1.4; 1.5; .9; 1.0; 1.3; 1.0; .7; .4; .4; (column 2) 1.3; 1.1; 1.2; 1.2; 1.0; .8; .8; 1.2; .7; .5; (column 3) .6; .6; .8; 1.1; .8; .9; 1.0; .8; 1.2; 1.3; (column 4) .3; .4; .5; .2; .3; .8; .8; .7; .8; 1.4 (column 5) .4; .3; .3; .2; .5; 1.0; 1.0; .8; 1.4; 1.5.

4.11   Overall Political Knowledge, by Methods of Instruction: ("Memorize," column 1) 2.5; 2.1; 1.8; 2.3; 2.4; (column 2) 1.2; 1.1; 1.0; 1.2; 1.2; (column 3) 1.4; 1.1; 1.1; 1.3; 1.9; ("Test," column 1) 2.9; 1.2; 1.8; (column 2) 1.4; .7; 1.2; (column 3) 1.6; .8; 1.5; ("Discuss," column 1) 1.2; 2.1; 5.1; (column 2) .6; .9; 1.7; (column 3) .7; .9; 1.7; 2.2; 2.5; ("Current events," column 1) 1.6; 2.0; (column 2) .9; 1.0; 1.2; (column 3) .8; 1.0; 1.7; 2.4.

4.12   Performance on the Presidential Responsibilities Essay, by Methods of Instruction: ("Memorize," column 1) .1; 1; (column 2) .1; 1; (column 3) .1; 1; ("Test," column 1) .1; (column 2) .1; 1; (column 3) .1; 1; ("Discuss," column 1) .1; 1; (column 2) .1; 1; (column 3) .1; 1; ("Current events," column) 1; (column 2) .1; 1; (column 3) .1; 1.

4.13 Opportunities to Learn Civics, by Type of School, Type of Community, and Region: (column 1) 1.7; 7.9; 5.1; 2.6; 2.4; 4.2; 2.5; 3.5; 4.0; 2.6; (column 2) 1.4; 7.2; 3.0; 2.1; 1.9; 2.4; 3.1; 1.6; 2.2; 2.7; (column 3) 1.4; 8.9; 6.3; 2.7; 1.8; 2.2; 3.4; 2.9; 3.5; 1.9.

4.14 Opportunities to Learn Civics, by Instructional Dollars per Pupil: (column 1) 13.4; 3.6; 3.2; 5.2; 5.4; 2.1; 28.8; (column 2) 7.0; 2.5; 2.6; 2.7; 6.0; .8; 1.9; (column 3) 3.2; 3.8; 4.1; 3.2; 4.5; 1.8; 3.7.

4.15 Opportunities to Learn Civics, by Student-Teacher Ratio: (column 1) 4.7; 2.9; 2.2; 3.4; 6.0; 1.2; (column 2) 4.7; 2.3; 2.3; 1.9; 2.0; 7.2; (column 3) 3.8; 2.4; 2.0; 3.4; 3.3; 3.5.

4.16 Opportunities to Learn Civics, by Minority Student Concentration: (column 1) 4.0; 2.9; 6.8; 4.4; (column 2) 2.4; 3.0; 11.3; 2.3; (column 3) 3.8; 2.7; 7.3; 4.0.

5.1 Overall Political Knowledge, by Amount of Television Viewing: (column 1) 1.1; .8; .8; .4; (column 2) .8; .6; .9; 1.2.

5.2 Ten Types of Political Knowledge, by Amount of Television Viewing: (column 1) .9; .7; 1.2; 1.6; 1.2; 1.4; 1.1; 1.2; 1.3; 1.8; (column 2) .8; .6; .9; .8; 1.1; 1.1; .7; 1.0; .9; 1.5; (column 3) 1.1; 1.1; .9; 1.6; 1.9; 1.6; 1.0; 1.6; 1.4; 2.3; (column 4) 1.8; 2.3; 1.5; 2.6; 2.3; 1.9; 1.5; 1.9; 2.7; 2.8.

5.3 Performance on the Presidential Responsibilities Essay, by Amount of Television Viewing: (column 1) 1.7; 2.5; 2.5; 2.9; (column 2) .9; 2.2; 2.3; 2.1; (column 3) 1.1; 2.9; 3.1; 2.3; (column 4) 4.2; 5.0; 5.2; 3.2.

5.4 Government Responsiveness, by Amount of Television Viewing: (column 1) 1.3; 1.6; 1.3; .8; 1.5; 1.5; (column 2) .9; 1.4; 1.2; .7; 1.3; 1.3; (column 3) 1.1; 1.8; 1.7; 1.1; 1.5; 1.6; (column 4) 3.8; 3.7; 3.7; 3.2; 3.2; 3.6.

5.5 Overall Political Knowledge and Presidential Responsibilities Essay, by Participation in Mock Elections, Councils, Trials: (column 1) 1.3; 1.1; .6; (column 2) .7; .6; .9; (column 3) 1.2; 1.1; 2.0; (column 4) 2.2; 1.9; 3.8; (column 5) 2.0; 2.1; 4.4; (column 6) 2.1; 1.7; 4.0.

5.6 Government Responsiveness, by Participation in Mock Elections, Councils, Trials: (column 1) 1.2; 1.2; .9; .7; 1.1; 1.0; (column 2) 1.4; 1.6; 1.4; .7; 1.4; 1.5; (column 3) 2.2; 3.0; 2.5; 1.2; 2.8; 3.0.

5.7 Overall Political Knowledge, by Interest in American Government/Civics: 1.2; .5; .6.

5.8 Ten Types of Political Knowledge by Interest, in American Government/Civics: (column 1) .9; .6; .7; 1.0; 1.2; .9; .8; 1.0; 1.2; 1.5; (column 2) .8; .6; .7; .9; 1.1; 1.1; .7; 1.0; 1.0; 1.6; (column 3) 1.4; 1.2; 1.5; 2.2; 2.0; 2.0; 1.5; 1.9; 1.7; 2.4.

5.9 Students' Performance on the Presidential Responsibilities Essay, by Interest in American Government/Civics: (column 1) 1.1; 2.0; 1.5; 1.8; (column 2) 1.0; 2.3; 2.5; 1.8; (column 3) 2.6; 3.5; 4.3; 5.0.

5.10 Government Responsiveness, by Interest in American Government/Civics: (column 1) 1.1; 1.2; .9; 1.0; 1.5; 1.3; (column 2) 1.3; 1.3; 1.0; .6; 1.0; 1.2; (column 3) 2.4; 2.4; 2.8; 1.7; 3.6; 3.7.

5.11 Students Responding Correctly to Items about Political Parties and Lobbying, by Gender: (Female) 1.6; 1.6; 2.0; 1.9; 1.6; 1.6; 2.4; 1.5; 1.8; 1.3; 2.1; 1.7; 2.0; 1.9; 2.1; (Male) 1.4; 1.9; 1.9; 1.9; 2.0; 1.8; 1.8; 1.9; 2.0; 1.5; 1.8; 2.2; 2.0; 1.6; 1.7.

5.12 Students Responding Correctly to Items about Elections and War and Foreign Affairs, by Gender: (column 1) .8; 1.1; 1.4; 1.5; 1.9; 2.1; 2.0; 2.2; 1.6; 1.7; 1.8; 1.3; 1.4; 1.4; 1.4; 1.5; 2.0; 1.6; 2.0; 1.6; 1.8; (column 2) 1.0; 1.1; 1.4; 1.8; 1.9; 2.3; 1.9; 1.9; 2.0; 2.1; 1.7; 1.6; 1.8; 1.5; 1.8; 1.5; 1.8; 1.4; 1.9; 2.2; 2.5.

5.13 Students Responding Correctly to Items Requiring Inferences from Text, Tables,

Student Background Questionnaire from the 1988 NAEP Civics Assessment

Questions 1–4. Did you take or do you expect to take a course in American government or civics in the following grades? Fill in one oval for each question.

	Yes	No	I don't know
1. Ninth	A	B	C
2. Tenth	A	B	C
3. Eleventh	A	B	C
4. Twelfth	A	B	C

5. Since the beginning of ninth grade, how much American government or civics course work have you completed up to now?
  A None
  B Less than ½ year
  C ½ year
  D Between ½ year and 1 year
  E 1 year
  F More than 1 year

6. Have you taken or are you now taking Advanced Placement American government and politics?
  A Yes
  B No

Questions 7–16. Since the beginning of ninth grade, how much have you studied the following topics in American government or civics? Fill in one oval for each question.

	A lot	Some	Not at all
7. United States Constitution and Bill of Rights	A	B	C
8. Congress	A	B	C
9. How laws are made	A	B	C
10. Court system	A	B	C
11. President and the cabinet	A	B	C
12. Political parties, elections, and voting	A	B	C
13. State and local government	A	B	C
14. Principles of democratic government	A	B	C
15. Other forms of government	A	B	C
16. Rights and responsibilities of citizens	A	B	C

17. How much do you like studying American government or civics?

   A It is one of my favorite subjects.

   B It is interesting.

   C I like several other subjects better.

   D I have never studied American government or civics.

18. How often have you participated in mock or imitation elections, governmental bodies (like a council, legislature, or Congress), or trials?

   A Several times

   B Once or twice

   C Never

19. How much do you feel that having elections makes the government pay attention to what people think when it decides what to do?

   A A good deal

   B Some

   C Not much

20. Over the years, how much attention do you feel the government pays to what people think when it decides what to do?

   A A good deal

   B Some

   C Not much

Questions 21–34 are about your current or most recent American government or civics class. If you have never studied American government or civics, fill in the appropriate oval for Question 21 and do not answer any more questions in this part.

21. Have you ever had an American government or civics class?

   A Yes (ANSWER QUESTIONS 22–34)

   B No (DO NOT ANSWER ANY MORE QUESTIONS IN THIS PART)

22. How much time have you usually spent each week on homework for your American government or civics class?

   A I usually haven't had homework assigned.

   B I have had homework, but I usually haven't done it.

   C Less than 1 hour

   D 1 hour

   E 2 hours

F 3 hours
G 4 hours
H 5 hours or more

23. What kind of grades have you gotten in your American government or civics class?
A Mostly A
B About half A and half B
C Mostly B
D About half B and half C
E Mostly C
F About half C and half D
G Mostly D
H Mostly below D

Questions 24–33. How often has your American government or civics teacher asked you to do the following things for class? Fill in one oval for each question.

	Almost every day	Once or twice a week	Once or twice a month	A few times a year	Never
24. Read material from your textbook	A	B	C	D	E
25. Read extra material not in your regular textbook	A	B	C	D	E
26. Memorize the material you have read	A	B	C	D	E
27. Discuss and analyze the material you have read	A	B	C	D	E
28. Write short answers to questions (a paragraph or less)	A	B	C	D	E
29. Write a report of three or more pages	A	B	C	D	E
30. Work on a group project	A	B	C	D	E
31. Give talks about what you are studying	A	B	C	D	E
32. Discuss current events	A	B	C	D	E
33. Take a test or quiz	A	B	C	D	E

34. How much difficulty have you had reading your American government or civics textbook?
A A lot
B Some
C None

Coding and Distribution of Variables Used in the Multivariate Analysis and Supplementary Regression Results

Whole Sample

Description of Variable Coding	Percentage of Students
Amount and recency of civics course work	
None (1)	9.1 (0.6)
Last in grade 9, 10, or 11 (2)	30.6 (2.0)
Grade 12 (3)	60.3 (2.2)
Raw *N* = 4,205 Weighted *N* = 517,317	
Variety of topics studied	
Studied 0 a lot (0)	24.8 (1.1)
Studied 1–5 a lot (1)	40.0 (0.9)
Studied 6–10 a lot (2)	35.2 (1.3)
Raw *N* = 4,231 Weighted *N* = 520,613	
Discussed current events in class	
Never (0)	11.6 (1.0)
A few times a year (1)	8.4 (0.7)
Once or twice a month (2)	12.6 (0.7)
Once or twice a week (3)	31.4 (1.1)
Almost every day (4)	35.9 (1.3)
Raw *N* = 3,802 Weighted *N* = 472,731	
Participation in mock elections, councils, trials	
Never (0)	52.1 (1.3)
Once or twice (1)	36.3 (1.1)
Several times (2)	11.6 (0.6)
Raw *N* = 4,242 Weighted *N* = 522,362	
How much you like to study government	
Never studied it (0)	2.1 (0.3)
Like others better (1)	46.5 (1.3)
It is interesting (2)	41.3 (1.0)
My favorite subject (3)	10.1 (0.5)
Raw *N* = 4,244 Weighted *N* = 522,291	

Four-year college planned
No (0)   46.1 (1.7)
Yes (1)   53.9 (1.7)
   Raw *N* = 4,211   Weighted *N* = 518,189

Reading and reference materials in the home
None (0)   0.8 (0.2)
One (1)   2.8 (0.3)
Two (2)   8.7 (0.6)
Three (3)   24.3 (0.7)
Four (4)   63.4 (0.9)
   Raw *N* = 4,251   Weighted *N* = 522,588

Language spoken at home
Always or sometimes other than English (0)   25.4 (0.9)
Always English (1)   74.6 (0.9)
   Raw *N* = 4,265   Weighted *N* = 524,380

Two-parent household
Only one parent (0)   23.6 (0.8)
Both parents at home (1)   76.4 (0.8)
   Raw *N* = 4,171   Weighted *N* = 513,492

Educational level of parents (highest of mother/father)
Grade shcool (0)   7.5 (0.5)
High school (1)   24.5 (1.1)
Some college (2)   24.5 (1.1)
College graduate (3)   43.5 (1.7)
   Raw *N* = 4,164   Weighted *N* = 512,446

Amount of television viewing
None (0)   2.9 (0.3)
1 hour or less (1)   24.9 (1.0)
2 hours (2)   25.4 (0.8)
3 hours (3)   19.0 (0.8)
4 hours (4)   14.0 (0.7)
5 hours (5)   7.2 (0.4)
6 hours or more (6)   6.6 (0.4)
   Raw *N* = 4,261   Weighted *N* = 523,908

African-American
All others (0)   88.2 (0.6)
African-American (1)   11.8 (0.6)
   Raw *N* = 4,275   Weighted *N* = 525,727

Hispanic
All others (0)   91.6 (0.4)
Hispanic (1)   8.4 (0.4)
   Raw *N* = 4,275   Weighted *N* = 525,727

Gender
Female (0)   51.6 (1.6)
Male (1)   48.4 (1.6)
   Raw *N* = 4,275   Weighted *N* = 525,727

Note: Throughout the analysis, we used the variables DRACE (imputed race or ethnicity) and DSEX (imputed sex or gender). DRACE relied mostly on student reports of their race (white; African-American; Hispanic; Asian or Pacific Islander; American Indian or Alaskan Native; other) and ethnicity (not Hispanic; Mexican, Mexican American or Chicano; Puerto Rican; Cuban; other Spanish or Hispanic background). When students provided illegible information or no information, test administrators' classifications were used. DSEX was taken from school records. For a few students, this information was missing and was imputed by ETS after the assessment. For complete descriptions, see Johnson, Zwick, et al. (1990, 681–82).
Standard errors are in parentheses.

By Race or Ethnicity

Description of Variable Coding	White	African-American (Percentages)	Hispanic
Amount of recency of civics course work			
Never studied it (0)	2.2 (0.3)	2.3 (0.5)	0.8 (0.4)
None (1)	6.9 (0.8)	5.7 (1.1)	8.4 (1.4)
Last in grade 9, 10, or 11 (2)	31.7 (2.3)	32.9 (3.8)	19.2 (4.0)
Grade 12 (3)	59.2 (2.5)	59.1 (3.6)	71.6 (4.5)
Variety of topics studied			
Studied 0 a lot (0)	25.8 (1.2)	17.1 (1.5)	24.7 (1.1)
Studied 1–5 a lot (1)	39.8 (1.1)	41.5 (2.1)	38.7 (0.9)
Studied 6–10 a lot (2)	34.5 (1.4)	41.4 (1.8)	35.5 (3.2)
Discussed current events in class			
Never (0)	11.8 (1.1)	10.2 (1.2)	11.9 (1.9)
A few times a year (1)	8.0 (0.8)	11.8 (2.0)	8.8 (1.9)
Once or twice a month (2)	12.5 (0.8)	18.5 (1.8)	13.4 (1.8)
Once or twice a week (3)	31.9 (1.3)	31.4 (2.3)	26.3 (2.4)
Almost every day (4)	35.8 (1.5)	33.0 (2.0)	39.5 (3.0)
Participation in mock elections, councils, trials			
Never (0)	49.9 (1.5)	59.3 (2.5)	65.5 (3.6)
Once or twice (1)	38.1 (1.3)	30.8 (2.3)	25.0 (2.4)
Several times (2)	12.0 (0.6)	9.9 (1.1)	9.5 (2.0)
How much you like to study government			
Never studied it (0)	2.2 (0.3)	2.3 (0.5)	0.8 (0.4)
Like others better (1)	47.9 (1.4)	43.3 (2.8)	38.6 (2.9)
It is interesting (2)	40.2 (1.2)	44.1 (2.3)	51.2 (3.2)
My favorite subject (3)	9.8 (0.6)	10.3 (1.3)	9.4 (2.1)
Four-year college planned			
No (0)	45.6 (1.9)	47.5 (3.0)	53.8 (4.1)
yes (1)	54.4 (1.9)	52.3 (3.0)	46.2 (4.1)
Reading and reference materials in the home			
None (0)	0.7 (0.2)	1.5 (0.5)	2.0 (0.8)
One (1)	2.0 (0.3)	4.4 (0.8)	8.0 (1.3)
Two (2)	6.4 (0.5)	14.7 (2.0)	20.7 (2.3)
Three (3)	22.3 (0.8)	33.3 (1.6)	28.7 (2.3)
Four (4)	68.6 (1.1)	46.2 (2.4)	40.6 (2.8)
Language spoken at home			
Always or sometimes other than English (0)	18.7 (0.9)	22.8 (1.4)	86.6 (2.1)
Always English (1)	81.3 (0.9)	77.2 (1.4)	13.4 (2.1)
Two-parent household			
Only one parent (0)	19.1 (0.9)	48.8 (2.2)	28.9 (2.5)
Both parents at home (1)	89.9 (0.9)	51.2 (2.2)	71.1 (2.5)
Educational level of parents (highest of mother/father)			
Grade school (0)	5.7 (0.6)	9.2 (1.6)	28.6 (2.5)
High school (1)	23.9 (1.3)	31.8 (2.2)	25.0 (1.9)
Some college (2)	24.8 (1.3)	27.2 (1.9)	20.9 (2.7)
College graduate (3)	45.6 (1.8)	31.8 (2.2)	25.5 (3.2)
Amount of television viewing			
None (0)	3.0 (0.4)	1.3 (0.4)	1.9 (0.7)
1 hour or less (1)	27.8 (1.2)	10.2 (1.1)	19.6 (2.7)
2 hours (2)	26.7 (0.9)	14.5 (1.8)	26.4 (2.5)
3 hours (3)	18.8 (0.9)	18.4 (1.6)	22.6 (3.4)

4 hours (4)	12.3 (0.8)	19.6 (1.7)	15.2 (2.3)
5 hours (5)	5.7 (0.4)	17.0 (1.5)	8.6 (1.8)
6 hours or more (6)	4.7 (0.5)	19.0 (1.7)	5.8 (1.7)
Gender			
Female (0)	51.6 (1.7)	52.6 (2.8)	50.0 (3.1)
Male (1)	48.8 (1.7)	47.4 (2.8)	50.0 (3.1)

Note: Numbers of unweighted cases are approximately 3,064, 710, and 350 for whites, African-Americans, Hispanics, respectively, with slight variations owing to missing data. Standard errors are in parentheses.

Numbers of Items per Respondent for the Categories Used in Chapter 6

As noted in chapter 1 and Appendix A, respondents were not all given the same set of political-knowledge items. This means that in the categories below, respondents have different numbers of items pertaining to that category. Nonetheless, as can be seen from the number of items per respondent, students' scores are based on relatively large numbers of test questions.

Category	Number of items per respondent	Frequency
Citizens' rights (combines items in tables 2.1 and 2.2)	12	615
	14	621
	15	608
	17	601
	18	628
	21	588
	27	614
Total = 4,275		
State and local government (items in table 2.3)	7	615
	9	608
	12	1,189
	13	614
	16	621
	19	628
Total = 4,275		
Miscellaneous (combines items in tables 2.4, 2.5, 2.7, 2.8)	14	621
	15	588
	17	628
	18	608
	23	615
	24	614
	29	601
Total = 4,275		
Structures and functions (items in table 2.6)	18	588
	23	608
	24	615
	25	621
	26	614
	31	601
	33	628
Total = 4,275		

Table E.1 Effects of Structural and Individual Characteristics on Twelfth Graders' Knowledge of Presidential Responsibilities

Variable	Presidential Responsibilities
Constant	1.90**
	(0.15)
School and civics curriculum	
Amount and recency of course work (0–2)	0.03
	(0.04)
Variety of topics studied (0–2)	0.09**
	(0.04)
Discussed current events in class (0–4)	0.01
	(0.02)
Individual achievement	
Participated in mock elections or government (0–2)	0.05
	(0.04)
Likes to study government (0–3)	0.09**
	(0.03)
Four-year college planned (0–1)	0.28**
	(0.05)
Home environment	
Reading and reference materials at home (0–4)	0.07*
	(0.03)
Only English spoken at home (0–1)	0.01
	(0.06)
Two-parent household (0–1)	0.05
	(0.07)
Educational level of parents (0–3)	0.06*
	(0.02)
Amount of television viewing (0–6)	0.01
	(0.02)
Background/demographics	
Male (0–1)	−0.14**
	(0.05)
Hispanic (0–1)	−0.06
	(0.09)
African-American (0–1)	−0.32**
	(0.08)
Adjusted R^2	.11
Raw N = 1,793 Weighted N = 221,900	

Note: Standard errors are in parentheses.
**p<.01; *p<.05.

Table E.2 Effects of Structural and Individual Characteristics on Knowledge of American Government/Civics (Listwise Deletion of Missing Data)

Variable	Civic Knowledge
Constant	36.2**
	(1.9)
School and civics curriculum	
Amount and recency of course work (0–2)	2.3**
	(0.5)
Variety of topics studied (0–2)	1.2**
	(0.4)
Discussed current events in class (0–4)	0.8**
	(0.3)
Individual achievement	
Participated in mock elections or government (0–2)	2.7**
	(0.5)
Likes to study government (0–3)	3.7**
	(0.4)
Four-year college planned (0–1)	9.8**
	(0.7)
Home environment	
Reading and reference materials at home (0–4)	1.7**
	(0.5)
Only English spoken at home (0–1)	1.9**
	(0.9)
Two-parent household (0–1)	2.7**
	(0.7)
Educational level of parents (0–3)	1.7**
	(0.4)
Amount of television viewing (0–6)	−0.7**
	(0.2)
Background/demographics	
Male (0–1)	2.9**
	(0.7)
Hispanic (0–1)	−5.8**
	(1.5)
African-American (0–1)	−8.9**
	(1.0)
Adjusted R^2	.31
Raw N = 3,597	
Weighted N = 447,717	

Note: Standard errors are in parentheses.
**p<.01; *p<.05.

Notes

Chapter 1: Civic Education and Students' Knowledge

1. See, for example, Page (1978) for a study of the clarity of the messages in presidential campaigns, and Neuman, Just, and Crigler (1992) for a study of the effect of various types of media exposure on political knowledge. A general review of media effects can be found in Semetko (1996: 269–78).

2. Converse (1964), among others, has argued that levels of political knowledge take on a scalar form, where it is logically impossible to be at the second level without passing through the first. Neuman (1986: 18) makes a similar point with a more mundane reference: "Watching politics without understanding the rules of the game is like watching a sporting event without any knowledge of its rules or traditions: it may seem to be a competition of some sort, but there is no way to know who is competing with whom over what."

3. The 1989 Survey of Political Knowledge of a random sample of the adult U.S. population is an exception to this general rule. See Delli Carpini and Keeter (1996).

4. For example, Zaller suggested that the average citizen can probably name more members on the starting line-up of the major-league home baseball team than justices on the U.S. Supreme Court (Zaller, 1992: 16). James Michener contributed the following. While researching voters' feelings about the Electoral College, he received this response: "Every boy and girl should go to college and if they can't afford Yale or Harvard, why, Electoral is just as good, if you work" (1969, 43).

5. This concern is not new. At the second annual meeting of the American Political Science Association in 1905, Professor W. A. Schaper of the University of Minnesota reported on a study of students in ten eastern and midwestern universities. After reading "350 papers covering 1,400 pages of manuscript," he concluded that "the want of information about the government and the utter want of

comprehension of our political system may be the rule, not the exception among this much favored class of the rising generation" (1906, 218).

6. There may be significant exceptions to the generally lower levels of knowledge among young people. Research by Jennings (1996) shows that high school seniors were more knowledgeable about certain factual matters about government than their parents, and the seniors' knowledge declined as they moved into adulthood.

7. Page and Shapiro (1992: 388) point out that collective decisions can be good even if many individuals judge only imperfectly the relevant information. The authors concede, however, that at times the public can be misled (chaps. 9–10).

8. We use the expressions "political knowledge," "knowledge about government and politics," and "civic knowledge" synonymously to encompass a wide range of information about political institutions, processes, and principles. The Civics Assessment on which we draw for our basic data is similarly broad in scope (see the description below).

9. Apropos of this point, the group that is planning the next NAEP Civics Assessment regards it as essential to inquire about *knowledge of* "civic dispositions" even though NAEP, as a matter of policy, "does not [now] collect information on individual students' personal values or attitudes" ("Policy Statement," 1996: 4; cf. Jones, 1980). Civic dispositions are defined as the "traits of private and public character essential to the preservation and improvement of American constitutional democracy" (*Civics Framework*, 1996, 31).

10. In addition, some scholars would argue that civics instruction and learning is fundamentally about attitudinal development and not about the acquisition of facts. As noted, this is something that NAEP avoids addressing.

11. Two additional features of the 1988 NAEP Civics Assessment are relevant. First, the assessment included several questions intended to assess interpretive skills and ability to reason logically about social and political matters. Although more such items would have been desirable, those that are included allow us to look at least one step beyond the ability to recall factual information. Second, although open-ended or constructed-response questions have their merits, the length of and difficulty in coding the extended verbatim answers to these questions necessarily reduce the number of items that can be included. In contrast, a format of closed-ended, multiple-choice questions can include more items, thereby increasing the reliability of the assessment. Moreover, as we shall see, the large set of items will allow us to study the acquisition of knowledge about various kinds of subjects rather than civic knowledge treated as a single, undifferentiated entity.

Chapter 2: What High School Students Know (and Don't Know)

1. Weighted *N*s are very large, inasmuch as they are intended to show the numbers of students in the population from which the sample was chosen (Kaplan, 1990, 346). We show the unweighted *N*s as well because they give greater insight into the reliability of the estimates.

2. The NAEP history assessments were conducted in 1986 and 1988. The former, limited to eleventh graders, is reported in Ravitch and Finn (1987). The latter, very similar in design to the civics assessment, is reported in Hammack et al. (1990). We draw on both of them in this chapter.

3. In our opinion, however, the table is poorly presented. The insertion of row totals (showing 100 percent) would help indicate that the percentaging was by rows rather than columns. Percentage signs (%) at the beginning of each row instead of on the top of each column would also be more appropriate for row percentaging. Still, the numbers in the first column clearly add to less than 100, and it is not difficult to confirm that the percentages add to 100 in each row.

4. *The Civics Report Card* provided verbatim responses of twelfth graders for the categories "elaborated" and "minimal." Below are verbatim answers for the categories described as "adequate," "minimal," and "unacceptable" for eighth graders.

Adequate
I think being a president has a lot of responsibilities. He or she has to keep peace between other countrys. They sometimes have to make up laws and get it passed. They also have to make long speeches on national t.v. and that takes a lot of self confidence. That is why I think it is hard to be a President.

His jobs are to keep us out of wars, veto laws, decide what to do with the governments money. If we get into a war, he tells us what to do. Another important function is to appoint Supreme Court Judge. He has got to make the right decision for our country. He has to trade and meat with the other countries. So he really, basically controls the U.S.

The president has many jobs to do as the president like passing laws if he likes them or vetoing them. But there aren't a lot of things he can't do like declare war. A President gets elected every four years and can serve two terms, our president now has served two terms already and cannot be elected again. He is considered chief in command of all of the Armed Forces. But there are alot of things the president can't do without the Congress and all the other branches.

Minimal
His purpose of being a president is to pass the laws and to abide by them. His purpose also is to try avoid wars and to govern the world, to make other citizens feel as tho the United States is a fair country, and as for me his final duties are to treat all men equal.

The president has many very important responsibilities. The president has to run the country, deal with other countries and keep out of trouble. Reagan has done a good job forming relationships (good) with Russia. But however he can't keep out of trouble.

Unacceptable
He could try to get home that we live on the street and could try get jobs. If I was president, I get people the street get them job and new clothes and a house. And then my mother will be proud of me.

Chapter 3: How Students Learn about Government

1. On an abstract level, these features are relevant to learning in general. Shortly, however, we discuss specific manifestations that are particularly relevant to learning about civics and government.

2. However, it has been argued with respect to math interest and ability that the observed differences between males and females in this regard are the result of behavior on the part of teachers and parents, who *expect* girls to be uninterested in certain subjects. As a result, parents and educators consistently (and usually unconsciously) treat girls in such a way as to create this response. See *The AAUW Report: How Schools Shortchange Girls* (1995).

Chapter 4: Exposure to Learning

1. We draw these course titles from our survey of social studies curriculum specialists and from Legum et al. (1997).

2. Recall that in 1988 the civics test was administered to some students in grades 9–11 as well as grade 12. Hence the form of the question.

3. Students were also asked whether they had taken (or were now taking) an Advanced Placement course. However, it is clear that students misunderstood this question (even ninth graders reported taking such a course), so we do not use it.

4. In Appendix C, we give standard errors for the estimates shown in all tables in this chapter.

5. In the 1988 NAEP data, 41 percent reported taking a civics class in ninth grade, 31 percent in tenth grade, 52 percent in eleventh grade, and 61 percent in twelfth grade. "Don't know" responses were counted as "no."

6. For mathematics, in contrast, the more semesters of mathematics students have had, the higher their test scores, up through eight semesters (Trevor Williams et al. 1995: A-1–26).

7. This estimate varies slightly from that in table 4.3 owing to rounding.

8. There is a certain amount of ambiguity in the responses used to distinguish the bottom two categories. All of these students reported having had no civics courses when asked in questions 1–5 of the civics questionnaire (Appendix D). When instructed later (before question 21) to check "no" to question 21 "if you have never studied American government or civics," the eighty-nine students in the bottom category did so. Here we interpret this further response as indicating an almost complete absence of civic material in the student's curriculum. However, note that question 21 itself, as opposed to the instructions before the question, refers to civics *classes,* so that, strictly speaking, all students in the bottom two categories should have answered no. Because of this ambiguity, we shall err on the side of caution when we interpret in chapters 6 and 7 the overall effects of civics course work. See chapter 6, note 5 for more details.

In addition, even those students who claimed to have no specific courses in civics might, nonetheless, have had some exposure to civics. For one thing, they might have been in their first civics course at the time of the survey and therefore not have *completed* any course, which was the operative word in the "course" question. More likely, they might not have regarded a small amount of civic instruction in a history or other class as having constituted civics *course work.*

9. A further breakdown revealed that students who claimed to have had a civics course in each of grades 9–12 were not all that knowledgeable (though more so than students with no course work); indeed, these students were less knowledgeable than those who had civics only in the twelfth grade or only in the ninth and twelfth grades. We suspect that many of the students claiming course work in

every grade misinterpreted the question (specifically, what constitutes a civics or American government course). If so, these errors may be part of the explanation for why the total amount of course work does not seem to explain increasing knowledge levels. Such error would also suggest that the differences by amount and recency *underestimate* true differences, since those reporting civics in each grade appear in the "12th grade latest" category, lowering the score of this group.

10. Instructional Dollars per Pupil (IDP) refers to district-level school expenditures, exclusive of teacher salaries and benefits. It is closely related to state-level per pupil expenditures that do include payments to teachers (Trevor Williams et al., 1995: A-1–24).

Chapter 5: Selection and Retention

1. There is also a possibility that some unmeasured factor is the cause of both a measured factor and knowledge, making the observed relation entirely spurious. Elementary school classes and teachers, for example, could be the source of students' interest in civics and of much of their knowledge. Were we able to do so in some reliable and manageable way, it would be useful to decompose the effects of every factor into its component parts so that we knew precisely the chain of causation. But the important point here is that there is such a chain and that these factors are a part of it. Parents' education, student interest, and each of the other factors are assumed to be direct as well as indirect causes of students' knowledge and attitudes.

2. Although these are not inherent differences, boys and girls and African-Americans and those of other races may react differently to what they observe because of their sex or race and ethnicity. As a columnist asked rhetorically on a recent July 4 (Williams 1996), can a black child read about American presidents (all white males) and still believe that any child in America can grow up to be president?

3. There were only about 110 students who said they were "best described" as Asian or Pacific Islander, too few on which to make reliable estimates.

4. The average score of the Asian and Pacific Islander students over all items was 67 percent correct. They are excluded from the remainder of the analyses in this chapter.

5. In the NAEP study, the mean and median values are quite close, and group differences for means and medians are almost identical. Therefore, comparison of mean differences with median values given by Delli Carpini and Keeter (1996) is warranted.

Chapter 6: What Makes Students Learn

1. In previous chapters, where we considered each item separately, we had to be concerned only with the smaller number of respondents, which was consistently large enough, at over 1,800. Here it is necessary to aggregate across items to develop a score for each individual, so we need to be concerned simultaneously with the number of questions of a given type answered by each individual and with the number of individuals remaining after establishing a minimum number of items of a given type.

2. Because of the data limitations noted above, some of the categories used here necessarily differ from those used in earlier chapters; however, they are closely connected in that they are formed by combining certain of the sets used previously. This has the advantage of tying together the results of this and previous chapters while making the results more meaningful and generalizable than they would be if we tried to determine the distinct causes of a set of more finely specified categories.

3. Because our primary interest is in broad comparisons of structural, individual, and background characteristics, we represented method of instruction by a single variable in the regressions—discussion of current events in civics classes. For this variable, students who said that they had never had a class in civics or American government were assigned a score of zero; students who skipped the question (in error) were assigned, as a replacement value, their response to a similar question on whether teachers in American government and civics classes discussed and analyzed the course material.

4. All of the regression models in this chapter are estimated with pairwise deletion of missing data. We chose this method because the cases on which data are unobserved appear to be randomly missing; there is no systematic selection bias in which students received or answered the questions. Moreover, in parallel regression analyses specifying listwise deletion of missing data, the substantive results do not diverge significantly. Appendix E gives ordinary least squares estimates with listwise deletion.

5. An important difference from the bivariate analyses reported in earlier chapters is that we do not attempt to distinguish here between those who have had no course work in American government or civics and those who have had no civic instruction at all. That is, in the regression analysis reported in this chapter, we use a three-category version of the amount and recency measure. Although this decision is undesirable from the perspective of reducing the variation in the measure, there are two reasons for it. First, we wanted to give less weight to the distinction between the lowest two categories because of concerns about the construction of the questionnaire and inconsistencies in student answers (see chapter 4, note 7). Second, the relatively small number of students in the lowest category is further reduced in the regressions because of missing data. Since the coefficient for this variable remains basically the same whether we use a three- or four-category version of the variable, our decision reduces the apparent effect by about 2 percentage points. We believe that it is appropriate to opt for the more conservative coding.

6. This is determined by multiplying the lowest and highest values of each measure by the estimated coefficients (with the "bottom" end for television viewing being 6). The total amount of the difference is 22.2.

7. In assessing the importance of the measure of language spoken in the home, it is important to note that the model also included a measure for whether or not the student is Hispanic.

8. The reference group is technically white students along with other non-Hispanic and non–African-American students. This group includes Asian and Native American students. Although it would have been ideal to estimate the exposure-selection model while accounting separately for these groups, the small number of Asian and Native American students included in the sample precluded such analysis.

9. We also estimated a regression predicting students' understanding of the responsibilities of the president (scored 1–4) with the same set of independent variables. The results, shown in Appendix E, are prone to greater measurement error and are less reliable because they are based on a smaller number of respondents. Nevertheless, they suggest that school factors are an important part of the extent to which students understand presidential responsibilities. Of the school and curriculum factors, the variety of civics topics studied is significantly associated with better answers, and its effect is as large as that of parental education. In addition, both interest in government and future educational plans also have a strong effect on the answers. Apart from parental education, none of the factors in the home environment contributes unambiguously to more elaborate discussions of the president's job. Unlike the results for overall political knowledge, females are better able to answer the question on presidential responsibilities. But consistent with earlier findings, African-American students are less likely to score well on this item.

10. Distributions by group on all structural and individual characteristics are given in Appendix E.

11. Results by subject area presented in chapter 4 also tend to undermine the redundancy hypothesis set forth by Langton and Jennings. Civics courses appeared to make a difference in each of the subject matter categories (see table 4.5). Where students already knew a lot—judging by those who had had no civics at all or at least no course work—gains were perhaps slightly less, but students made gains even in those areas. If a saturation point was reached, it appears to have been at much higher levels than suggested in the earlier study. Conversely, when students began with relatively low levels of knowledge, they did not learn much more.

12. In the history data, the extent of discussion and analysis of material was substituted for the measure of discussing current events, which was available only in the civics data. Similarly, the measure of participation in mock trials and elections was excluded from the model predicting knowledge of American history.

13. Individual analysis of the six items shows the following results (percentage correct):

	Number of civics courses in grades 10–12			Extreme difference
	None	One	Two or more	
Years in a senator's term	45	53	61	+16
Number of members on Supreme Court	34	42	45	+11
Tito is leader of what country?	25	28	32	+7
Country with WWII concentration camps	86	85	88	+2
FDR was a Democrat or Republican	65	67	67	+2
Name of state governor	90	90	88	−2
Number of cases	420	814	114	

Note: The number of cases is usually reduced by one or two after eliminating missing cases (coded "not ascertained").

Consistent with the argument in the text, the largest differences are on the first two items. Also, more than 85 percent of the respondents correctly answered two of the remaining items. In contrast, 85 percent or more of the students answered correctly on 18 percent of the items in the NAEP test.

14. We are reminded of Converse's (1962) demonstration of the large difference in attitude stability between respondents who were completely shut off from politics and those who had a small amount of political information.

Chapter 7: The Future of Civic Education

1. One can also add to this estimate the 5 percent contributed by participation in mock elections and government, which we have classified as a matter of individual achievement but which takes place within the school.

2. See chapter six, note 5. Note, too, that when the schools omit a topic from the curriculum, students do not spontaneously learn about it, as we see in the matter of political parties and lobbying. These subjects are largely ignored in civics courses and, consequently, the students' level of knowledge in this area is low compared that in with topics that get more coverage in classes.

3. Although the findings from our analysis of the NAEP data do not provide conclusive evidence that civics course work has a significant impact on a range of democratic attitudes and values, they do provide important counter evidence against the null findings in some previous work (e.g., Langton and Jennings, 1968). In addition, other studies (e.g., Avery et al., 1992; Brody, 1994) have demonstrated that course work has the potential for creating significant alterations in levels of political tolerance among high school students.

4. A remaining issue, which we cannot address adequately with the NAEP data, is whether the effects of civics classes are long-lasting. This is obviously important, all the more so because Jennings (1996) finds that "textbook knowledge" of politics declines as high school seniors age. In line with our analysis of individual items from that study, we reproduced the table in chapter 6, note 13, with the percentages of correct answers the same individuals gave in 1973, eight years after the students had graduated from high school. The extreme differences, shown in the same order as in the earlier note, were +5, +8, +6, −3, +3, and 0. Thus, where there were more than minimal differences in 1965, differences remained in 1973. To be sure, the differences were smaller in two of the three cases, but one could still detect the effects of civics classes well into young adulthood.

5. Kinds of theoretical and comparative topics that might reasonably be introduced at the high school level are discussed in the national standards proposed by the Center for Civic Education (1994).

6. However, "how to study" books, such as Riker's (1966) small guidebook for college students, might be appropriate and useful.

7. Efforts such as Project '87, a joint initiative with the American Historical Association, are occasional at best.

8. In 1996 the president-elect of the American Political Science Association, Elinor Ostrom, announced the formation of a task force, "Civic Education for the Next Century." Its charge, among other things, is to evaluate existing instructional materials and develop new works for teachers at the eleventh- and twelfth-grade levels, the community college level, and the undergraduate university level. The plan calls for work over the next several years, with a final report in 2005. On earlier activities, see Sheilah Mann (1994).

References

The AAUW Report: How Schools Shortchange Girls. 1995. New York: Marlowe and Company.

Abramson, Paul R. 1977. *The Political Socialization of Black Americans.* New York: Free Press.

Abramson, Paul R. 1983. *Political Attitudes in America.* San Francisco: W. H. Freeman.

Achen, Christopher H. 1975. "Mass Political Attitudes and the Survey Response." *American Political Science Review* 69:1218–31.

Adelson, Joseph, and Robert P. O'Neill. 1966. "Growth of Political Ideas in Adolescence: The Sense of Community." *Journal of Personality and Social Psychology* 4:295–306.

Almond, Gabriel A., and Sidney Verba. 1963. *The Civic Culture.* Princeton: Princeton University Press.

Altbach, Philip G. 1968. *Student Politics and Higher Education in the United States: A Select Bibliography.* Cambridge: Center for International Affairs, Harvard University.

Allen, Russell, et al. 1990. *The Geography Learning of High-School Seniors.* Princeton: National Assessment of Educational Progress, Educational Testing Service.

Anderson, Lee, et al. 1990. *The Civics Report Card.* Princeton: National Assessment of Educational Progress, Educational Testing Service.

APSA Guidelines. "APSA Guidelines for Teacher Training." *PS: Political Science and Politics* 27:261–62.

Avery, Patricia G., et al. 1992. "Exploring Political Tolerance with Adolescents." *Theory and Research in Social Education* 20:386–420.

Bachman, Jerald. 1969. *Youth in Transition,* vol. 1. Ann Arbor, Mich.: Institute for Social Research.

Barnes, Samuel H., Max Kaase, et al. 1979. *Political Action: Mass Participation in Five Western Democracies.* Beverly Hills, Calif.: Sage.

Beck, Paul Allen. 1977. "The Role of Agents in Political Socialization." In *Handbook of Political Socialization,* ed. Stanley Allen Renshon. New York: Free Press.

Beck, Paul Allen, and M. Kent Jennings. 1982. "Pathways to Participation." *American Political Science Review* 76:94–108.

Berliner, David C., and Bruce J. Biddle. 1995. *The Manufactured Crisis: Myths, Fraud, and the Attack on America's Public Schools.* Reading, Mass.: Addison-Wesley.

Brody, Richard A. 1994. *Secondary Education and Political Attitudes: Examining the Effects on Political Tolerance of the* We the People . . . *Curriculum.* Calabasas, Calif.: Center for Civic Education.

Butler, David, and Donald Stokes. 1969. *Political Change in Britain.* New York: St. Martin's.

Button, Christine Bennett. 1974. "Political Education for Minority Groups." In *The Politics of Future Citizens,* ed. Richard G. Niemi. San Francisco: Jossey-Bass.

Butts, R. Freeman. 1980. *The Revival of Civic Learning: A Rationale for Citizenship Education in American Schools.* Bloomington, Ind.: Phi Delta Kappa.

Campbell, Angus, Philip E. Converse, Warren E. Miller, and Donald E. Stokes. 1960. *The American Voter.* New York: Wiley.

Carroll, James. D., et al. 1987. *We The People: A Review of U.S. Government and Civics Textbooks.* Washington, D.C.: People for the American Way.

Center for Civic Education. 1994. *National Standards for Civics and Government.* Calabasas, Calif.: Center for Civic Education.

Chaffee, Steven H., Jack M. McLeod, and Daniel B. Wackman. 1973. "Family Communication Patterns and Adolescent Political Participation." In *Socialization to Politics,* ed. Jack Dennis. New York: Wiley.

Civics: United States Government and Politics Objectives, 1988 Assessment. 1987. Princeton: National Assessment of Educational Progress, Educational Testing Service.

Civics Framework for the 1998 National Assessment of Educational Progress. 1996. Washington, D.C.: National Assessment Governing Board, Council of Chief State School Officers.

Coleman, James S., et al. 1966. *Equality of Educational Opportunity.* Washington, D.C.: U.S. Government Printing Office.

Committee on Pre-Collegiate Education. 1971. "Political Education in the Public Schools: The Challenge for Political Science." *PS: Political Science and Politics* 4:432–48.

Converse, Philip E. 1962. "Information Flow and the Stability of Partisan Attitudes." *Public Opinion Quarterly* 26:578–99.

Converse, Philip E. 1964. "The Nature of Belief Systems in Mass Publics." In *Ideology and Discontent,* ed. David E. Apter. New York: Free Press.

Converse, Philip E. 1972. "Change in the American Electorate." In *The Human Meaning of Social Change,* ed. Angus Campbell and Philip E. Converse. New York: Russell Sage.

Converse, Philip E. 1990. "Popular Representation and the Distribution of Information." In *Information and Democratic Processes,* ed. John A. Ferejohn and James H. Kuklinski. Urbana: University of Illinois Press.

Converse, Philip E., and Georges Dupeux. 1962. "Politicization of the Electorate in France and the United States." *Public Opinion Quarterly* 26:1–23.

Corbett, Michael. 1991. *American Public Opinion.* New York: Longman.

Cuban, Larry. 1991. "History of Teaching in Social Sciences." In *Handbook of Research on Social Studies Teaching and Learning,* ed. James P. Shaver. New York: Macmillan.

Delli Carpini, Michael X., and Scott Keeter. 1996. *What Americans Know about Politics and Why It Matters.* New Haven: Yale University Press.

Denver, David, and Gordon Hands. 1990. "Does Studying Politics Make a Difference? The Political Knowledge, Attitudes, and Perceptions of School Students." *British Journal of Political Science* 20:263–88.

Dewey, John. [1916] 1966. *Democracy and Education.* New York: Free Press.

Downs, Anthony. 1957. *An Economic Theory of Democracy.* New York: Harper.

Dry, Murray. 1996. "Review of National Standards for Civics and Government." *PS: Political Science and Politics* 29:49–53.

Easton, David, and Jack Dennis. 1969. *Children in the Political System.* New York: McGraw-Hill.

Ehman, Lee H. 1977. "Research on Social Studies Curriculum and Instruction: Values." In Francis P. Hunkins, et al., *Review of Research in Social Studies Education, 1970–1975.* Washington, D.C.: National Council for the Social Studies.

Ehman, Lee H. 1980. "The American School in the Political Socialization Process." *Review of Educational Research* 50:99–119

Ehman, Lee H., and Carole L. Hahn. 1981. "Contributions of Research to Social Studies Education." In *The Social Studies: Eightieth Yearbook of the National Society for the Study of Education,* ed. Howard D. Mehlinger and O. L. Davis. Chicago: University of Chicago Press.

Erikson, Robert S., and Kent L. Tedin. 1995. *American Pubic Opinion,* 5th ed. Boston: Allyn and Bacon.

Ernst, Randy, and Peter Petrossian. 1996. "Teachers of Psychology in Secondary Schools (TOPSS): Aiming for Excellence in High School Psychology Instruction." *American Psychologist* 51:256–58.

Erskine, Hazel Gaudet. 1963. "The Polls: Textbook Knowledge"; "The Polls: Exposure to Domestic Information"; "The Polls: Exposure to International Information." *Public Opinion Quarterly* 27:132–41; 491–500; 658–62.

Farnen, Russell F. 1990. *Integrating Political Science, Education and Public Policy.* Frankfurt: Peter Lang.

Farnen, Russell F., and Dan B. German. 1972. "Cross-National Research on Political Socialization and Educational Processes." In *Public Opinion and Political Attitudes,* ed. Allen R. Wilcox. New York: Wiley.

Feldman, Kenneth A., and Theodore A. Newcomb. 1969. *The Impact of College on Students.* San Francisco: Jossey-Bass.

Ferguson, Patrick. 1991. "Impacts on Social and Political Participation." In *Handbook of Research on Social Studies Teaching and Learning,* ed. James P. Shaver. New York: Macmillan.

Fiorina, Morris P. 1990. "Information and Rationality in Elections." In *Information and Democratic Processes,* ed. John A. Ferejohn and James H. Kuklinski. Urbana: University of Illinois Press.

Gallagher, A. F. 1987. "How Law-Related Education Fits into the Curriculum." *International Journal of Social Education* 2:37–44.

Garcia, F. Chris. 1973. *Political Socialization of Chicano Children: A Comparative Study with Anglos in California Schools.* New York: Praeger.

"General Knowledge of Historical Events." 1993. *Public Perspective* 4(5):34.

Glazer, Nathan, and Reed Ueda. 1983. *Ethnic Groups in History Textbooks.* Washington, D.C.: Ethics and Public Policy Center.

Goldenson, Dennis R. 1978. "An Alternative View about the Role of the Secondary School in Political Socialization: A Field-Experimental Study of the Development of Civil Liberties Attitudes." *Theory and Research in Social Education* 6:44–72.

Graber, Doris. 1994. "Why Voters Fail Information Tests: Can the Hurdles Be Overcome?" *Political Communication* 11:331–46.

Green, Donald Philip. 1989. "On the Dimensionality of Public Sentiment toward Partisan and Ideological Groups." *American Journal of Political Science* 32:758–80.

Gurin, Patricia, Shirley Hatchett, and James S. Jackson. 1989. *Hope and Independence: Blacks' Response to Electoral and Party Politics.* New York: Russell Sage.

Gutmann, Amy. 1987. *Democratic Education.* Princeton: Princeton University Press.

Hahn, Carole L. 1991. "Controversial Issues in Social Studies." In *Handbook of Research on Social Studies Teaching and Learning,* ed. James P. Shaver. New York: Macmillan.

Hammack, David C., et al. 1990. *The U.S. History Report Card.* Princeton: National Assessment of Educational Progress, Educational Testing Service.

Hess, Robert D., and Judith V. Torney. 1967. *The Development of Political Attitudes in Children.* Chicago: Aldine.

Hirsch, E. D., Jr. 1987. *Cultural Literacy: What Every American Needs to Know.* Boston: Houghton Mifflin.

Holland, Alyce, and Thomas Andre. 1987. "Participation in Extracurricular Activities in Secondary School: What Is Known, What Needs to Be Known." *Review of Educational Research* 57:437–66.

Hunter, R. M., and M. J. Turner. 1981. *Law-Related Education Evaluation Project: Final Report.* Boulder, Colo.: Social Science Education Consortium.

Hursh, David. 1994. "Civic Education." In *International Encyclopedia of Education,* ed. Torsten Husten and T. Neville Postlethwaite. 2d ed. London: Pergamon.

Hyman Herbert H., and Paul B. Sheatsley. 1947. "Some Reasons Why Information Campaigns Fail." *Public Opinion Quarterly* 11:412–23.

Hyman, Herbert H., and Charles R. Wright. 1979. *Education's Lasting Influence on Values.* Chicago: University of Chicago Press.

Hyman, Herbert H., Charles R. Wright, and John Shelton Reed. 1975. *The Enduring Effects of Education.* Chicago: University of Chicago Press.

Jacob, Philip E. 1957. *Changing Values in College: An Exploratory Study of the Impact of College Teaching.* New York: Harper and Row.

Jennings, M. Kent. 1996. "Political Knowledge over Time and across Generations." *Public Opinion Quarterly* 60:228–52.

Jennings, M. Kent, Lee H. Ehman, and Richard G. Niemi. 1974. "Social Studies Teachers and Their Pupils." In M. Kent Jennings and Richard G. Niemi, *The Political Character of Adolescence.* Princeton: Princeton University Press.

Jennings, M. Kent, and Richard G. Niemi. 1974. *The Political Character of Adolescence.* Princeton: Princeton University Press.

Jennings, M. Kent, and Richard G. Niemi. 1981. *Generations and Politics.* Princeton: Princeton University Press.

Johnson, Eugene G., Rebecca Zwick, et al. 1990. *Focusing the New Design: The NAEP 1988 Technical Report.* Princeton: Educational Testing Service.

Jones, Ruth S. 1980. "Democratic Values and Preadult Virtues: Tolerance, Knowledge, and Participation." *Youth and Society* 12:189–220.

Kaplan, Bruce A. 1990. "Statistical Summary of the 1988 NAEP Samples and Estimates of the Proficiencies of American Students." In Eugene G. Johnson, et al., *Focusing the New Design: The NAEP 1988 Technical Report.* Princeton: Educational Testing Service.

Katz, Ellis. 1986. "Federalism in Secondary School American History and Government Textbooks." *In Teaching about American Federal Democracy,* ed. Stephen L. Schechter. Philadelphia: Center for the Study of Federalism, Temple University.

Kinder, Donald, and David O. Sears. 1985. "Public Opinion and Political Action." In *Handbook of Social Psychology,* vol. 2, ed. Gardner Lindzey and Elliot Aronson. New York: Random House.

Krosnick, Jon A. 1991. "The Stability of Political Preferences: Comparisons of Symbolic and Nonsymbolic Attitudes." *American Journal of Political Science* 35:547–76.

Kuklinski, James H., and Norman L. Hurley. 1994. "On Hearing and Interpreting Political Messages: A Cautionary Tale of Citizen Cue-Taking." *Journal of Politics:* 56:729–51.

Langton, Kenneth, and M. Kent Jennings. 1968. "Political Socialization and the High School Civics Curriculum in the United States." *American Political Science Review* 62:862–67.

Legum, Stanley, et al. 1997. "The 1994 High School Transcript Study Tabulations: Comparative Data on Credits Earned and Demographics for 1994, 1990, 1987, and 1982 High School Graduates." Washington, D.C.: National Center for Educational Statistics, U.S. Department of Education.

Leming, James S. 1985. "Research on Social Studies Curriculum and Instruction: Interventions and Outcomes in the Socio-Moral Domain." In *Review of Research in Social Studies Education: 1976–1983,* ed . William B. Stanley. Washington, D.C.: National Council for the Social Studies.

Liebschutz, Sarah, and Richard G. Niemi. 1974. "Political Attitudes among Black Children." In *The Politics of Future Citizens,* ed. Richard G. Niemi. San Francisco: Jossey-Bass.

Litt, Edgar. 1963. "Civic Education Norms and Political Indoctrination." *American Sociological Review* 28:69–75.

Luskin, Robert C. 1987. "Measuring Political Sophistication." *American Journal of Political Science* 31:856–99.

Luskin, Robert C. 1990. "Explaining Political Sophistication." *Political Behavior* 12:331–61.

McClosky, Herbert, and John R. Zaller. 1984. *The American Ethos: Public Attitudes toward Capitalism and Democracy.* Cambridge: Harvard University Press.

Mann, Sheilah. 1994. "Political Scientists Examine Civics Standards: Introduction." *PS: Political Science and Politics* 29:47–49.

Mann, Thomas E., and Raymond E. Wolfinger. 1980. "Candidates and Parties in Congressional Elections." *American Political Science Review* 74:617–32.

Merelman, Richard M. 1971. *Political Socialization and Educational Climates.* New York: Holt, Rinehart, and Winston.

Merelman, Richard M. 1996. "Symbols as Substance in National Civics Standards." *PS: Political Science and Politics* 29:53–57.

Merriam, Charles E. 1931. *The Making of Citizens: A Comparative Study of Methods of Civic Training.* Chicago: University of Chicago Press.

Merriam, Charles E. 1934. *Civic Education in the United States.* New York: Scribners.

Michener, James. 1969. *Presidential Lottery: The Reckless Gamble in Our Electoral System.* New York: Random House.

Milbrath, Lester, and M. L. Goel. 1977. *Political Participation,* 2d ed. Chicago: Rand McNally.

Miller, Jon D. 1985. "The Influence of High School Social Studies Courses on Political Participation by Young Adults." Paper presented at the annual meeting of the American Educational Research Association, Chicago. (ERIC Reproduction Service Document No. ED 265 086)

Miller, Warren E., Arthur H. Miller, and Edward J. Schneider. 1980. *American National Election Studies Data Sourcebook, 1952–1978.* Cambridge: Harvard University Press.

Moore, Stanley W., James Lare, and Kenneth A. Wagner. 1985. *The Child's Political World.* New York: Praeger.

Morduchowicz, Roxana, Edgardo Catterberg, Richard G. Niemi, and Frank Bell. 1996. "Teaching Political Knowledge and Democratic Values in a New Democracy: An Argentine Experiment." *Comparative Politics* 28:465–76.

Morin, Richard. 1996. "Who's in Control? Many Don't Know or Care." *Washington Post,* January 29:1.

Morrison, A., and D. McIntyre. 1971. *Schools and Socialization.* Harmondsworth, G.B.: Penguin.

Murphy, Joseph, ed. 1990. *The Educational Reform Movement of the 1980s.* Berkeley: McCutchan.

National Center for Education Statistics. 1995. "Community Service Performed by High School Seniors," Education Policy Issues Series No. 95–743. Washington, D.C.: National Center for Education Statistics.

National Commission on Teaching and America's Future. 1996. "What Matters

Most: Teaching for America's Future." New York: Teachers College, Columbia University.

A Nation at Risk: The Imperative for Educational Reform. 1983. Washington, D.C.: United States Department of Education, National Commission on Excellence in Education.

Neuman, W. Russell. 1986. *The Paradox of Mass Politics.* Cambridge: Harvard University Press.

Neuman, W. Russell, Marion R. Just, and Ann N. Crigler. 1992. *Common Knowledge: News and the Construction of Political Meaning.* Chicago: University of Chicago Press.

Newcomb, Theodore M. 1943. *Personality and Social Change: Attitude Formation in a Student Community.* New York: Dryden.

Newcomb, Theodore M., Kathryn K. Koenig, Richard Flacks, and Donald P. Warwick. 1967. *Persistence and Change: Bennington College and Its Students after Twenty-Five Years.* New York: Wiley.

Nie, Norman H., Jane Junn, and Kenneth Stehlik-Barry. 1996. *Education and Democratic Citizenship in America.* Chicago: University of Chicago Press.

Niemi, Richard G., and Mary Hepburn. 1995. "The Rebirth of Political Socialization." *Perspectives on Political Science* 24:7–16.

Niemi, Richard G., John Mueller, and Tom Smith. 1989. *Trends in Public Opinion.* Westport, Conn.: Greenwood.

Niemi, Richard G., and Anders Westholm. 1984. "Issues, Parties, and Attitudinal Stability: A Comparative Study of Sweden and the United States." *Electoral Studies* 3:65–83.

Owen, Diana, and Jack Dennis. 1988. "Gender Differences in the Politicization of American Children." *Women and Politics* 82:3–43.

Page, Benjamin I. 1978. *Choices and Echoes in Presidential Elections.* Chicago: University of Chicago Press.

Page, Benjamin I., and Richard A. Brody. 1972. "Policy Voting and the Electoral Process: The Vietnam War Issue." *American Political Science Review* 66:979–95.

Page, Benjamin I., and Robert Y. Shapiro. 1992. *The Rational Public: Fifty Years of Trends in American's Policy Preferences.* Chicago: University of Chicago Press.

Patrick, John J. 1972. "The Impact of an Experimental Course, 'American Political Behavior,' on the Knowledge, Skills, and Attitudes of Secondary School Students." *Social Education* 36:168–79.

Patrick, John J. 1977. "Political Socialization and Political Education in Schools." In *Handbook of Political Socialization,* ed. Stanley Allen Renshon. New York: Free Press.

Patrick, John J., and John D. Hoge. 1991. "Teaching Government, Civics, and Law." In *Handbook of Research on Social Studies Teaching and Learning,* ed. James P. Shaver. New York: Macmillan.

"Policy Statement on Redesigning the National Assessment of Education Progress." 1996. Washington, D.C.: National Assessment Government Board.

"Polling on the Holocaust." 1993. *Public Perspective* 4(5):31–33.

Popkin, Samuel L. 1991. *The Reasoning Voter: Communication and Persua-sion in Presidential Campaigns.* Chicago: University of Chicago Press.

"Pop Quiz: What Do Students Know?" 1988. *Newsweek on Campus,* March: 18.

Powell, Pearl M., and Jack V. Powell. 1984. "An Investigation of Political Apa-thy among Selected High School Students." *Journal of Social Studies Re-search* 8:53–66.

Preston, Ben. 1993. "Survey Finds Tenth of Teenagers Have No Idea Where UK Is." *Times* (London), September 20: Home News Section.

Prothro, James W., and Charles M. Grigg. 1960. "Fundamental Principles of Democracy: Bases of Agreement and Disagreement." *Journal of Politics* 22:276–94.

Ravitch, Diane, and Chester E. Finn, Jr. 1987. *What Do Our Seventeen-Year-Olds Know?* New York: Harper and Row.

Remmers, H. H., and D. H. Radler. 1957. *The American Teenager.* Indianapo-lis: Charter.

Remy, Richard C. 1981. "Treatment of the Constitution in Civics and Govern-ment Textbooks." In *Teaching about the Constitution in American Sec-ondary Schools,* ed. Howard D. Mehlinger. Washington, D.C.: Project '87 of the American Historical Association and the American Political Science Association.

Riker, William H. 1966. *The Study of Local Politics: A Manual.* New York: Random House.

Robinson, James A., Lee F. Anderson, Margaret G. Hermann, and Richard C. Snyder. 1966. "Teaching with Inter-Nation Simulation and Case Studies." *American Political Science Review* 60:53–65.

Rodgers, Harrell R., Jr. 1973. "Civics Curricula and Southern Schoolchildren: The Impact of Segregated and Integrated School Environments." *Journal of Politics* 35:1002–07.

Schaper, W. A. 1906. "What Do Students Know about American Government, before Taking College Courses in Political Science." *Proceedings of the American Political Science Association.* Lancaster, Pa.: Wickersham.

Schug, Mark C., and William B. Walstad. 1991. "Teaching and Learning Eco-nomics." In *Handbook of Research on Social Studies Teaching and Learn-ing,* ed. James P. Shaver. New York: Macmillan.

Schumaker, Paul, and Nancy Elizabeth Burns. 1988. "Gender Cleavages and the Resolution of Local Policy Issues." *American Journal of Political Science* 32:1070–95.

Semetko, Holli. 1996. "The Media." In *Comparing Democracies: Elections and Voting in Global Perspective,* ed. Lawrence LeDuc, Richard G. Niemi, and Pippa Norris. Thousand Oaks, Calif.: Sage.

Shaver, James P. 1984. "The Law-Related Education Evaluation Project: A Methodological Critique of the 'Impacts on Students' Findings." Prepared for the Rocky Mountain Regional Conference of the National Council for the Social Studies. (ERIC Document Reproduction Service No. ED 252 459)

Sidelnick, Daniel J. 1989. "Effects of Ability, Grade, and Gender on Three Measures of Citizenship with High School Students." *Social Studies* 80:92–97.

Sigel, Roberta S., and Marilyn B. Hoskin. 1981. *The Political Involvement of Adolescents*. New Brunswick, N.J.: Rutgers University Press.

Smith, Eric R. A. N. 1989. *The Unchanging American Voter*. Berkeley: University of California Press.

Sniderman, Paul M., Richard A. Brody, and Philip Tetlock. 1991. *Reasoning and Choice: Explorations in Political Psychology*. New York: Cambridge University Press.

Sniderman, Paul M., et al. 1989. "Principled Tolerance and the American Mass Public." *British Journal of Political Science* 19:25–45.

Somit, Albert, Joseph Tannenhaus, Walter H. Wilke, and Rita W. Cooley. 1958. "The Effect of the Introductory Political Science Course on Student Attitudes toward Personal Political Participation." *American Political Science Review* 52:1129–32.

Stanley, Harold, and Richard G. Niemi. 1995. *Vital Statistics on American Politics,* 5th ed. Washington, D.C.: CQ Press.

Steiner, David M. 1994. *Rethinking Democratic Education: The Politics of Reform*. Baltimore: Johns Hopkins University Press.

Stouffer, Samuel. 1955. *Communism, Conformism, and Civil Liberties*. Garden City, N.Y.: Doubleday.

Stretcher, Brian. 1988. *Instructional Effects of the National Bicentennial Competition on the Constitution and Bill of Rights*. Pasadena, Calif.: Educational Testing Service.

Study Group on Law-Related Education. 1978. *Final Report of the U.S. Office of Education Study Group on Law-Related Education*. Washington, D.C.: U.S. Government Printing Office. (ERIC Document Reproduction Service No. ED 175 737)

Sullivan, John L., James E. Piereson, and George E. Marcus. 1982. *Political Tolerance and American Democracy*. Chicago: University of Chicago Press.

Targ, Harry R. 1975. "Elementary Social Inter-Nation Simulation: Impacts on Developing Orientations to International Politics." *Teaching Political Science* 2:200–220.

Television Audiences Report. Various Years. New York: Mediamark Research.

Tolley, Howard, Jr. 1973. *Children and War*. New York: Teachers College, Columbia University.

Torney, Judith V., A. N. Oppenheim, and Russell F. Farnen. 1975. *Civics Education in Ten Countries*. Stockholm: Almqvist and Wiksell.

Vandermyn, Gaye. 1974. "Assessing Students' Political IQ." *American Education* 10(5):22–25.

Verba, Sidney, Kay Lehman Schlozman, and Henry E. Brady. 1995. *Voice and Equality: Civic Voluntarism in American Politics*. Cambridge: Harvard University Press.

Westholm, Anders, Arne Lindquist, and Richard G. Niemi. 1990. "Education and the Making of the Informed Citizen: Political Literacy and the Outside World." In *Political Socialization, Citizen Education, and Democracy,* ed. Orit Ichilov. New York: Teachers College, Columbia University.

Wilen, William W., and Jane J. White. 1991. "Interaction and Discourse in Social Studies Classrooms." In *Handbook of Research on Social Studies Teaching and Learning,* ed. James P. Shaver. New York: Macmillan.

Williams, Armstrong. 1996. "Can Any Child Become President?" *Rochester Democrat and Chronicle,* July 4:8A.

Williams, Paul L., Stephen Lazer, Clyde M. Reese, and Peggy Carr. 1995. *NAEP 1994 U.S. History: A First Look.* Washington, D.C.: Office of Educational Research and Improvement, U.S. Department of Education.

Williams, Trevor, Nadir Atash, Kenneth Burgdorf, and Bradford Chaney. 1995. "Legislating Achievement: Graduation Requirements, Course Taking, and Achievement in Mathematics and Science." Paper presented at the annual meeting of the American Education Research Association.

Wirt, Frederick M. 1986. "The Uses of Blandness: State, Local, and Professional Roles in Citizenship Education." In *Teaching about American Federal Democracy,* ed. Stephen L. Schechter. Philadelphia: Center for the Study of Federalism, Temple University.

Wittebrood, Karin. 1995. *Politieke Socialisatie in Nederland.* Amsterdam: Thesis Publishers. (Summary in English.)

Wormald, Eileen. 1988. "Political Literacy in a Newly Independent Country: Papua New Guinea." Paper presented at the triennial meeting of the International Political Science Association, Washington, D.C.

Young, John T., and Kelly D. Patterson. 1994. "Political Knowledge and Public Opinion about Congress: Does What Citizens Know Matter?" Paper presented at the annual meeting of the American Political Science Association, New York.

Zaller, John R. 1992. *The Nature and Origins of Mass Opinion.* Cambridge: Cambridge University Press.

Index

Abramson, Paul, 71, 146
Achen, Christopher, 7
Achievement, individual: relationship to political knowledge, 96–102, 120, 123–24
Adelson, Joseph, 156
Advanced Placement courses, 158, 186n
African-Americans. *See* Race or ethnicity
Allen, Russell, 24, 60
Almond, Gabriel, 16, 19
American Association of University Women, 186n
American Political Science Association, 158–59, 183n, 190n
Anderson, Lee, 13, 19, 23–24, 45, 60, 67, 74, 76, 78, 161, 163
Andre, Thomas, 15, 96
Asians and Pacific Islanders, 187nn, 188n
Attitudes, impact of education on, 19. *See also* Trust in government
Avery, Patricia, 19, 71, 190n

Barnes, Samuel, 7
Beck, Paul Allen, 15–16, 96
Berliner, David, 17
Biddle, Bruce, 17
Brady, Henry, 15, 104
Brody, Richard, 7–8, 19, 71, 190n

Burns, Nancy Elizabeth, 105
Butler, David, 7
Button, Christine Bennett, 19
Butts, R. Freeman, 157

Campbell, Angus, 3, 6
Carroll, James, 71, 75
Catholic schools. *See* Schools: types of
Center for Civic Education, 11, 12, 190n
Chaffee, Steven, 16
Citizenship, and political knowledge, 1–2
Civic instruction: amount of, 64–67, 84–88; in the eighth grade, 73–75; "hidden" curriculum in, 15 (*see also* Extracurricular activities); and how students learn, 53–60; importance of, to democratic citizenship, 3; state requirements for, 63–64; timing of, 65–69, 156; topics studied, 75–77, 150–54, 157. *See also* Civics courses
Civic knowledge. *See* Political knowledge
Civics courses, 55–57, 63–67; impact on political knowledge of, 3, 14–19, 67–70, 112, 120–23, 130–40, 142–46, 148–49; impact on political trust of, 71–73, 140–42; instructional approaches, 77–82, 156–57; reform